the
joker
is
wild

the joker is wild

the Story of Joe E. Lewis

BY ART COHN

Random House • *New York*

First Printing

© Copyright, 1955, by Art Cohn

All rights reserved under the International and
Pan American Copyright Conventions. Published in
New York by Random House, Inc., and simultaneously in
Toronto, Canada, by Random House of Canada, Limited.
Library of Congress Catalog Card Number: 55-10633
Manufactured in the United States of America
by H. Wolff, New York
Design: Betty K. Crumley

GRATEFUL ACKNOWLEDGMENT IS MADE FOR PERMISSION TO QUOTE FROM THE FOL-
LOWING SONGS:

"In Room Two Hundred and Two," copyright, 1919, by Mills Music, Inc.
Copyright renewed, 1946—Bert Kalmar, Edgar Leslie, and Dave Harris. Used
by permission.

"Chicago," copyright, 1922, Fred Fisher, Inc. Copyright renewed and assigned, 1949, to Fred Fisher Music Co., Inc. Used by permission.

"Dardanella," copyright, 1919, McCarthy and Fisher, Inc. Assigned to Mills
Music, Inc. U.S. copyright renewed and assigned, 1947, to Fred Fisher Music
Co., Inc. Used by permission.

"Paper Doll," by Johnny S. Black, copyrighted by Edward B. Marks Music
Corporation. Used by permission.

"As Time Goes By," copyright, 1931, by Harms, Inc. Used by permission.

"Diamonds Are a Girl's Best Friend," words by Leo Robin, music by Jule
Styne. Copyright, 1949, Consolidated Music Publishers, Inc., 240 West 55th
Street, New York 18, N.Y. Used by permission of the publisher.

The parody lyrics (pages 245-46) were written to be sung to the tune of
"Thanks for the Memory," and are used by permission of the Paramount
Music Corporation.

Who but Marta?

"YOU'RE ONLY YOUNG ONCE.
BUT IF YOU WORK IT RIGHT,
ONCE IS ENOUGH."

Joe E. Lewis

ENTRANCE

We were slogging through the New Guinea jungle in 1943, Joe E. Lewis as an entertainer and I as a war correspondent.

"When the war is over," I said, "let's get together on a book."

"Okay," he said.

Ten years later I got around to it. "How about the book?" I asked Joe.

He stared at me incredulously. "After what Kefauver did to Costello, Erickson and Harry Gross? Where have you been?"

"Not that kind of a book," I said. "A book on your life."

"Why?"

"People want to read about great men. Look at the biographies on Napoleon, Lincoln, Toots Shor, Willie Sutton and Fulton Lewis, Jr."

Joe was flattered. "Twenty years ago I was a nobody," he said humbly, "but today I am a nonentity."

"No phony autobiography 'as told to' or 'edited by' or 'imagined by' some spook," I said. "If I write it, it will be without handcuffs. And I'll put in the scars, all of them. Will you hold still for it?"

"If nobody gets hurt."

"Innocent people sue. I've never been sued."

"Go ahead," he said, "but it's two to one they'll think it's about Joe Louis, the fighter."

This is the story of Joe Lewis, the fighter.

Burns Mantle called him "a genius." Damon Runyon said

he is "peerless." Robert Ruark wrote that he is "a symbol of his age." Quentin Reynolds ranked him, without reservation, "the funniest man who ever lived, and the fact that he comes close to being the nicest man who ever lived has nothing to do with it." George Jessel, in the early '40's, extolled him as "the only comedian with originality to come up within the last ten years." Westbrook Pegler hailed him as "a character unique in this world . . . a real good political satirist." Earl Wilson lauded him "the greatest café entertainer of our time." Abel Green said he is "a show business phenomenon whose work almost literally is his play and vice versa." Ashton Stevens stated that "he unfailingly expresses nobody but himself, a clean guy whose heart is pure even when his lyrics aren't." Florabelle Muir said he is "the best-loved comedian of our time."

His personal friends and aficionados have included Franklin D. Roosevelt, Bernard Baruch, Averell Harriman, Herbert Bayard Swope, Jock Whitney, Winthrop Rockefeller and Morgan. That is, Swifty Morgan.

At one of the perennial Lewis love festivals, a testimonial banquet at the Waldorf-Astoria Hotel, after he had drawn $328,000 in six weeks at a New York cave called the Copacabana, Joe responded, "If I had known you were going to talk about me this way, I would have done the decent thing and died first."

Many have loved him with devouring violence.

Machine Gun Jack McGurn tried to kill him. Al Capone tried to become his padrone. Dutch Schultz tried to buy him. He missed being in the St. Valentine's Day massacre by a few minutes.

And Martha Stewart tried to domesticate him.

All failed. Joe E. remains himself, a triumph of the individual against conformity.

This book is as unconventional as its subject. It is not objective, impersonal or unprejudiced. It is a dramatized biography, a portrait not an inventory. Most of it is written in the third person. The chapters relating Joe's life with Martha are written in the first person, hers. Other parts, particularly his odyssey to the South Pacific, and the evolution of this story in New York, Chicago and Hollywood, are interpolated in the first person, by me. "In all creation," said Emerson, "there should be one rule: ask the fact for the form."

I wanted to call it *The Other Cheek*. Joe came up with *The Worms Are Waiting and Laughing*. We left the choice to Bennett Cerf, the publisher.

"I like *The Joker Is Wild*," said Cerf.

I turned the Other Cheek. Otherwise, I have pulled no punches. Within the law and good taste, I believe that anything that has been lived should be written about without equivocation. Joe disapproves of many passages. We are friends, but when truth and friendship were at odds, I chose truth in the name of friendship.

It is Joe's life. It is Cerf's title. It is my book.

Art Cohn

Rome, Italy
1955

contents

THE FORTIES—Joe's and The World's

THE FIFTIES—Joe's

ILLUSTRATIONS

the twenties

JOE'S AND CAPONE'S

"I'm not a hoodlum—I'm an entertainer"

JOE E.

Joe knew Danny would take it hard. "Danny," he began haltingly. "My contract . . . it's up the end of the month and—"

"Don't worry," Danny Cohen assured him without looking up from the night's take he was counting in his small office. "I'm renewing for another year."

Joe hesitated. From the cabaret stage came the voices of the Williams Sisters and the chorus line winding up the late floor show. "I'm giving notice, Danny."

The owner of the Green Mill stopped counting. "I told you," he said, a note of irritation in his voice, "I'm renewing for another year."

"Thanks—but I'm leavin'."

Danny Cohen's jaw hardened. "You ungrateful punk," he seethed. "You were a two-bit comic on the Levee when I picked you up and gave you a break. Who made you a master of ceremonies? Who upped you to six hundred and fifty a week? I *made* you—and this is how you pay me back."

Joe did not blame Danny but he rationalized, as he surveyed the stacks of currency that covered the desk, he did not owe Danny anything: he had earned his six-five-o, he had packed the Green Mill for a solid year.

"I'm giving you three more weeks, Danny . . ."

"You're giving me nothing. You're through right now."

It had been a good year and Joe was sorry to see it end this way. But he did not intend to stay in the Green Mill all his life. Anyway, he had been offered a thousand a week plus a cut of the cover charges and the gambling to move over to the New Rendezvous Café.

The little comedian sighed and walked out, before Danny changed his mind.

The next day, a handsome, raven-haired young man, dapper and debonair, was waiting for Joe outside his hotel, the Commonwealth. "Hiya, Joe," he greeted him affably.

Joe looked up in surprise. "Hello, Jack."

They walked half a block down Diversey Parkway without exchanging a word. At last the man called Jack broke the silence. "What's the beef with Danny?"

Joe shrugged. "No beef. My contract's up . . . I'm not renewin'."

"We're renewing."

"We?"

"Now, Joe," his companion smiled forebearingly, "you know I got a piece of the joint."

Joe stopped. "But not of me. I start at the Rendezvous November second."

"You'll never live to open." Jack's gentle voice had not risen above a whisper.

The comedian faced his judge. Jack, born Vincent Gebardi in Italy, had been a professional boxer and a professional golfer. Now he was a professional killer, the most lethal marksman with a Thompson submachine gun spawned by the tragic folly of Prohibition. On this mid-October afternoon, as he passed the death sentence on Joe Lewis, the man known as Machine Gun Jack McGurn was twenty-three years old.

The judge glared at the condemned. Lewis, born Joseph Klewan on New York's East Side, looked like a mug and talked like one. He regarded hoodlums neither with deference nor disdain. To him they were customers: as long as they behaved themselves and paid their tabs he would try to entertain them. In less than two years, at the age of twenty-five, he had become the biggest name in Chicago show business: he was gangland's favorite jester.

"You'll never live to open . . ." It was preposterous. Mc-

Gurn should have known better. "I'll reserve a table for you." Joe grinned and walked away, toward the New Rendezvous in the next block.

McGurn turned and walked in the opposite direction.

The man who had lured Joe from the Green Mill was a leathery, six-foot tough who packed a gun every day in the expectancy of using it. John Fogarty, born in Chicago's tenderloin, graduated from bootlegging to speakeasies in the early '20's, and had been doing well at the Rendezvous on North Clark Street at Diversey until Joe started jamming the Green Mill. After that, Fogarty was lucky to get the overflow, even when he brought in Van and Schenck. Business fell off until no alternative remained: he had to get Lewis or get out. He knew that meant trouble but he was used to trouble, and prepared.

"Anything new?" Fogarty was edgy.

Joe nodded. "Hannah Williams and her sister want to come over too."

"What about McGurn?"

"He's been happier."

Fogarty's face darkened. "I'll let you off the hook, if you want."

Joe threw him a withering look. "Trying to renege?"

"You know how much I want you, Joe. I told you, you can have any part of the joint. But I don't want to see you hurt. McGurn is a killer . . ."

Joe had turned his back and walked toward the stage. "Let's try the lights!" he shouted to the electrician.

Fogarty followed him. "If McGurn wants you," he said, wrapping his long arm around Joe's shoulders, "he'll have to get me first."

"I can take care of myself."

If you were born a Jew, raised with seven brothers and sisters in the poverty of a tenement house on Jefferson and Cherry streets in New York, and your father died when you were ten, you were bred to fight. Joe never looked for a scrap but he never backed away from one. At the age of sixteen he had been in World War I. Where was McGurn—and his machine gun—then?

McGurn—little Vincent Gebardi then, age fourteen—was serving his apprenticeship in the jungle of Chicago's Little Hell. When Prohibition came, his father became an alky cooker on the North Side, until the day he made a mistake and sold two gallons of alcohol to an enemy alien from the South Side. That night Papa Gebardi was executed by a North Side firing squad.

Four sons stood beside Papa Gebardi's deathbed as a priest gave the last sacrament of the Catholic Church. Frank, John, Michael and Vincent Gebardi intoned the Requiem Aeterna in the words they had memorized as children, *"Dominis domine lux perpetua lux et coeli, requiescat in pace amen . . ."* even as, a few years previously, four sons of another immigrant—Albert, Murray, William and Joe Klewan—had stood beside the deathbed of their father, Abraham, who had come from Russia to New York's East Side to manufacture corks for bottles such as Papa Gebardi filled, and had prayed to their God in the ancient words of their people, *"Yisgadal, v'yiskadash, sh'mai rabau . . ."*

Young Vincent remained with the corpse of his father after the others left and, by the tapers that illuminated the seamed, tired face, the boy took a terrible oath to avenge his death. He stole his first gun, a Daisy repeating air rifle, and he learned how to shoot by blasting sparrows off telephone wires. As Machine Gun Jack McGurn, he would one day turn on the North Side, become the deadliest of Al Capone's torpedoes on the South Side and simultaneously carry on his own vendetta by killing North Side mobmen like sparrows.

He would kill without pity or remorse, climaxing his gory carnival with a masterwork, the conception and execution of the mass murder of seven members of the North Side mob on St. Valentine's Day, 1929.

This was the psychopathic killer who told Joe Lewis he would not live to open at the New Rendezvous Café.

Was there more to it than Joe quitting the Green Mill? There was talk that Joe had been trespassing in McGurn's stable. Joe denied it but the gossip persisted. They had shared women, though not concurrently, an inevitability in their orbit. There was a lovely piece in particular, a show girl named Gloria. She had been Joe's girl for a few months. The affair ended and, after an interlude, she became McGurn's girl and still was. Joe had not seen Gloria in a long time. Kathy would not have permitted it, even if McGurn had.

Kathy loved Joe with a possessive, unreasoning jealousy. She was waiting in his room at the Commonwealth when he came back from Fogarty's place. "Gloria called twice," she said icily and handed him a slip of paper. "The tramp says it's urgent."

Joe called the number on the paper. Gloria answered. "I got to see you, hon," she pleaded. "Come up to my place—right away."

"Sorry, Gloria," Joe replied, "but I won't be able to see you until November second, when I open at the Rendezvous." He put down the receiver and stared at it, genuine concern in his face. This was McGurn's first move, the second would be less subtle.

"What's with you and Gloria?" Kathy demanded.

Joe told her about McGurn's threat. "He'd like to trap me in her apartment. Then . . ."

Kathy did not believe a word, and when he suggested that she visit her family in Pennsylvania for a few weeks, she was positive he wanted to move her out for Gloria or a more alluring successor. Joe attracted more women than he could handle.

The phone rang. "Don't be a sucker, Joe," an anonymous man's voice warned. "You better be back at the Green Mill tonight or—" Joe slammed down the receiver.

"Who was it?" Kathy asked.

"Trouble." There was a long pause. The phone rang again. Joe did not answer it. "Let it ring," he said.

Kathy's jealousy gave way to alarm.

"I can take care of myself," Joe said, "but I can't be responsible for you." He pulled out a wad of bills and forced them into her hand. "You have to clear out of here."

Kathy, now convinced that he was in jeopardy, became even more adamant about remaining. "I'm not leaving—*ever!*" she cried, and clasped him fiercely. "Joe, let's get married. Please."

Joe had thought of it. Kathy was a good girl, honest, sweet and loyal. If he had signed up for another year at the Green Mill he probably would have made it legal. "Not now, Kathy. We'll see—when you come back."

Kathy sobbed most of the night but she took the morning train east.

The threats continued. "You can't win, Joe," an unknown man's voice admonished him on the phone. "What's the use fighting?"

Fogarty picked up Joe's clothes at the Green Mill and on the way acquired a hoodlum called Big Sam, an ex-heavyweight fighter. From now on Big Sam would be Joe's bodyguard.

Fogarty was acquainting Big Sam with his duties when Cap Goldberg arrived. Joe Goldberg, a captain on the Chicago police force, had been a nightly visitor at the Green Mill, at first as a cop and then as a friend.

"Joe," Cap announced exuberantly, "we're going hunting!"

"For who?"

"Pheasants. I got a pal over in Dubuque, Iowa. The county

sheriff. He invites me every year. This time I'm making it —and you're going along."

Fogarty threw Cap a look of gratitude and turned to Joe. Great idea. It'll do you good, Joe."

"And McGurn," Cap added. "Give him time to cool off."

"I don't need police protection," Joe said testily. "Anyway, I got to rehearse."

Cap grabbed Joe's arm. "You can rehearse in Dubuque. It'll be *quieter* there." It was an order.

Joe went. He was up at dawn, walked for miles and stayed in the open all day. He went on the wagon and trained down to a lean 165 pounds.

Cap did not mention McGurn until the second week. "No percentage, Joe," he said as they sat in the stillness of the autumn night and stared into a crackling campfire. "You can't buck the Outfit."

"I'm opening November second."

"They made you. They can break you."

Joe stiffened. "I'm not a hoodlum!" His voice rose defiantly. "I'm an entertainer."

"You're a piece of property. *Their* property. A valuable piece. You can fill a night club . . . or empty one across the street."

Joe said nothing. He did not consider himself a part of the criminal world but he conceded, to himself if to no one else, that he was not an alien in it either.

"Why don't you go to New York for a while?"

Joe smiled sardonically. "You can't beat the odds by ducking 'em."

Cap hesitated. "I thought it was all over between you and Gloria."

"It is."

"Not according to McGurn. I hear that's his real burn."

"McGurn is playing games."

"McGurn doesn't play games." Goldberg's eyes drilled Joe's. "Jack *has* to go through with it. He declared himself."

"So have I," said Joe, with finality.

Flamboyant advertisements appeared in the Chicago Sunday newspapers, October 30th, reading:

THE NEW RENDEZVOUS ANNOUNCES ITS OPENING, NOVEMBER 2! THE MOST ELABORATE AND SNAPPY GIRL REVUE EVER ATTEMPTED! STARRING JOE LEWIS, AMERICA'S GREATEST CAFÉ ENTERTAINER! AND TWELVE (12) UNADORNED DAUGHTERS OF EVE!

Anonymous warnings and threats, by telephone and notes, continued until Wednesday, November second. Goldberg, having failed to dissuade Joe, had moved in with him at the Commonwealth, sleeping in the other twin bed, with his gun holster hanging from the bedpost. Big Sam slept in an adjoining room, a .45 revolver under his pillow.

Joe did not leave his room all day Wednesday. At last he dressed. He adjusted his black tie and put a red carnation in the buttonhole of his white tuxedo.

Ten P.M. The phone rang. Joe answered it. "There's still time, Joe," an anonymous male voice exhorted. "Don't go or you'll be—"

Joe put down the receiver. "Let's go," he said.

The comedian, five feet seven and a half, was dwarfed by Fogarty, Goldberg and Big Sam as they cautiously marched the two blocks down Diversey Parkway to the brilliantly illuminated Rendezvous.

A crowd was fighting to get in and, inside, not an inch of standing room remained. The word had gotten around.

Captain Goldberg checked the room. His plainclothesmen were at their stations, at the head of every aisle and exit.

Fogarty checked the room. His armorers were inside and

outside. Three of them were perched on the roof of the gasoline service station across the street, one in mechanic's overalls keeping an eye on the entrance to the Rendezvous through the sights of a sawed-off shotgun.

Backstage, Joe peered through a slit in the curtain. Every table was occupied but one, the one he had reserved for Machine Gun Jack McGurn.

2   *A Rendezvous with Death*

Fogarty's twelve "unadorned daughters of Eve," as bereft of talent as of costumes, pranced off the stage. "And now, ladies and gentlemen," the leader of the Rendezvous band announced, "we are proud to present to you, in person, the comedy kid with the fastest patter routine in show business —Joe Lewis!"

A tumult of applause brought him on, the house lights dimmed and he was alone in the disk of glaring light. What a target I am, he thought, especially in this white suit. His eyes searched the room and focused on the lone unoccupied table at ringside. He began singing.

In case McGurn showed up with his machine gun, he had a pistol in the right side pocket of his jacket. A .22.

Halfway through his second song there was a shattering report from a ringside table. Joe stopped singing, his face ashen, his hand in his gun pocket. Captain Goldberg and his plainclothesmen sprang from the shadows and converged on the source. Fogarty and his strong-arm boys closed in, their rods out.

Joe was safe. The commotion had been caused by a clumsy busboy who had dropped a tray.

No one tried to kill Joe that night. But he killed business at the Green Mill.

Thursday . . . Friday . . . Saturday . . . Sunday . . . Monday . . . Tuesday. The Rendezvous was sold out every night and the week ended without incident. Fogarty was jubilant. "You were right, Joe," he chortled. "McGurn was bluffing." But he continued to walk Joe to and from the Commonwealth Hotel.

They were slightly mulled this early morning—almost 5 A.M., Wednesday, November 9th—and were half a block from the hotel when a black limousine pulled up. Three men came out, their hands in their pockets.

Fogarty moved fast. He shoved Joe into a doorway, shielding him as he whipped out a gun in each hand.

The three visitors moved in. The one in the middle was McGurn.

Joe forced his way from behind Fogarty and faced McGurn. "What do you want, Jack?"

McGurn's smile was as gentle as his voice. "I came to see you, Joe."

"I kind of figured that out."

"You and I always got along together." There was a note of conciliation in McGurn's voice.

"Who said we didn't?"

McGurn sighed. "We miss you, Joe. The old Mill's a morgue without you."

"You'll get another act."

McGurn's penetrating black eyes never left Joe's. "You made your point, Joe. You said you'd open—and you did."

He paused and looked at him as if he was an errant child.

"It's time to come back now."

"Not a chance, Jack."

McGurn hesitated, then smiled and extended his open right hand. "No hard feelings, Joe."

Joe shook his hand.

Then McGurn turned to Fogarty and held out his hand. "No hard feelings, John."

Fogarty measured McGurn. He slipped one gun in his right hip pocket but kept the other trained on McGurn's heart as he clasped his hand.

"Shake hands with Joe Lewis and John Fogarty," McGurn ordered his companions. They took their hands out of their pockets and complied. The social amenities concluded, the three hoodlums went back to their car.

Before stepping inside, McGurn turned. "I almost forgot, Joe. Gloria says hello."

A moment later the car was hurtling down Diversey.

"You're coming to my hotel," Fogarty said, as he put away his second gun. He lived at the Parkway on North Lincoln Park West, ten blocks south of the Commonwealth. His room would be safer.

"Nothing is going to happen," Joe said.

Fogarty glowered. "One night he'll come by and he'll be shaking hands with a Tommy gun. You're coming to the Parkway with me."

"I'm not moving."

Fogarty knew that overtone too well. "All right," he gave in. "But this has gone far enough. I'm going to see Bugs." Bugs was George Moran, boss of the North Side rum runners. Fogarty was confident he would get a square rattle from him. "I'll see Bugs between nine and ten in the morning." Fogarty accompanied Joe through the deserted lobby of the Commonwealth. *"Don't leave your room until I get there,"* he said.

Joe grinned. "You know I don't get up before one o'clock." He shook Fogarty's hand.

"Good evening, Mr. Lewis!" Casey, the elderly elevator operator, greeted him.

"Good morning, Mr. Casey," Joe responded. It was a daily ritual.

As the elevator slowly ascended, Joe thought of Schemer. Schemer Drucci. Fogarty's mention of Bugs Moran . . . five o'clock in the morning . . . the Commonwealth elevator . . .

Joe and Schemer had come up this elevator at this time of the morning many times, Schemer getting off at the eighth floor and Joe on the tenth. Joe knew Schemer's reputation but he took a man as he found him, and he knew Drucci only as a pleasant, mild-mannered man who closed the Green Mill more nights than he didn't. Joe was his favorite comedian. After the joint folded, they often went next door for ham and eggs, picked up the morning papers and walked to the hotel. Some nights they would have dames but they never took them to the Commonwealth. Mrs. Vera (Mama) Lauterman, the manager, would have broken their heads. She ran a respectable place. Kathy was an exception. Kathy was a kind of respectable girl.

Joe was doing his early show at the Mill one night when he saw Drucci come in. He cut his routine, raced through the finale and did not come back for the demanded encore.

"Nice sun tan, Schemer," he said, slipping into a chair at Drucci's table.

"Imported from Florida, Joey."

Joe looked furtively around the crowded room. "Get back there fast," he whispered, "if you want to keep it." As the mobsters' comic, it was his business to know the temperatures of his devotees: who was hot, who would soon be cold, et alii.

"Now I'll give you a tip," said Schemer, feigning resentment. "Don't cheat the second show."

Joe stood up. "Stay off the streets," he warned.

Drucci was truly irritated now. He did not have to stay off the streets, not on the North Side. Since Hymie Weiss had fallen dead with twelve slugs in his body in front of the Holy Name Cathedral, he was Headman on the North Side. "You need a drink, kid," he said, pouring a shot.

Joe threw down the drink. "Stay off the streets, Schemer," he repeated.

Schemer went out and glared down North Clark Street. He patted the automatic strapped to his waist and nodded to his two bodyguards.

They had walked two blocks when a police squad car pulled up. A cop and two detectives were inside. The cop, Leo Healy, came out and thumbed the three gangsters into the car. A few minutes later they were being booked, photographed and fingerprinted. Drucci was furious but unworried. He had made a phone call.

Within an hour Officer Healy was ordered to deliver Drucci to the Criminal Courts Building where Schemer's lawyer had secured a writ of habeas corpus.

Officer Healy handcuffed his prisoner and led him back into the squad car. Cop and criminal looked at each other with mutual contempt. In a little while the hoodlum would be free. Suddenly, according to Healy, Drucci began taunting him. A moment later, according to Healy, Drucci attempted to seize his service revolver.

The cop gave it to him. In the belly, four times.

Tiers of flowers encased his silver-trimmed coffin. Bugs Moran, his chief of staff and successor, led the mourners. The Schemer had been Number One only three months but everyone who was loyal to the North Side turned out, including the comedian who had warned him to keep off the streets.

Joe would have warned anyone in the same circumstance. Drucci had not been wanted by the police. The only reason they picked him up was because a blanket order had been issued to round up all known gangsters as a safeguard against possible frauds in the municipal election the following day. Joe had heard of the order and he thought he was doing everyone a favor, including the police, by cautioning Drucci to stay out of circulation.

"Don't feel sorry for him," Cap Goldberg told him as they drove back from the funeral.

"They didn't have to kill him," Joe said.

There was a silence.

"Dapper guy, wasn't he?" Goldberg commented.

"Yeah."

"Had his hair cut every day. Same barber."

Joe looked at Cap quizzically.

"Went in one day and saw a friend of his getting a shave. Sam Amatuna. Sam had been president of the Unione Siciliano only a few weeks but the North Side wanted to get rid of him. Schemer got rid of him. Didn't move him from the barber chair. Two slugs did it. Year ago last month." Cap paused. "Neat man, Vincent Drucci. He told the barber to finish shaving Sam."

"Here's your floor, Mr. Lewis."

He walked into the empty corridor, lost in thought. Vincent Drucci . . . Vincent Gebardi . . . Joe had warned Drucci just seven months ago . . . and McGurn had warned Joe tonight. "You made your point," his words echoed. "It's time to come back now." McGurn had opened the door . . . "Not a chance, Jack." Joe had slammed the door, and he remembered the cold, vindictive look in McGurn's eyes that moment.

Joe noiselessly unlocked the door to his room. Cap Goldberg was asleep. Joe started undressing. He pulled out a sheaf of hundred-dollar bills, his first week's pay, and his eyes glistened.

This was the big year. 1927. The year Babe Ruth slammed sixty home runs. The year Tunney licked Dempsey in Chicago. The year Joe Lewis' salary went into four figures. He was on his way. Another year or two like this one and he would be up there with Sophie Tucker and Harry Richman.

Dawn was breaking over Chicago when Joe fell asleep.

The shrill ring of the telephone awakened him. Joe sleepily fumbled for the receiver. "Hello . . ."

"Don' open da door," a man's voice warned him in a heavy Italian accent.

Joe roused himself. "Who is this?"

"Don' open da door—fa *nobody*." An instant later, Joe heard the click of the receiver.

The other bed was empty. Cap had gone to work. Joe looked at this watch on the table next to his bed. It was 9:15 A.M., the middle of his night. He turned over. But he could not sleep.

"Gloria says hello." That was the last thing McGurn had said. Did McGurn really believe he had gone back for a rematch? . . . What would McGurn and his two men have done if Fogarty had not drawn both guns as fast as he had? . . . Why had an anonymous friend, someone afraid to give his name, called to warn him?

Joe slowly sat up. Everything was suddenly different. He had, for the first time in his life, a premonition of disaster.

"Don' open da door—fa *nobody*." Joe stared at the door, and waited.

The knock came at 10:30 A.M.

Joe, still in pajamas, clambered out of bed and, without hesitation, went to the door and unlocked it. The action was almost reflex: it did not occur to him not to open it or even to ask who was there.

Three men, none of whom he recognized, brushed past him. Joe automatically closed the door.

"Just one favor, Joe," the spokesman asked. "Don't yell."

The spokesman drew a .45 revolver. One of his helpers pulled out a .38 and moved behind Joe.

Joe braced himself for the first bullet. It did not come.

An horrendous blow struck him from behind. He turned as he fell and saw the man with the .38 raising his arm to clout him again.

The third assailant was unsheathing a hunting knife.

Pain coiled around his brain, tighter, tighter, and sank its fangs deeper and deeper. A searing, blinding flash, and he felt his head being torn apart.

The two gunmen used the butts of their revolvers. They hammered his skull until he was unconscious, and they continued pounding.

The knifeman went to work. He punched the blade into Joe's left jaw as far as he could, ripped his face open from ear to throat, and went on cleaving impassively, like a butcher.

Joe did not yell.

3   *The Joker*

His first reaction was an impression that he was drowning. He was lying on the floor, his face immersed in a pool of blood. He remained in a state of shock for several seconds. He could not see.

Joe tried to lift his right hand to his eyes. The arm was devoid of feeling or strength. He tried his left hand. It obeyed his will, with difficulty. In a moment the first beam of light pierced the darkness. He had wiped the film of blood from his eyes. He could see but everything was blurred and out of focus.

Without turning his head, he investigated his surroundings. His attackers had gone. He was alone, as far as he could see. At last he attempted to move his legs. It was futile. He seemed paralyzed.

With tortured effort, he slowly turned his head. In the full-length mirror of the closet door he saw the horrifying image of a man, his left jaw hanging loose in a great raw flap, the splintered bones and slashed muscles exposed.

His trembling fingers inched their way to the top of his head. Blood was spurting from a gaping wound.

I might as well lay down and die, he decided, it will only be a few minutes. He remained motionless for several minutes. The blood clogged his throat and flooded his eyes. Slowly, every movement an agony, he lifted his good hand to wipe his eyes again.

His vision cleared momentarily and two faces came into focus, the photographs that had and always would be propped up on the dresser of every hotel room he called home, the faded pictures of his father and mother. The soft brown eyes of Pauline Klewan looked down upon her sixth child as he lay dying. Soon he would join Abe, his father.

Joe thought of his mother and father, his brothers and sisters, but only for a moment. They were different. They lived quiet lives, they were foreign to violence. He had been almost a stranger to them, and they to him, since he left home. They swiftly receded into his past as other voices intruded—

"You'll never live to open . . ." Great kidder, McGurn. He had meant he would not live to open the second week.

"No percentage, Joe. You can't buck the Outfit." Cap Goldberg was right, as usual.

"**Don'** open da door—fa *nobody*." He was going to die without knowing the name of the unknown friend who had tried to save his life.

He looked up at the clock. 11:18. He wasn't dying as fast as he figured . . . Maybe I ought to give myself a chance, he thought. Johnny Torrio walked away with three bullets in him. I'm as tough as Torrio. *Was,* anyway. It's worth a try . . .

The telephone. He had to get to the phone. He focused on it. It was fifteen feet away, maybe twelve. I should be able to make it. Hell, I *got* to make it.

Joe tried to stand up. It was impossible. He began crawling. A current of pain shot through his body. Both legs and his right arm remained helpless. The left arm had to support all of his weight as he dragged himself across the room. Every inch was a new torment. It took fifteen minutes and he nearly passed out several times but at last he reached the table next to his bed.

He tried to reach the phone with his right hand. The right one's gone, the right one's gone, he repeated to himself. He stretched his left hand but the table was too high. He pulled the cord and the phone crashed to the floor.

Joe picked up the receiver. The voice of an operator was on. "Number, please!"

"Help!" His slashed lips formed the word but no sound came out.

"Number, please!" the operator repeated.

Joe again cried for help but he was mute. He thought his line was dead and put the receiver back in the cradle. He did not realize that his vocal cords had been severed.

He tried to find an alternative but the terrible concussion had clouded his brain. There must be a way out, he thought. *I got to get help!* How? He was trapped on the tenth floor of a hotel and he could not lift himself to the window sill. Hopelessness engulfed him.

Where was Mary? Mary Keane, the housemaid. As if he didn't know. Mary had strict orders not to disturb him until 2 P.M. He would be gone by then.

The door. That was the last means of escape. If he could only reach the door . . .

He dragged himself on all fours to the door, leaving a trail of blood across the carpet. At last he made it. He reached for the knob, nearly blacking out before he touched it. The knob refused to turn. His hand was slippery with blood.

It took him five minutes to open the door. His strength was almost spent.

The hallway was deserted. He could not crawl any more. There was not time. He had to get on his feet if it killed him.

He clawed the wall with his left hand, clung to the door knob and pushed his body up. He swayed, lost his balance and fell to the floor. He kept trying—over and over again—until his nails were torn, until it seemed impossible that he had strength left to rise once more.

But he did.

Now, hugging the wall, he inched his way along the corridor. Every step was a hell. He knocked on the door next to his. Big Sam's. No answer. Where the hell was Big Sam? He kept on. Someone had to show up. He heard the elevator at the other end. Sooner or later Casey had to stop at the tenth floor.

At last the outline of a woman became visible. As she came into focus his eyes lighted up. Mary Keane! Good old Mary, the floor maid, a bundle of fresh linen under her arm, was making her rounds.

"Mary!" Joe tried to call out, not knowing that he was incapable of speech.

Mary did not see him. He could tell by the preoccupied look on her face. Please God, he prayed, lift her head just an inch. Don't let her go into a room before she sees me. Oh, Mary!

Mary lifted her head an inch and saw Joe.

He was overjoyed. Mary would bring help.

An instant later, Joe was plunged into fathomless despair. Mary, on seeing him, had fainted . . . It's only me, Mary. Joe Lewis. I wouldn't hurt you . . .

Joe clawed, pushed, dragged and drove himself along the fifty-foot purgatory, past the prostrated floor maid, he fading out of and back into consciousness almost on alternate seconds . . . Where is everybody who lives on this floor? Won't *anyone* come? Big Sam . . . Now he remembered. He had gotten rid of Big Sam. "I look ridiculous with that ape following me around," he had told Fogarty. Fogarty . . . Where's Fogarty? . . . At that moment, Fogarty was shaking hands with Bugs Moran in a garage on North Clark Street, Moran's headquarters. "From now on," Bugs assured Fogarty, "Joe has nothing to worry about."

Joe reached the elevator at last. He tried to push the button but his left hand was now useless too. He could not raise it from his side.

Instinct took over. He bowed his head and, with his last bit of strength, he fiercely butted the elevator button. He listened to the buzzer signal, the most beautiful sound he had ever heard. He pushed it as long as he could and then slid to the floor, completely out, a triumphant smile on what was left of his face.

The elevator doors rolled open and Casey waited. At last he looked out. Casey blanched and slammed the door.

A moment later, Casey burst into the manager's office and, after partially composing himself, managed to inform Mrs. Lauterman that Joe Lewis was lying on the tenth floor, either dying or dead.

Mama Lauterman sighed. "Ach, Casey, old as you are! Still being fooled by Cho Lewis and his chokes." She looked at Casey with disdain and turned away.

"This isn't a joke, Mrs. Lauterman," Casey cried hysterically, drawing his finger across his neck. "He's been slashed from ear to ear!"

She nodded indulgently. "Look again. You'll see it's from ketchup or red ink . . . I know."

"It's blood—real blood! Casey persisted. "Call an ambulance—right away!"

Mrs. Lauterman recalled the countless practical jokes Joe had played on her, Casey and almost everyone else in the hotel. They were harmless, and some of them were hilarious, but she was busy and, admittedly, a little weary of being the butt of his pranks.

"Like a week ago Saturday. Remember, Casey?" Casey remembered. Police Headquarters had called her on the phone. "Mrs. Lauterman?" The caller asked in a thick Irish brogue. "This is Police Sergeant O'Rourke. I'm sorry to have to break the news but we just found Joe Lewis' body in Lake Michigan, dead. Will you please pack all of his clothes? I will be right over for them."

Mrs. Lauterman and Casey tearfully superintended the packing of Joe's effects. Fifteen minutes later, there was a knock on the door of his room.

"Who is it?" Mrs. Lauterman asked in a sob-choked voice.

"Sergeant O'Rourke," replied the man with the Irish accent.

Mrs. Lauterman opened the door. Joe Lewis, in an over-sized sergeant's uniform, stood outside. "And it's a foine evening for boating, Mrs. Lauterman," he greeted her in an impeccable Corkian dialect.

"I'm not bidink *this* time," she told Casey. "Maybe it will be a lessing to him."

Casey was shaking. "Mr. Lewis is hurt," he said grimly. "Real bad."

Mrs. Lauterman's eyes moved to the clock on the wall. She became pale. Something terrible *was* wrong. Joe Lewis had not been up *before* noon since he had moved into the Commonwealth. She was out of the office before Casey. "Get an ambulance—emerchency!" she shouted to the telephone operator as she ran past her. "And the bolice!"

The police arrived first. "He's a goner." The younger cop shook his head. "I'll call the morgue."

The second cop got down on his knees and examined Joe more closely. "He's still breathing . . ."

"The ambulance should be here any minute," Mrs. Lauterman told them.

"No time," said the elder cop. "Give me a hand, Mac." The two cops picked up Joe, piled him in their patrol car and rushed him to Columbia Memorial Hospital, three blocks away.

The interne looked at the little man on the stretcher. "A black pill," he requested. Not much chance of this one reaching Surgery alive. The Sister at his side nodded and her lips moved in prayer.

A call was put in for Dr. Harvey Cushing, the eminent brain surgeon. He was unavailable.

An emergency call was put in for *any* surgeon in the hospital.

Fogarty, Cap Goldberg and a dozen newspapermen paced the hospital corridor. Now and then, one of them would unroll a newspaper he was carrying and reread the headlines in the afternoon extras:

CABARET STAR'S THROAT SLASHED!

VICIOUS KNIFING SILENCES COMEDIAN!

JOE LEWIS STABBED, NEAR DEATH!

Six hours had passed since Joe had been wheeled into Surgery. He was still on the operating table, clinging to a spark of life that had almost been extinguished countless times, only to be revived each time by a man he had never seen, an obscure general practitioner, Dr. Daniel Orth, performing the most miraculous operation of his career.

As Joe fought for his life, the wheels of the law— Gang Law, the only law that was enforced in Chicago during the anarchy of Prohibition—began moving. Fogarty inserted advertisements in the morning newspapers offering a reward of $10,000 cash for information leading to the identities of Joe's attackers. Bugs Moran, speaking for the North Side mob, pledged an additional $20,000 and, more realistically, assigned his ace torpedoes, Pete and Frank Gusenberg, to help Fogarty maintain a round-the-clock guard at Columbia Memorial Hospital. That is, if Joe beat the rap.

Moran knew what he was doing. If Joe lived, he would still be under a death sentence. McGurn would *have* to finish him, in self-defense, because he alone could identify his attackers.

That night, a Chicago correspondent for *Variety,* the theatrical scratch sheet, optimistically wired his office in New York: "Joe Lewis may survive minus his voice, one arm and his mind. He was slashed from one end of his body to the other. The deepest of twelve gashes is in his throat, another deprives him of the use of his right arm and hand, while the most serious is his skull fracture. His brain is clouded, his tongue is ripped and useless."

McGurn's knifeman was positive he had killed Joe. He made a slight miscalculation: he missed the jugular vein by the breadth of a hair.

Fogarty blocked the door to Joe's room. "I said *nobody* goes in there."

"I told you, I'm Joe's brother," the stranger insisted, "his oldest brother."

Fogarty eyed him suspiciously. "You don't look like Joe's brother to me."

The stranger fished in his pocket and pulled out a business card.

AL'S MEN'S SHOP—ENGLEWOOD, N.J.
AL KLEWAN, PROP.

Fogarty studied the card. "Joe's brother—with a monicker like that? What do you take me for?"

"A violinist," the stranger replied, noting the violin case gripped in Fogarty's right hand.

Fogarty smiled. The hick looked as if he came from New Jersey and he sounded a little like Joe, you couldn't tell whether he was ribbing or on the square. But he wasn't taking any chances. He handed back the card.

"You'll need more proof than that, mister."

The stranger searched his wallet and found a snapshot of the four Klewan brothers, one of them unmistakably Joe. Fogarty put down the violin case and shook his hand.

"I read about it in the newspaper," Al said. "I grabbed the first train."

Joe's room was small and bleak.

"Joe . . ." Al's voice called out hopefully.

Joe's head was swathed in bandages.

Al drew closer. "Joe . . ."

Joe was still unconscious.

"Joe . . ." Al could not hold back the tears any longer.

Fogarty took his arm and led him to his room across the corridor. He poured a drink and told him to relax, Joe would be all right.

"He always wanted to be in show business . . ." Al sighed. "And I always tried to discourage him."

"You can't discourage guys like Joe—from anything."

Al nodded. He was twelve years older than Joe but he was closer to him than anyone else in the family. "Nobody could change Joe . . ."

He quit DeWitt Clinton High School after two years, and no amount of threats, promises and cajolery by the family could make him return. A few days later, he enlisted in the U.S. Marine Corps but was discharged after his elder sister Henrietta intercepted his travel orders and exposed his falsification of age.

"I'll be in uniform tomorrow," he told Henrietta a week later.

"No, Joe," she cried, embracing him. "You'll be killed!"

Joe loved to tease Henrietta. "Who's the Western Union fighting?" He had become a messenger boy.

Out of respect to his mother, who had wept at the prospect of her fifteen-year-old son going to war, Joe waited until 1918 to join the Merchant Marine. He was en route to France on a troop ship at the ripened age of sixteen, an officers' messman, no class.

The war was over in a few months and Joe came back with a consuming ambition to get into show business. He had wanted to amuse people as long as he could remember. At P.S. 184 he had been the first to volunteer for all entertainments. In his early teens he had entered every amateur contest he could find: he had made the rounds of the neighborhood theatres, fraternal organizations, dance halls and cabarets nightly. Any place with a stage. Anyone who would listen to him.

Now, with his schooling behind him, he could give his undivided time to being an entertainer. The pickings were lean. After singing for a few months—in Church choirs, synagogues, at Elks smokers, B'nai B'rith initiations, from the sidewalks of Harlem to picnics at Far Rockaway—he had nothing to show for his efforts except a tiny gold medal, first prize in an amateur contest conducted by the Fylo Club on 115th Street, and two one-dollar bills for winning an amateur competition at the Regent Theatre in Harlem with a current song hit—

In Room Two Hundred and Two
The walls keep talking to you . . .

"Soon you will be good enough maybe Murray will take you in his act," Al commented wryly when he saw him at Yom Kippur services. Their brother Murray, four years older than Joe, was the only other member of the family who had been attracted to the stage. He was a blackface comedian, not a very good one, and his vaudeville career had ended in Muncie, Indiana, where he was stranded. He had walked back to New York and his feet had never been the same. Joe did not want to be reminded of Murray and his fallen arches.

Mama Klewan was concerned about Joe but she did nothing until Henrietta, the family radar, heard that he was rehearsing for a third-rate burlesque show in Hoboken. "I will not have it," Mama said. Becoming an actor in those days, to use Joe's words, "was a death worse than fate."

He would not think of defying his mother, let alone hurting her, but he had to be honest with himself. He left home and the burlesque show.

Al, who ran a clothing store in Easton, Pennsylvania, offered him a job. Joe needed eating money and he took it. He remained in Easton ten months, selling men's haberdashery during the day and haunting the dance halls at night.

His patience ultimately was rewarded. A friend who sang in the Honey Boy Jazz Band was stricken with laryngitis and he persuaded the leader to let Joe go on for him. Joe almost balked when he was obliged to appear in blackface but he corked his face and, judging from the response, he was convinced that he had not surpassed his brother Murray's performance in Muncie. Actually, no one was aware of him. It was January 15, 1920. Prohibition went into effect at midnight.

Joe did so well as a haberdashery salesman that he received an offer to manage a clothing store in Norristown, Pa., at fifty dollars a week. He remained in Norristown six months, until he had saved $200, and then left for Atlantic City. He was eighteen years old, a war veteran and a successful merchant but he was not in show business. The time had come.

He spent freely in the dives along the boardwalk, mostly at the Columbia Beer Garden, hoping to attract attention. One night he recognized Roscoe (Fatty) Arbuckle, the famous movie comedian. He followed him for several hours, too shy to introduce himself. In ten days Joe was broke. No one was hiring singers, especially amateurs. He wanted to go back to New York but he did not have the fare and he was too proud to ask Al.

He applied for a job at a department store and was put to work at fifteen dollars a week. He lasted three hours. A floor-walker called him a "Jew bastard" and Joe belted him unconscious.

He looked for work, any kind of work, the rest of the day without success. In the evening he walked past the Columbia Beer Garden many times. It was after midnight before desperation drove him inside.

"Buy me a beer," he begged the bartender, digging into the free lunch. "I haven't eaten since yesterday morning." It was the first time he had ever asked for a handout.

The bartender drew a beer. Joe had given him a buck tip three days previously.

"I got to find work," Joe told him. "There must be something I can do here."

The leader of the band came to the bar for a whiskey. Joe grabbed his arm. "Give me a break. Let me sing just one song!"

The leader did not bother to reply.

The bartender interceded. "Let him work out his beer."

A few minutes later, Joe was singing "Macushla," the ballad that had won him first prize in the Fylo Club amateur night. It would not affect the phonograph sales of John McCormack, the famed Irish tenor, but the crowd at the Columbia Beer Hall liked it and wanted more. He came back with "County Downs" and "Stumblin' All Around," a currently popular song which he dramatized by stumbling across the floor, unknowingly casting the die of a character that would make him the greatest night club entertainer of his time.

Joe stumbled off stage but he ran back to pick up the coins that the customers were throwing.

He counted the money on the bar, twelve dollars and thirty-six cents, and he stared in astonishment at the stacks of silver and copper. Ten minutes ago he had been a nobody. Now he was in show business.

The bartender, an Irishman, was misty-eyed. "You're a fortunate lad," he sighed enviously, "to be blessed with a voice like that . . ."

Al finished his drink in Fogarty's room. "That night spoiled him," he said. "I tried to get him back in the clothing business but there wasn't a chance. 'I pick up ten to fifteen bucks a night—and free beer,' he told me. 'And I can sleep all day . . .' " Al stopped. The thought of Joe lying helplessly across the hall with his throat slashed, strangled Al and he broke down.

Joe regained consciousness the following day. He stared at Al and Fogarty, who were sitting at his bedside. He tried to speak but it was impossible. He lifted his left hand and weakly made a sign that he recognized them, then lapsed into unconsciousness.

Al and Fogarty hugged each other. It had been only a moment of awareness but that moment was sufficient cause for celebration.

Dr. Orth chanced to pass Fogarty's room long after midnight as the Gusenberg brothers were hauling in a couple cases of whiskey, reinforcements for Joe's coming-out party that had been in progress since the previous forenoon. Through the door he saw eight or ten men persuading two nurses, already well lubricated, that they would perform the Charleston with greater efficacy if they removed their uniforms.

"Out—all of you!" Dr. Orth caught the startled nurses unbuttoning and buttoning themselves simultaneously. Everyone complied with Dr. Orth's order except Fogarty and the Gusenbergs.

"I said *all* of you!"

Fogarty put his hand on Dr. Orth's shoulder. "Doc," he said gently, "you did a great job on Joe—and all of us are grateful—but he ain't saved yet."

Dr. Orth stared at him. "He isn't even conscious yet!"

Fogarty became grim. "You can only save him from what they *did,* but you can't save him from what they *will* do. That's why we're here—and why we're staying."

"This is a hospital, Mr. Fogarty, not a bawdy house."

"Sorry about the dames." Fogarty was contrite. "After this I'll see that the boys bring their own."

Hoodlums continued to drop in at all hours of the day and night to inquire about Joe's condition and, while they were there, drink a few toasts to his health and take a hand in Fogarty's continuous poker and crap games.

The newspapers demanded police action and the police went through the motions of an investigation, as they had and would in the murders of more than 5,000 citizens in Chicago during Prohibition, a saturnalia of crime in which they would establish an unparalleled record of detection unblemished by a single conviction.

Danny Cohen, questioned by the press, gave his version of the story: "Lewis told me he was going on the stage and make more money. He told the customers he was leaving. I didn't like that so I fired him." When a reporter insinuated that McGurn was a partner in the Green Mill and had engineered the attempted killing with Cohen's knowledge if not at his instigation, Danny exploded indignantly. "McGurn hasn't a nickel in my place," he declared. "If he went after Joe it wasn't on my account. McGurn is just a customer . . ."

The Chicago *Tribune* conjectured, with Detective Sergeant John J. Sullivan as its authority, that "Lewis had the sort of a face that women love, and the man who stabbed him may have done so to punish the singer for philandering with his wife or sweetheart."

Assistant State Attorneys Emmett Byrne and Joe Nicolai were assigned to the case. May Mack, an entertainer at the Rendezvous, was picked up and questioned. A few hours later she was released.

Many theories were advanced, among them that Joe had attempted suicide.

Joe emerged from his coma in another twenty-four hours but he was incapable of uttering a sound. He struggled to speak for two weeks. At last, on Thanksgiving Day, he heard his voice again. It was a faint, hoarse whisper, strange and unintelligible, like the cry of a wounded animal. His speech center, behind the frontal lobe of his brain, had been destroyed.

He recognized Al but he could not remember his name. Noticing Al's naïve familiarity with the Gusenbergs, he wanted to warn him that they were killers, but he did not know how. Al would find out that night. Fogarty, hearing strange footsteps near Joe's door, opened his violin case for the first time in his presence. Al saw the sawed-off shotgun inside and fainted.

A new terror took hold of Joe. Not only was he physically incapable of articulation but he was powerless to think in terms of language. His subconscious groped for another tongue. He had learned a smattering of Hebrew before his Bar Mitzvah and had heard Yiddish in his home, he cudgeled his brain for a word but none came.

Joe was in a panic. He remembered the lyrics of "Macushla" but he did not know the names of the objects in his room—the bed, table, chair, curtains, mirror or light.

He wanted a pencil but did not know what it was called. At last he pointed to one in Fogarty's pocket. Once he had it, he could not write. His right hand was still useless and his left hand could not form a letter any better than his lips had.

Frantic, he pointed to a newspaper on the table. Fogarty handed it to him. Joe stared at the front page. It might as well have been printed in Singhalese. The letters of the alphabet had been erased from his memory, along with all other learning—except "Macushla."

Joe turned his head and sobbed. His greatest fear was confirmed. He was crippled mentally as well as physically.

Days passed. There was no change in his condition. "He seems to have lost the will to live," Dr. Orth admitted.

Joe had given up.

The door opened and a middle-aged priest appeared in the doorway. "Oh, pardon me," he excused himself. "Wrong room." The door closed. A moment later the door swung open again and the priest reappeared. "Aren't you Mr. Lewis?" he asked.

Joe nodded.

The priest entered the room. "My sister has been telling me about you," he said. "She is in room 323. I always confuse it with yours, 332." He was beside Joe's bed. "I am Father Heitzer." He touched Joe's hand. "Can I help you, son?"

Joe stared at him. Help? What was that?

Father Heitzer pulled a chair close to the bed and sat down. "You must not be afraid," he said, speaking slowly and enunciating each syllable carefully.

Oh, God, Joe thought, he's going to give me religion—and it isn't even my brand.

"What has happened to you, son," the priest went on prosaically, "has happened to thousands of people after certain kinds of accidents. You have forgotten how to speak and read and write."

Joe gaped at him through the heavy bandages that almost covered his face. Who had sent him? And why did he toss off his inability to speak as lightly as if he had merely lost a handkerchief? What was he selling?

"I am an English teacher—at Notre Dame." The priest opened a book he had carried under his arm. "You must have confidence in me, son. I am going to teach you how to speak and read and write again."

It was an old story to Father J. A. Heitzer. He had been called to the bedsides of lawyers and truck drivers, prize fighters and statesmen, poets and peasants. The human brain reacted identically under certain types of shock. His sister was at Columbia Memorial Hospital but it was not an accident that he opened Joe's door that Sunday morning.

"The first letter of the alphabet is *a,*" he said, pointing to the symbol on the opening page of his book, *The First Reader*.

Joe looked at the letter. He had no recollection of having seen it before.

"You open your mouth like this . . . A . . . A . . . A . . . A . . . Repeat after me—A . . . A . . . A . . . A."

Joe tried. A croaking sound came out.

The priest beamed. *"Wonderful,* Joe! Once more. A . . . A . . . A . . ."

5   *Down on the Levee*

Father Heitzer came up from South Bend every Sunday. He brought large cards with letters printed on them and he held them up for Joe to study. Slowly, with patient, painstaking effort, he retaught Joe the alphabet. Light filtered through the blacked-out areas of Joe's mind and he began to remember.

The letter *t* was the most difficult. It always came out *s*. For ten years he would lisp *bass* when he meant *bath*. He would never be able to pronounce *District Attorney*. The fastest-talking comedian in Chicago now struggled with *cat* and *dog*. Often he lost confidence, positive that he would never be able to speak again, but Father Heitzer always restored his faith and gave him the courage to go on.

"You *will* speak again," the priest reassured him over and over.

"Sing?"

Father Heitzer nodded. "You will sing too, Joe."

Joe looked at his teacher and his doubts surrendered to the reliance reflected in the priest's strong, serene face. He believed Father Heitzer. They had been born of different faiths but they were of the same faith.

It was a Sunday late in December. Father Heitzer had just complimented him on his progress and Dr. Orth had promised to discharge him before Christmas. For a man who could not move his right hand, who had a hole the size of a dollar on top of his head, who was stitched from his left ear to his jugular vein and whose memory was obliterated by vast expanses of darkness, Joe was at peace with the world and grateful.

A series of miracles had enabled him to survive the ordeal. He would not have made it without the remarkable constitution he had inherited from his mother, an amazing woman today hardy and alert in her ninety-seventh year. He could not have picked himself off the floor had he not been in perfect physical condition. He had Cap Goldberg and his Iowa hunting trip to thank for that. His blood would have run out if an anonymous cop had not had the presence of mind to rush him to the hospital in a squad car instead of waiting for the ambulance. He would have taken a one-way ride to Surgery if Dr. Orth, a general practitioner who called himself a corn doctor, had not performed a masterpiece in his seven-hour battle with death. And he would not be able to speak if Father Heitzer had not come unbidden to his room.

Never again would he repeat the words he had said to Fogarty the day McGurn threatened him, "I can take care of myself." In room 332 he had learned that no man takes care of himself. For the rest of his life, wherever he was, he would rise each day, lift the window shade, look out and murmur in wonderment, "What do you know? . . . I made it again."

Weeks passed and the complaints against Fogarty's all-night gambling and drinking parties became so vehement that Dr. Orth organized a group of his confreres, armed with surgical instruments, to rout the hoodlums from their hospital.

Fogarty, caught by surprise without his violin case, shook off his pursuers long enough to take refuge in Joe's room. It took the vigilantes almost an hour to discover that the man curled under the covers of Lewis' bed was Fogarty and the figure huddled in a chair at the window, with a shawl over his head, was Joe.

The mob was evicted and Columbia Memorial was quiet again.

One day, Big Sam shuffled in, a doleful look on his fight-scarred face. "Bad news, Joe," he whispered. "McGurn's in the hospital."

Joe tightened. "Here?"

Big Sam nodded. "Went into a booth to make a call. Slugs bounced back. A couple went into his guts." Big Sam shook his head mournfully. "Bad news. The sonofabitch is gonna live."

Joe's friends were busy.

Cap Goldberg came in with Chief of Detectives Schumacher. "We picked up one of 'em," Cap whispered excitedly after he had thumbed Big Sam out.

Joe's eyes, peering out from his bandages, betrayed no reaction. "We *know* he's one of the three," Chief Schumacher added, "but we'll need your identification—to make it official."

Joe shook his head.

"Don't be a damn fool," Cap growled. "This rat tried to kill you. He's a public menace as long as he's free."

Joe shook his head.

"You're not putting the finger on him." Chief Schumacher's

patience was running out. "We've nailed him. All we're asking is a little co-operation."

Joe continued to shake his head.

Cap Goldberg knew it was futile to argue with Joe when he could speak; in his present state it was insane. He nodded to Chief Schumacher, who left the room. "I think we're pretty good friends, Joe." Cap's voice quavered. "I've done you a couple favors and I think I got a right to ask you for one. I'm asking you to help us."

Joe promised nothing, by word or expression.

Across the hall, Fogarty, the Gusenbergs and a couple other North Side rum runners took time out from their poker game to watch Chief Schumacher lead a squat Italian, about five feet three inches tall, into Joe's room.

The hoodlum froze when he saw Joe. The last time he had seen him was the morning he had ripped his throat open.

Joe looked at him without a flicker of recognition.

At last, Schumacher took the hoodlum out and Goldberg pulled up a chair close to Joe. "He *was* one of 'em—wasn't he?"

Joe shook his head.

"You're lying, Joe. He nearly passed out when he saw you. He would have if he hadn't been full of coke." Cap leaned closer. "Help us do our job, Joe," he begged. "Was he one of the three who attacked you?"

Again Joe shook his head.

Cap lost his temper. "You're a bigger sucker than I thought you were." He stood up. "The 'code,'" he lashed contemptuously. "The good old 'code.' Everything goes— rape, arson, murder—everything except helping a cop do his duty. Maybe McGurn'll give you a medal for Christmas." Cold with rage, he turned and walked away without saying good-bye.

"C-C-Cap . . . !" It took all of Joe's strength to cry out.

Goldberg was halfway out of the door when he heard Joe's

croaking voice. He turned to see Joe desperately trying to lift himself out of bed. Cap rushed to him.

Joe held out his trembling left hand and clutched Cap's arm. He tried to speak but no words came.

"I'm sorry, Joe, I lost my head." Goldberg gently forced him to lie back. "I shouldn't have bullied you. . . . I just wanted to get that little bastard for what he did to you."

Joe, still holding on to his arm, shook his head.

"Why, Joe?" The policeman spoke no longer in anger but in sadness. "Why do you want to save that dirty little killer? Why don't you let us put him away where he belongs?"

Joe reached for the pad and pencil Father Heitzer had given him. With his left hand he grimly and laboriously formed a crude, childishly blocked letter and another and another. At last he gave Cap Goldberg his answer:

WANT GET HIM MYSELF.

Someone beat him to it. Six days later, the knifeman was found in an alley, shot to death. Within a few months his two helpers were also liquidated by "a person or persons unknown."

Joe was released from the hospital four days before Christmas. He stood on the sidewalk outside Columbia Memorial, Fogarty holding his arm, and he took a deep breath. "Let's take a walk, John," he said.

Fogarty understood, or thought he did. "I'll pick up a couple dames."

"I said we're taking a walk." There was a hard note in Joe's voice.

They walked a long way, hardly exchanging a word. Joe was lost in thought. "Where are we going?" Fogarty asked at last.

"South Side."

Fogarty stopped. "Are you crazy?"

"I hear McGurn switched to the South Side."

"It's suicide crossing the line!"

"No guts?"

"Listen to reason, Joe."

Joe smiled and his long jagged scar glistened in the harsh light of a corner street lamp. "McGurn took his best shot. He can't do anything more to me."

Fogarty grabbed his arm. "It's no good. Let's go home."

"Hands off, John. This is my business."

Fogarty felt the .45 in his shoulder holster. "Let's go," he said.

They were coming out of a South Side honky-tonk a few hours later when two plainclothesmen, friends of Joe, stepped up. "You've walked enough for your first night," one of them said. "My buddy and I have been tailing you more than an hour—and *we're* getting tired."

"Thanks, Mac," Joe said. "John and I are going to have a java and then hit the sack."

"Don't worry about McGurn," the plainclothesman added, noting a familiar bulge on Joe's hip. "He'll be taken care of."

Joe suppressed a bitter smile. The law would never take care of McGurn. This was not the State of Illinois versus McGurn. This was Lewis versus McGurn. McGurn lived outside the law and, if he had anything to do with it, McGurn would die outside the law. McGurn had tried to kill him. Why shouldn't he try to kill McGurn? Didn't the Bible say an eye for an eye?

"I'll get him home right away," Fogarty assured the plainclothesmen. Satisfied, the officers waved good night and walked away.

Ten minutes later, on the next block, a newcomer on the police force who did not recognize Joe or Fogarty investigated the bulge on Joe's hip and, the following morning, he

was back on the front pages of the Chicago newspapers.
The *Tribune* reported:

"Joe Lewis, the well-known café entertainer, still bandaged
from his near-fatal slashing six weeks ago, was arrested last
night on leaving the Midnight Frolics Club with John
Fogarty. Lewis was charged with carrying a concealed
weapon."

Cap Goldberg was incredulous. "What the hell were you
doing on the South Side?" he asked.

"Lookin' for McGurn."

"But Twenty-second Street and Wabash! You *really* asked
for it."

"I started on Twenty-second and Wabash," Joe reminded
him. Nineteen twenty-five. Was it only two years ago?

Two years . . .

Roy Mack, who produced the floor show at the Midnight
Frolics, had caught his act with John Black and had told him
to look him up if he ever needed a job. He needed one a
week later and for the next year he sang and clowned at the
Frolics, four shows a night, starting at $115 a week.

He sang everything he knew on opening night, from
"Macushla" to "Dardanella" to "Eddy Steady," and the customers yelled for more. As they got stiffer, they became louder
and more insistent in their requests. By the fourth show, at
5 A.M., he had sung most of the notable arias of the day,
including "Barney Google," "Yes, We Have No Bananas,"
"Lovin' Sam," "The Sheik of Alabam'," "Ain't We Got Fun?"
and an Eskimo love call, "Oogie Oogie Wa Wa."

"Great opening, Mr. Lewis!" the doorman, Red McCann,
greeted him when the club ultimately closed at dawn. "Can
I get you a cab?"

"No, thanks," Joe said, slipping McCann a bill. "I feel like
walking."

It was the biggest night of his life and he had to walk three miles to his hotel. He had given the doorman his last dollar.

Joe almost starved the first week until he received his check but he drank more than a hundred dollars' worth of whiskey. Everyone wanted to set him up a drink and no one offered to buy him a sandwich. He would find this to be true wherever he played as long as he lived.

The Midnight Frolics was in the heart of the Levee, the most notorious red-light district in the country, with 50,000 official, authorized prostitutes and an almost equal number of procurers. Around the corner, at 2222 Wabash Avenue, was the Four Deuces, Big Jim Colossimo's joint. Joe hung out there between shows with Roy Mack and his younger brother Austin, a pianist who had the band at the Frolics.

Early one morning, Al Capone and his bodyguards stopped at Joe's table. "I hear you got a good act," the Big Guy, as he was called, told Joe. "Save me a table tomorrow night."

Roy Mack knew he could not keep Joe long at the Frolics. The underworld financed, directly or through dummies, most of the speakeasies, supplied them with liquor, protected them from the police and helped to support them with their patronage. The entertainers they liked remained, the others were dispatched to less discriminating communities. Joe Lewis would soon be out of the $115 league.

Austin Mack touched Joe's arm and whispered, "If you ever need a piano player . . ."

Joe nodded but the Four Deuces jazz band was playing so loud Austin was certain he had not heard him.

Capone became a regular customer at the Frolics. It was around the corner from the Metropole Hotel, his headquarters. It had sixteen chorus girls and dancing until dawn. And it had Lewis. Joe made the Big Guy laugh. There were not many who could.

One night Capone came in unannounced and went to a

rear table where Joe was talking to Ralph Gillette, one of the owners of the Frolics.

Gillette jumped to his feet, bowed and held a chair for his unexpected guest.

Capone fixed his pig eyes on Joe. "Are you having trouble with Gillette?" he asked, ignoring Gillette as if he were not there.

Joe was astounded. He and Gillette had been wrangling over money but how did Capone know? Joe had not yet learned that Capone knew everything that happened in Chicago. "No, Al," he said, "everything is okay."

Capone's face darkened. "If Gillette gives you any trouble, you tell me."

Gillette stood paralyzed with fear. At last he found his voice. "What kind of trouble could there be? We just decided to give Joe a raise . . . a nice raise." He turned to Joe. "You said three hundred, didn't you, Joe boy?"

"I said *four* hundred, Ralph—per week."

Gillette smiled apologetically. "Of course, Joe boy. And four hundred it is."

Capone still took no notice of Gillette. "If Gillette gives you any trouble, Joe," he went on, *"I'll* be your partner. You can pick out any joint in the Loop. I'll give you fifty G's to open and I don't want a nickel profit."

"Thanks, Al, but I think I'll stick with the Frolics . . ." Joe paused. "For a while, anyway."

"The fifty's ready any time," Capone said and walked out.

Gillette slumped in his chair and wiped the sweat from his neck.

"That's the second offer I've had this week," Joe said. "Danny Cohen wants me up on the North Side."

Gillette swallowed hard. "Go as far north as you can," he said.

This way of life—rum running, bootlegging, hijacking and the incidental murder and corruption that followed through thirteen years of organized anarchy after the Eighteenth Amendment—had its birth at 2222 Wabash Avenue with Colossimo, a cunning, ambitious dock-walloper from Palermo, Sicily, who had become the first of the Prohibition lords. He had brought Johnny Torrio, a relative of his wife, from New York to help him run his organization, and Torrio had brought Capone, a young thug who was on a hide-out from Brooklyn.

Capone started as a twenty-five-dollar-a-week mop-boy at the Four Deuces in 1919. In a few months he was making seventy-five dollars opening the door to Colossimo's car and acting as a bouncer at the club. Big Jim took a liking to him and made him his personal bodyguard. On an afternoon in May, 1920, Big Jim was shot to death in the Four Deuces by "a person or persons unknown," who also divested him of $150,000 pocket money that he carried in a sheaf of thousand-dollar bills. Capone was on an errand at the other end of town.

Torrio took over and Capone became his bodyguard. "There's no need for all this killing," Torrio told him. "This is a good business and it ought to be run right—like the shoe business or the soap business. There's enough for all of us." One day, a car pulled up alongside Torrio's and raked it with gunfire. Torrio's chauffeur was killed and Torrio escaped with a bullet-perforated hat. Two days later, Torrio and his wife were trapped in a fusillade of fifty-one machine gun bullets. Three slugs, poisoned with garlic, tore through Torrio's body. On both days Capone was otherwise engaged on the other side of Chicago.

Torrio left and Capone seized control, first of the Unione Siciliano, the whiskey industry and the underworld—7,500 speakeasies, 8,000 other spigots in drug stores, gin flats and bootleggers on call, 2,500 brothels and 2,000 horse-racing handbooks in addition to two hundred major gambling clubs. He may have been the lousiest bodyguard in the history of

Chicago but he now controlled its heart and nerve centers—
the Loop, the City Hall and the Police Department—under
his official seal, "Al for All and All for Al."

"The Eighteenth Amendment is an unenforceable law and
a bad law," thundered Clarence Darrow, the celebrated criminal lawyer. "It should be treated with contempt."

The public needed no urging. The measure of its contempt was one hundred million dollars a year, the income of
Capone's syndicate.

Commerce of these proportions stimulated competition
and, when ambition or avarice inspired business practices
generally regarded as dishonorable, the victims, unable to
appeal to any legal authority, substituted justice for the law.
Accordingly, arrests, trials and executions were held coin-
stantaneously on any street or alley that happened to be ex-
pedient. There was no alternative. Legal jurisprudence
provides for the official shooting, hanging, cooking or gassing
of those found guilty of certain crimes but it is not equipped
to prosecute crime within the criminal empire. Notwithstanding, barbarians of all ages, Eolithic to Atomic, have required
laws and penalties governing right and wrong. Each man set-
tles his accounts in his own way, with or without legal authority. As long as he lives up to his code of morality, whether
it is high or low by others' standards, *he* can have no sense of
guilt.

Capone was faithful to his code. "A crook is a crook and
there's something healthy about his frankness in the matter,"
he contended. "But any guy who pretends he's enforcing the
law, and steals on his authority, is a snake. The worst type
of these punks is the big politician. You can only get a little
of his time because he spends so much time covering up so
nobody will know he's a thief. A hard-working crook hates
'em and won't depend on 'em."

"Maybe I break the law . . ." Capone would look around
a speakeasy at the leaders of Chicago industry, society, cul-

ture and government. "So do they—with every drink. At
least I don't drink." Capone, the teetotaler, had no difficulty
rationalizing. "Chicago voted six to one against Prohibition.
The only reason the Eighteenth Amendment was passed
was because the Drys had been organized for fifty years.
The drinkers had no organization at all, they were too busy
drinking. There were seventy-five hundred saloons in Chicago
before Prohibition and they took in a hundred million bucks
a year at the old prices. Someone had to throw liquor on
that thirst . . ."

"I can't change conditions," Capone told Joe one night,
"I just meet them without backing up."

"That's all I'm trying to do, meet conditions without
backing up," Joe told Cap Goldberg after the police picked
him up.

There was no sympathy in Cap's face. "And you claimed
you were an entertainer," he said, "not a hoodlum."

Joe could not answer. He had begun to hemorrhage.

6   *A Study in Black*

Chicago, Chicago,
That toddlin' town . . . that toddlin' town.

Joe listened to the clamorous chorus as it came over the
portable radio Fogarty had brought him.

Chicago, Chicago,
I'll show you around . . . show you around.

He propped himself up on his pillow and looked out of his hotel window over the twinkling lights to Lincoln Park, Picnic Island and the beaches along the lake.

> *Bet your bottom dollar*
> *You'll lose the blues*
> *In Chicago . . . Chicago . . .*

King Joe Oliver and a young protégé from New Orleans, Louis Armstrong, were losing the blues at the Savoy Ballroom; Earl (Fatha) Hines was playing "Sweet Lorraine" on his magical piano at the Sunset Café on Thirty-fifth Street; Duke Ellington was holding court at the Lincoln Tavern; Ben Bernie was at the College Inn, Paul Ash was packing the Oriental Theatre; Al Jolson was smashing all records in Artists and Models; Kid Ory, Jelly Roll Morton and Johnny Dodds were making it tough for King Joe and Satchmo; Buck and Bubbles were hoofing on the South Side . . .

Joe could hear the wonderful symphony, hot and sweet, blaring and whispering from numberless joints in this brawling, sprawling town and, lying alone on the tenth floor of the Commonwealth Hotel, unable to walk or talk normally, he wondered why one act out of those thousands—Lewis and Black—had been doomed to such a violent finish.

Lewis and Black . . .

John Stewart Black, a Scotch Indian, was an artist of diversified talents. He invented a trumpet mute, a dime manicuring machine and an apparatus to land an airplane on a mountainside. He could assemble an automobile or a watch, he was proficient in chemistry and criminal law, he was an accomplished violinist, pianist and trombonist. He composed "Dardanella," the first example of boogie-woogie in American music, a song that sold 1,600,000 copies of sheet music and 6,000,000 phonograph records. He was a libertine and a lush.

Black was playing a Philadelphia honky-tonk in 1923 when his current partner, Gil Mack, quit the act. Losing partners was an occupational disease with Black and he took it philosophically. He knew that the world was densely populated with stage-struck youths who would be grateful for the opportunity to work cheaply for the man who had written "Dardanella." That night, while swilling in a dive called Dad's Hotel, on Eighth and Race streets, he found Gil Mack's successor.

"My aunt opened a millinery shop but closed down in two weeks," the young man on stage cracked. "She sold only eight bottles."

Black groaned at the alleged humor inspired by the Volstead Act and continued to dose himself until the agony was finished. Then he invited the young "comedian"—Joe Lewis at twenty-one—to his table. "You have a good voice," he told him. "Why do you waste it telling stale jokes?"

"Seventy-five bucks a week," Joe snapped. It was good money for Philadelphia—and for a semiprofessional. The three years since he had broken in at Atlantic City had been hard years. He had remained at the Columbia Beer Garden until he saved $300. He was ready to invade New York and conquer Broadway. So was his roommate, who left without him but not without Joe's $300 and Joe's clothes. Joe started in the sticks, vaudeville in northern Pennsylvania, upstate New York and the Borscht Circuit of the Catskills, often as low as $1.25 a day. A friend, the drummer in the band at the old Columbia Beer Garden, recommended him to Jimmy Irish, the owner of Dad's Hotel. Joe began at forty dollars a week, he had almost doubled it in a year and a half and he was proud of himself, stale jokes or not.

Black studied him through bloodshot eyes. This was his pigeon. "I'll give you a hundred to sing my songs." He punctuated the proposition with a ripe belch.

Joe hesitated. John Black was a man of infinite charm who

would allay the fears of a belligerent theatre manager as adroitly as those of a conscientious wife or, in this case, an apprehensive novice. "Do you want to play Philadelphia all your life?" he prodded him. "Especially a crummy joint like this?"

Dad's Hotel was a crummy joint, a hangout for hoodlums. Joe crossed his legs and his eyes lighted on a small hole in the cuff of his trousers, the only suit he owned. A few nights previously, three customers had opened gunfire on one another. It did not occur to Joe to drop to the floor or hide under a table or run for the door. He remained standing on the stage, his head turning from one side to the other following the crossfire, like an announcer at a tennis match. More than a hundred shots were fired and two of the men fell dead.

"This can't go on," Joe complained to Irish after the barrage. "They drowned out all the laughs."

Not until he went home and undressed did he discover that one of the bullets had passed through his trouser cuff.

Yet, it was a steady job and John Black was something less than a steady man.

"Tell you what I'll do." Black became magnanimous, noting Joe's indecision. "I never did this before in my life—but I like you, kid." He choked up and his palsied fingers found Joe's arm. "I'm going to give you top billing." It was the voice of a martyr making his supreme sacrifice.

Joe offered a half-hearted protest which Black dismissed. "I'm an old man. I've had my fame." He indulged in a shrug of self-pity. "I'm alone. I don't have anyone—no son of my own to leave anything to. The least I can do, in the few years I have left, is to help some deserving lad up the ladder —and teach him show business, real show business." He clamped a firmer grip on Joe's arm. "I'll take you to New York! I'll put you on Broadway! Can't you see it, son? Up there in big lights: Lewis and Black!" He almost shouted

Joe's name and reduced his own to a humble whisper. "LEWIS and black—in the top spot at the Palace!"

That did it. Joe eagerly grasped his hand to seal the bargain and, a few hours later, he was still clutching it as he guided, supported and finally carried Black to his hotel. Black's room was shabby and dismal, littered with empty bottles, song sheets and divers impedimenta, including a surveyor's tripod and level. "Is that in the act?" Joe asked, pointing to the telescope. Black nodded torpidly. "But I thought we just did songs," Joe questioned.

"Be a good boy," Black sighed as he collapsed on the bed, "and help me off with my shoes." In an instant he was snoring in the carefree slumber of the sodden. As Joe unlaced Black's shoes and picked up the sheets of music he had to learn, he realized why he had been given first billing: he was the one who could see. From now on he would be a singing seeing-eye dog.

> *Oh, sweet Dardanella, I love your harem eyes,*
> *I'm a lucky fellow, to capture such a prize.*
> *Oh Allah knows my love for you,*
> *And he tells you to be true,*
> *DAR-DA-NEL-LA, oh hear my sigh!*

Lewis and Black, billed as "The Writers of 'Dardanella,'" opened not at the Palace or on Broadway but at the Rose Tree Club—in Philadelphia, a few blocks from Dad's Hotel, and an even more tawdry trap if possible.

"I want to introduce a card who sings like the deuce—my partner, Joe Lewis!"

For the next year and a half, Lewis and Black played every vaudeville circuit, speakeasy, banquet, stag, tent show, carnival, summer resort, wedding and walkathon that would book them, toting John's fiddle and trombone without cases, and his pet canary on all trains, busses and highways.

Joe at 23 and the late Johnny Black (left), his first and last partner, in Chicago, 1925, as vaudeville's Dardanella Boys. Joe started out with a rose, today carries four, distilled.

"You'll never live to open the Rendezvous," Vincent Gebardi (above left), better known as Machine Gun Jack McGurn, threatened Joe in 1927. P.S. Joe opened. P.P.S. McGurn was subsequently murdered. *International News Photo.*

The man in frightening repose, Al Capone (above right), handed Joe an envelope with $50,000 cash. "With me as your partner," he said, "you'll make a million. I'll see to it." *International News Photo.*

They were frequently stranded in the hinterlands, a familiar crisis against which Black had made several provisions, among them the surveyor's outfit salvaged from a forgotten chapter in his checkered career. In these periodic emergencies they would assemble their equipment at a strategic site in the countryside, usually in close proximity to an impressive-looking home. With Black's rheumy eye squinting through the revolving telescope and Joe solemnly pacing off imaginary distances, they invariably attracted clusters of curious spectators.

In the idiom of the surveying science, compounded with a coded patois of their own, Lewis and Black carried on solemn conversations in "links . . . chains . . . poles" until one of the onlookers had the temerity to inquire whom they represented. Black, among his sundry hobbies, collected data on railroad and bus lines, highway projects and the most desirable locations for service stations in each territory they played and, out of his encyclopedic knowledge, he told his interrogator, sotto voce, in the strictest confidence, that a new railroad or highway would eventuate if and when the necessary rights of way could be purchased. In a matter of minutes, the owners of land and property within a radius of several miles of their surveyor's level converged upon them in quest of additional information.

Black, by now preoccupied with surveying the length of Joe's trousers at a hundred feet, made himself unavailable until lunch-time or dinner. The landowners, envisioning the sales of their realty at fabulous profits, vied with one another for precedence in feting the surveyors. Black possessed a clairvoyant talent in divining the bank balances of total strangers, as well as the quality of their hospitality and their larders, and he assigned priorities with uncanny accuracy. Lewis and Black ate sumptuously if not regularly.

A man of remarkable attainments and undisciplined hungers, Black was a source of constant fascination and grief.

When Joe was not trying to sober him sufficiently to lead him on the stage and prop him on the piano bench, he was rescuing him from homicide at the hands of jealous husbands.

They were playing a vaudeville matinee at the Auditorium Theatre in Quebec. Black, attracted by two beautiful girls in the third row, directed an unceasing broadside of suggestive asides to them, the most subtle being an assurance that he and his young partner would be pleased to entertain them privately later in the afternoon. He repeated the number of their hotel room half a dozen times in case they had faulty memories, unaware that the two burly lumberjacks seated directly behind them were their husbands.

Two infuriated Canucks were waiting for Lewis and Black at the stage door. Joe was terrified when the offended spouses declared their intentions but Black, who had overslept that day and consequently was behind in his drinking, lost none of the aplomb that was his as long as he remained on his feet. "My friend," he protested, when one took his right arm and rendered it useless with a lethal hammerlock, "you are making a grave mistake."

"And you were trying to make my wife, you lecherous bastard!"

"It was part of the act," Joe gasped as his assailant demonstrated the relative effectiveness of a hold celebrated by another Lewis, Strangler Ed.

"You weren't kidding," Black's captor bellowed. "I checked the number of your hotel room."

Black drew himself up with as much dignity as a man can who is doubled under a viselike hammerlock. "I will have you know, sir, that a woman's chastity is sacred to me. I have five daughters of my own."

"And I ought to know," Joe sputtered, "I'm married to one of them."

"It was just patter, as we say in show business," Black said with a look of injured innocence, thereupon improvising a routine of double-entendre to the satisfaction of the lumberjacks, with the inevitable outcome: the foursome went on a roisterous drunk, the husbands picking up the check.

The next afternoon there was a knock on the door of Black's hotel room. It was the wife of one of the lumberjacks, apologetic for being twenty-four hours late.

Lewis and Black incredibly reached New York alive, rich in experiences but bankrupt of funds, bookings or prospects. Black could not comprehend the cause of his fading popularity. "I wrote 'Dardanella'!" he exclaimed as if it were an eternal meal-ticket.

"Maybe you ought to write a second song," Joe said waspishly. He was hungry.

A man whose unharnessed ego precluded his ignoring a challenge, even in the realization that he was a one-shot wonder who had never written anything before or since "Dardanella" worthy of mention, Black sat down to compose a second song—but not until he had exhausted all other alternatives and had borrowed on, sold or pawned almost all of his possessions including his only overcoat, the patent rights to his trumpet mute, his automatic manicure machine, his emergency airplane landing apparatus and, with the greatest wrench of all, his trusty surveyor's outfit; everything except his fiddle and his canary. Even then, he would not write the first note until the last bottle of whiskey had been drained, and Joe could not hustle a pint anywhere, and his unquenchable thirst was driving him mad.

With Joe holding him a prisoner in his room, a meritorious feat in light of the fact that Black's desire to go out was equaled only by that of an inimical landlady to get him out, John ultimately began working. The song was finished in two days. "Now," he announced, waving the last sheet to dry, "it must be introduced in a setting worthy of its excellence."

"Make up your mind," Joe grumbled impatiently. "I'm hungry."

John Black's eyes lighted up. "That's it, Joseph! We'll give a dinner . . ." He beamed in anticipation. "A Chinese dinner. Let's see now, the guest list . . ."

Joe looked at him as if his senses had taken leave. "Wake up, John. We haven't the price of a hamburger."

Black did not hear him. "Ed Marks . . . Put it down, Joseph. I want Marks here at seven-thirty. Have Fred Fisher come at eight and . . ."

Joe shook his head. Fred Fisher? The man who wrote "Ireland Must Be Heaven Because My Mother Came From There" and "Oh, You Beautiful Doll"? Fisher was the biggest name in song business. "They won't come here, John."

"They'll come." Black nodded with certainty. Fisher had polished Black's original melody of "Dardanella," written the lyrics and had it published. Before it became a hit four years later, in 1919, Fisher bought all of Black's rights for $12,000, an investment on which he was said to have made a couple hundred thousand dollars. Fisher would come. So would Edward B. Marks, president of the Marks Publishing Company. " 'Dardanella' is his favorite song," Black said. "And he's a sucker for chow mein."

"It's better than 'Dardanella'!" Black announced.

Marks, the first guest to arrive, nodded courteously. He was accustomed to Black's opening gambit.

"It was inspired by an unrequited love . . ." Black tucked his fiddle under his chin. "It's about a guy who has had a million dolls or more. And now he's alone. Every one went away, like all dolls do . . ." He caressed his fiddle and began playing with astonishing virtuosity, his canary chirping on his shoulder and Joe singing the chorus.

I'm goin' to buy a paper doll that I can call my own,
A doll that other fellows cannot steal.
And then the flirty, flirty guys
With their flirty, flirty eyes
Will have to flirt with dollies that are real.

Marks listened attentively. At least it did not sound like "Dardanella," an asset Black's abortive efforts in recent years had not boasted, but the lyrics were childish.

Fisher arrived as Joe began the second chorus.

"Didn't I tell you it was better than 'Dardanella'?" Black shouted triumphantly when he had finished.

Fisher's face did not reflect Black's enthusiasm. "It isn't bad," he said, "but it sounds familiar . . ."

Black ignored Fisher and, noting the famished look in Joe's face, turned to Marks. "Mr. Marks," he said, "I didn't invite you to dinner to talk business . . . but a most embarrassing exigency has arisen. If you will be good enough to lend me twenty-five dollars, I will give you an option on this for . . ."

Marks had anticipated the bite and was happily surprised that it had not been for fifty.

Black handed the money to Joe, who passed it to a messenger waiting outside the door. Almost immediately, a succulent dinner for four was served by a file of Celestials from the chop suey joint downstairs.

The following day Black played his song for Marks again, this time on a piano in the publisher's office. Abruptly, in the middle of the last chorus, he stopped. "Mozart was buried in a pauper's grave because he didn't leave enough for his own funeral," he cried emotionally. "Schubert was so poor he never could afford a piano!" He grabbed the sheet of music from the piano and shook it in Marks' face. "This scrap of paper is all that stands between me and starvation. Everything else is gone. Soon I will join my masters and you will be kicking yourself in the ass because you didn't buy the rights to this hit when you could!"

Joe, who had come along at Black's insistence, walked out. John became pretty maudlin when he was sober.

The publisher was startled. "I didn't say I wouldn't buy it," he said, fearful of violence.

"But I didn't say I would sell it," stormed Black. "Rather than suffer these indignities, I'd rather destroy it." He started to tear it, on the margin. Marks stopped him.

"Fifty bucks," said the publisher. "You owe me twenty-five and I'll give you twenty-five."

Black looked at Marks with contempt. "The price is one thousand dollars. Take it or leave it."

After an hour of lachrymose entreaties, threats and cajolery by Black, the song writer capitulated and agreed to sell the song for eighty dollars against royalties. Marks produced a standard contract. "Sign," he said.

"I do nothing without my partner," Black said. "Joseph!" His roar echoed through the building. Joe, who had been waiting in the corridor, stuck his head in the doorway. "Come in, kid," Black commanded, "and put your John Henry down here."

"Why?"

"Why? Because our pal Marks bought our song!"

"Get the dough before he changes his mind," said Joe impatiently, showing no inclination to enter.

"But I want your name on the contract too." Black may have been a drunken trouper but he was a loyal trouper. "Who knows?" he chortled, to the publisher's discomfort. "Maybe somebody will like it—and you might get $2.25 in royalties."

"I'm starvin'," Joe snapped. "Let's go!" He disappeared outside and Black reluctantly signed the contract alone.

Marks studied the sheet of paper he had just purchased. "Where's the title?" he asked.

A moment's thought was all Black required. He hastily scrawled across the top, "I'm Going to Buy a Paper Doll."

Marks stared at what he had written. "Is this the title?" he asked.

There was no answer. He was already outside with Joe, chuckling. "Put one over on old Marks, didn't we?"

"Let's go eat," Joe said.

Black grinned. "I thought we were dead last night when Fisher said it sounded familiar. I'd forgotten he heard it."

"That's impossible," Joe said. "You just finished it yesterday afternoon."

Black shook his head. "I finished it ten years ago. Nineteen fifteen. That's when Freddy Fisher heard it—the first time." He sighed. "Nobody would publish it. So I forgot it and wrote 'Dardanella.'"

"And I thought you had written it in two days."

"I wrote it in one day . . . It took me two days to remember it."

The song was an immediate smash hit, an even more spectacular success when it was revived twenty years later during World War II. And, if Joe had deigned to take the two steps from the doorway of E. B. Marks' office to his desk to sign his name, as Black had begged him, his share of the royalties would have been more than $50,000.

> *When I come home at night she will be waiting,*
> *She'll be the truest doll in all this world.*
> *I'd rather have a paper doll to call my own,*
> *Than have a fickle-minded real live girl.*

Lewis and Black were back in business, back in the money and back off the wagon, thanks to the paper doll John had scissored out of his memory. America was singing, dancing and making love to his music again. He strode Broadway like a cockeyed Colossus and introduced Joe to the best people and the best places.

The day Black took him to the Friars Club was the most unforgettable. Joe stared in awe at the great names of the theatre who passed by and, on the wall, the portraits of the legendary giants of show business. "Stick with me," Black promised, "and someday you'll be a member."

All went well for a few weeks, until a fateful night when Lewis and Black were playing Proctor's Fifth Avenue Theatre. Joe was singing a parody on Dixie music, "Down Where the South Begins."

> Way down upon the Swanee River,
> I love to roam
> That's where they really make chopped liver
> Just like the old folks at home.

This was Black's cue to join Joe and, arms entwined, do a take-off on "Old Black Joe" as they shuffled into the wings. John came on cue, singing,

> I'm comin' . . . I'm comin' . . .
> But my rear end is bending low . . .

Here Joe would set up the finale by feeding Black the line, "You remember old Black Joe?"

"You remember old Black Joe?" he asked, gently patting Black on the back.

John Black did not remember. There was a silence. Then the crowd broke into unrestrained laughter. Joe turned and froze. Black had vanished as if he were Blackstone.

A groan came from below. Black lay crumpled on the floor of the orchestra pit, unhurt, lost in an alcoholic blackout. He had been sneaking drinks all evening and was out on his feet when Joe's feathery tap struck him like a mallet, sent him hurtling off the stage, out of vaudeville, and into—

Chicago, Chicago . . .
The town that Billy Sunday
Could not shut down . . .

Black had remembered an old chum who ran the Chez
Pierre, a garish deadfall on Fairbanks Court in Chicago. A
frantic SOS brought two railroad tickets and an offer of $200
a week for the act. "It's walking-around money," Black reasoned. "Three months and we'll be back up there . . ."

Joe doubted it but he went along. Within a few days he
realized his mistake. Black was drinking heavier than ever.

"I'm blowing," Joe told him at the end of the week.

There was honest dread in Black's eyes. He could not afford to lose Joe. He knew that he was running out his string
—fast. There would not be many more partners. "Give me
one more chance, kid," the old man of thirty-four begged the
young man of twenty-three.

Joe looked at him with pity and disgust. "You're a great
man, John, but you're a drunk. You're one to three to die in
the gutter and I don't want to be around when you do." He
tried to conceal his affection but could not.

Black sobbed. It was not an act and the tears had no alcoholic content. "I'll never touch another drop, Joe—as long
as I live. I swear on my mother's . . ."

Joe stopped him. "All right, John," he gave in. "We'll try
it—on one condition."

"Anything, kid—anything!"

"You show up drunk tonight and we're through." Joe held
out his hand and Black grasped it gratefully.

Black showed up falling-down drunk. That night Joe became a single.

Black wound up with a tavern, which he wistfully called
the Dardanella Club, near Hamilton, Ohio. One night in
June, 1936, during an argument over a twenty-five-cent
charge for a bottle of beer, a customer named Edward Moor-

man, a twenty-year-old boy, hit Black. Black hit the ground, never to rise. Joe's frail, gifted mentor had run his wild course in forty-five years.

He left an estate of $100 but eight years after his death, following the tremendous revival of his "Paper Doll," three women who claimed to be his legal widows fought a bitter court battle over $20,000 in royalties: his first wife, Mattie Shanks, a vaudeville trouper who claimed that she had helped him write "Dardanella"; his second wife, Willie Icia Kissick, who claimed that their divorce was invalid; and his third wife, Sally Baird, who was separated from him at the time of his death. The fifteen-year-old daughter of his father's landlady, Etta Mae Williams, and his eighty-year-old father also claimed the royalties.

> *Oh, sweet Dardanella, prepare the wedding wine,*
> *There'll be one girl in my harem*
> *When you're mine . . .*

John Black, in life, had left his greatest legacy to the young man he had picked up in Dad's Hotel, Philadelphia, a protégé destined for a career even more turbulent than his own.

Until Joe met Black he was unmolded, unsophisticated and unoriginal, a pleasant but crude amateur without poise, direction or know-how. Black made him a professional and, by his example, taught him that a man must have an act of his own, one that is not dependent upon anyone else, or he does not have an act.

> *On State Street, that great street,*
> *I just wanna say, just wanna say,*
> *They do things they don't on Broadway, say—*

Joe's reverie was broken by the sound of footsteps. Fogarty was making his midnight check.

Fogarty poured a fresh glass of water, opened the window and adjusted the shade. "Anything you need?" he asked.

Joe looked up. "Bulletin board still up?"

Fogarty nodded. He had posted daily reports on Joe's condition at the Rendezvous since the day he had been cut.

"Got a bulletin for you." His words were slow and studied.

Fogarty grinned eagerly. "I need a gag or two. Let's have it."

"It's not a gag. I'm opening in two weeks."

Fogarty was not sure he had heard correctly. It must be a joke or Joe's brain *had* been affected. "We'll talk about it in the morning," he said. "Good night, Joe."

"We'll talk about it now."

Fogarty saw that he was in earnest. "But you can't walk yet! You can't even—" He was a hard man but he could not finish the sentence.

"I can talk," Joe finished it for him.

Fogarty fixed his covers. "Go to sleep, Joe. We'll see what Doc Orth says . . ."

There was a silence.

At last, as Fogarty was leaving, Joe spoke again. "You didn't remember my birthday."

Fogarty scowled. "Birthday? When was your birthday?"

"Today."

Fogarty was skeptical. "You're kiddin'."

"Look in my wallet, inside the dresser . . . January twelfth."

Fogarty gripped his left hand. "Congratulations, Joe."

His weatherbeaten face wrinkled into a wry smile. "For a while there I wasn't sure you were going to make it. What is it—twenty-seven?"

"Twenty-six." Joe held on to his hand.

"You'll get your present tomorrow."

"Tonight."

Fogarty looked at him for understanding. "Don't ask me, Joe."

"I'm not asking—I'm insistin'." He released his hand.

Fogarty hesitated.

"Afraid to take a chance on me?"

"You know better than that."

Joe shook his head. "Show me."

Fogarty's tension mounted. "It's not the joint I'm afraid of, you stupid bastard—it's you!"

"I'm opening in two weeks." Joe looked up at his friend. "What do you want me to do, John . . . crawl back to the Green Mill and beg McGurn for my old job?"

Fogarty stared at the shrunken little man who did not have the strength to move his bedpan, who stuttered in a slurred tongue, whose horribly mutilated head was still in bandages. It seemed inconceivable that he could get on the stage in a year or two, if ever.

Joe read the doubt in his face. "They didn't think I'd ever get up off the floor either."

Fogarty knew when he was licked. "It's a deal—on one condition." He gave Joe his hand. "From now on we're partners—fifty-fifty on everything."

Joe choked up. "We'll drink to that."

Fogarty handed him his glass of water.

"I said we'd *drink* to it."

Fogarty scowled. "You know you can't have any booze."

Joe lifted himself higher on his pillow. "I've been on the wagon three months. Get the jug."

Fogarty obeyed.

There was a puzzled expression on Fogarty's face a while later as he poured their third drink. "I've gone over every step," he said, reconstructing the events of the morning of November ninth, "and I always come to a blank wall."

Joe looked up from his drink. "What do you mean?"

"You say you opened the door and the three punks were standing outside."

Joe nodded.

"Then, you say, they piled into the room—the three of them."

Joe nodded.

"How far did they come in?"

"All the way."

Fogarty went to the door, opened it and re-enacted the scene. "And you were standing at the door—like this?"

Joe nodded.

"Try to remember, Joe," Fogarty pleaded. "Didn't one or two of 'em or all three grab you—and then lock the door?"

Joe shook his head. "Not when they came in. They didn't touch me—until I closed the door."

Fogarty returned to his bedside, exasperated. "Please, Joe, give it to me straight—the way it happened."

"I *am*, John."

"You say they didn't touch you when they walked in and you were all alone at the door for a few seconds—is that right?"

Joe nodded. "That's right."

"Then *why* did you close the door? Why in hell didn't you run *out* in the hallway?"

"Because," Joe replied simply, "I didn't have my shoes on."

The Rendezvous was sold out within an hour of the announcement that Joe was coming back on January 28th, less than eleven weeks after his throat was slashed. Sophie

Tucker gave up a $5,000 theatre engagement to be on the show with him. When Ted Healy, the master of ceremonies, brought him on the stage, every person in the room rose and cheered. They craned to see his scars and they shuddered at the sight of his head bandages. They stared in awe and respect at the man who had defied Machine Gun Jack McGurn and who had survived three of his killers.

"Joe! Joe! Joe!" They kept shouting his name, clapping, whistling and telling him in every way they knew how happy they were to see him.

Joe held up his hands, the right one moving only a couple of inches, but the customers would not stop until they realized they were embarrassing him. At last they sat down and gave him an even greater tribute: absolute quiet.

"Thanks . . ." Joe was deeply moved and could hardly speak. The crowd understood. The orchestra played another chorus of his opening song. He stalled, fearful of the first note. "It was like this," he said. "Three of the boys came up to my room to talk over old times . . ." He knew what he wanted to say but his delivery was uncertain and inarticulate, he was lisping in a pathetic gibberish. "They told a few jokes and I laughed so much I thought I'd *die*."

Hardly anyone, even at the ringside tables, caught more than a few disjointed syllables of the macabre and incoherent jest but everyone laughed and applauded.

"After a while, the boys got a little rough," he continued in a pathetic, unintelligible rasp. "The next day I sent them a sharp note." He paused and the crowd surmised it was time to laugh again. Another gale of approval swept over the club.

"I'll say this about getting your brains beat out," he went on in a tongue known only to himself. "Once is all right, but not too often . . . My croaker, Dr. Orth, took one look at me and said he wanted to be paid in advance. He was a wonderful surgeon—except he didn't know what to do with an extra piece of skull."

Fogarty and Captain Goldberg, standing in the back of the room, looked at each other. They said nothing. Their worst fears were confirmed.

Joe tried to clear his throat, unaware that he would speak with an impediment the rest of his life. At last he went into a zany song called "Far Rockaway" that extolled the virtues of its sandy beach where "the matzoh trees gently sway . . . and the people watch the tomato herrings play all day."

The Rendezvous echoed with laughter and applause. He went through his repertoire, faltering hoarsely until he was almost inaudible, but they made him come back for encore after encore until he was compelled to beg off by pointing painfully to his throat.

Again the crowd rose as one man and gave him a deafening ovation. He ran off the stage. Another moment, and he would have broken down.

He was slumped in a chair at his dressing table, his head buried in his arms, when Fogarty came in. "You were great, Joe!" he shouted.

Joe looked up. "You're a lousy liar."

"They nearly tore the house apart. What more do you want?"

Joe stood up, disconsolate. "I'm finished, John."

"You're better than ever!" Fogarty lied.

"I talk like a drunken immigrant," Joe lisped. A drunken immigrant *fairy!*" He picked up a song sheet on the table. "The material is the same—but I'm not."

"You're nuts," Fogarty kept punching, "they were in hysterics!"

"Out of pity. That was a benefit show."

"No, Joe—it wasn't."

Joe turned on his friend. "I don't want charity—theirs or

yours!" He turned and walked out. By his lights pity was the cheapest of emotions, the bastard son of contempt.

Fogarty ran to the door after him. "You signed a contract, you ungrateful sonofabitch," he called, "and I'm holding you to it!"

Joe carried on for almost three weeks. His voice became weaker and the customers fewer. Only three or four tables were occupied the last night. Even with the waiters helping, the applause was a death rattle.

"Thanks for everything, John." He gripped Fogarty's hand.

"You'll be back," said the big fellow confidently.

Joe nodded. "As an acrobat."

A visitor was waiting for him at the hotel. "Joey!" Kathy rushed up, threw her arms around his neck and kissed him tearfully.

He had almost forgotten Kathy, along with everything else in his life before the slashing. "I thought you were in Pennsylvania . . ."

"I'm back . . . to stay."

"We'll talk about that . . . Hungry?"

"Starving—but I'm too tired to go out. How about ordering something up in the room?"

They were finishing the dessert. Kathy reached across the table and clasped his hand. "We're going to be happy, Joe."

"On what?"

"It'll be different when we're married."

"We're not getting married, Kathy." It was a flat statement, devoid of emotion.

"Don't say that, Joe," she implored in a strange voice.

"I'm washed up!" He stood up and turned away from her. "I can't even support myself, let alone the both of us!"

"All right . . ." her voice trailed off resignedly. "Goodbye, Joe . . ."

He turned to see Kathy grab his gun from the top of the

dresser and press the muzzle to her temple. "No!" he cried
as he lunged at her. "Haven't I got enough trouble, Kathy?"

She hesitated a moment and then dropped the gun on the
table. "I'm sorry, darling . . ." She put her head on his
shoulder and sobbed convulsively. "The least you could say
is that you love me . . ."

Joe stared out of the window at the blustering, snow-be-
sieged city. "What difference does it make now?" he asked.

He heard the door open and, a moment later, softly close.
He was alone.

Fogarty came to his room in the morning. "Here's reservations to Miami," he said, handing him a thick envelope,
"and enough dough to keep going a while."

"No loans." Joe pushed the money back. "I'll never get
caught up."

"It ain't a loan, it's an investment." He pressed the envelope in his hand. "The sun'll bake out that voice. You'll be
back at the Rendezvous in no time . . ."

Joe left for Florida, unaware that Federal Prohibition
agents had padlocked the Rendezvous a few hours previously.

8   *Brother, Can You Spare Ten G's?*

Harry (Swifty) Morgan, a salty Broadway character who inspired many Damon Runyon stories, lived by his wits, his
friends and a brief case of gaudy cravats that he peddled to
those who were as benevolent as they were affluent. This
visit to Miami Beach was strictly personal.

"You're not supposed to know it, Joe," he said, "but they're putting on a testimonial show for you—all the cabarets in Chicago."

"Testimonial . . ." Joe's voice was caustic. "The word is benefit."

"You need the dough." Swifty was a realist.

"Nice of 'em."

"Nice, my pratt!" Swifty looked around furtively and lowered his voice. "That's what I came to see you about, Joe . . . Mike Ottery will give you seventy-five G's—cash on the line—to run a benefit for you."

"Seventy-five *thousand!* You must have heard it wrong, Swift. Maybe Mike would go seventy-five *hundred*—but I don't know why."

"I said seventy-five *G's*—and it's a steal. Capone wants to do something for you. So does Moran's outfit. Every joint in town would have to buy a book of tickets. Mike knows what he's doing."

It was a temptation, a one-night offer of as much money as the President of the United States received for a year, but Joe said no. "I don't need it that bad."

"You're a sucker."

"That isn't news," Joe croaked.

Swifty was desolate, for Joe's sake. "As for this other benefit . . . you better get your ass up there before they steal everything."

If everyone who has since claimed to have been present at Joe's testimonial show actually was there, at least 150,000 people occupied the 1,514 seats in Chicago's Oriental Theatre. Al Jolson sang for almost an hour on a bill that included Sophie Tucker, Abe Lyman's band, Tom Mix and Hoot Gibson from the Hollywood sagebrush and Aviatrix Ruth Elder.

Joe received $14,000 in bonds.

"It isn't a fortune, Joe," Jolson said apologetically at

breakfast the next morning, "but it'll get you started again. You'll do all right . . ."

"Don't rib a ribber. I can't sing a note."

Jolson looked at him curiously. "I wasn't thinking of show business. The testimonial *was* to stake you to a haberdashery store, wasn't it?"

Joe swallowed hard. He would not admit to Jolson that this was the first time he had heard about it. He did not blame anyone for keeping it a secret. No one had the heart to tell him. "Didn't know I was a star salesman in Easton, P.A., did you?"

"You got all of my business, pal!"

Joe shook his head. "You belong to Swifty Morgan. I'm not cutting in on his trade . . . not for a while, anyway."

"Not for at least a year. You're spending the next year in California with me."

"Please, Jolie." His hoarse voice cracked. "I can't take any more charity!"

"Don't mix up charity and friendship. You're coming to California. It's settled."

"I'll see about it."

"I'll make the arrangements as soon as I get back to the Coast."

Joe knew Al's intentions were good but he did not take the invitation seriously. He regarded it as a Hollywood euphemism, like, "Let's have lunch next week."

He was sitting alone in a dismal bar on Cicero's Skid Row. He had been walking all day, and drinking, against Dr. Orth's orders. He had stopped in twenty or thirty bars, ordering the same drink, a straight rye, asking the same question, "Jack McGurn around?" and leaving the same message after buying the bartender a drink, "If you see him, tell him Joe Lewis is looking for him."

He was in McGurn's territory. He did not know what he would say to him or do to him when he saw him but he had to see him. This was the last stop. He had left an easy trail to follow. McGurn could not help knowing where he was.

After a while he continued drinking for another reason, to forget he was a cripple. He looked up eagerly as every customer entered, no longer searching for McGurn but hopeful of seeing a friendly face. None appeared. Joe had become a stranger on the South Side.

By 1:30 A.M. there was only one other drinker in the place and he was rising to leave. Joe stopped him as he passed his table. "Have a drink with me," he begged. He was desperate, he did not want to be left alone.

"Sorry," the stranger said, "I got a date."

"She'll wait." Joe held his arm and called out to the waiter, "Bring my friend a drink—the best in the house!"

"I shouldn't . . ." The stranger wavered.

"Sit down," Joe insisted.

The stranger reluctantly sat down. "I got a date. An important date . . ."

"Don't worry, pal." Joe brought out his address book. "I'll take care of you."

"It isn't that kind of date."

"I got *all* kinds!" Joe patted his little book with a knowing smile.

They drank steadily through the night. The stranger, suddenly aware of the morning sun, consulted his watch. "Now look what you made me do," he said. "I missed my date."

"I told you I'd take care of you."

"It's too late," the stranger blubbered. "The opportunity of a lifetime has come and gone." He focused his bleary eyes on Joe. "Sir, you have changed the course of my destiny."

Joe nodded. "You were drinking beer when you met me. I've been pouring bonded whiskey into you all night."

"I mean my date . . ."

"Quit whining." The repetition was boring him. "I told you I'd fix you up."

"You don't understand," the stranger wailed. "The guy I was going to meet would've staked me."

"Why didn't you say so?" Joe pulled out some bills and handed his drinking partner a dollar. "Here, pal . . . wait a minute." He peeled off another single.

The stranger looked at the two bills with disdain and shook his head. "You don't understand."

"Isn't my dough as good as your guy's?"

"It's not the quality. It's the quantity."

"How much you need?"

"More than you got."

Joe bristled. "I asked you how much you need."

The stranger finished his drink and stared into the empty glass. "Ten thousand bucks . . ."

Joe stood up, a little unsteadily. "Let's go," he said.

An hour later, they were standing in front of the First National Bank at Dearborn Street and Monroe. They had to wait an hour for the bank to open. Leaning against the building, the sun in his face, Joe began to sober up. "How much did you say you needed?" he asked, his eyes closed.

"Ten thousand bucks . . ."

"That's what I thought you said."

At last the doors were opened. Joe took the arm of his drinking partner and, each helping to support the other, they weaved a circuitous course to a teller's window. "I want ten G's," Joe demanded, clutching the grilled window to keep from falling down.

The teller looked at the two drunks and backed away from Joe's rye-laden breath. "One moment, sir," he said and whispered to the teller in the next cage.

Joe waited impatiently. A uniformed private officer came up and gripped Joe's arm. "This way, sir . . ."

Joe balked. "My pal needs ten G's," he croaked, slapping

off the officer's hands, "and I'm not leaving here until he gets it!"

The officer took a new grip on Joe's arm with one hand and, with the other, tightened his fingers around the .45 revolver in his hip holster. This could be a holdup. "No disturbance—please!"

"There won't be any disturbance," Joe retorted, breaking his hold with a sharp whack, "if my pal gets his dough."

Joe's companion, seeing the officer reach for his gun, became panicky. "Forget it!" he whispered to Joe. "Let's get out of here!"

"I won't forget it!" Joe shouted as loudly as he could.

"Mr. Lewis!" An assistant manager recognized him and broke through the gathering crowd.

Joe fixed an unsteady but indicting gaze on the junior executive. "Is this the way you treat all customers?"

The assistant manager apologized, dismissed the officer and the crowd disintegrated. "Now what can I do for you?" he asked.

Joe pointed to his eight-hour friend. "He needs ten thousand bucks."

The assistant manager nodded indulgently. "If he can give us sufficient collateral, we will be pleased to consider . . ."

"Why should he give *you* anything? *I'm* giving him the money!"

The assistant manager was perplexed. "Mr. Lewis," he said, taking another inventory of his condition, "I suggest that you—come back later . . ."

"Have I got ten G's in this bank—or haven't I?"

The assistant manager went to the teller's window and asked for Joe's balance. It was almost $11,000, his hospital and medical bills having taken approximately $3,000.

Joe turned to his friend. "How do you want it: in hundreds—or bigger bills?"

The assistant manager interrupted. "Mr. Lewis, your funds are in bonds. The—the Committee insisted that—"

"Cash 'em!" Joe ordered.

"This is a great deal of money, Mr. Lewis," the banker persisted. "I suggest that you think it over a few hours—soberly—and . . ."

Joe glared at him. "I didn't ask you when I should put that money in here—and I'm not asking you when I should take it out." He jerked his thumb toward the teller. "Tell Rothschild to start counting."

Joe took the ten crisp thousand-dollar packets and handed them to the stranger.

The stranger took the money, uncertain whether this was a dream or a delusion—or he was still drunk. "You didn't even ask me what it's for," he said to his benefactor.

"What difference does it make?" Joe shrugged. "You said you needed it."

"But—but you don't even know who I am. I'll make you out a note. Let's get a blank note and . . ."

"A note won't help you." Joe looked at the stranger unemotionally. "That's my case dough. If you don't pay it back, I'll kill you."

The stranger, a man named Leonard Sachs, took the $10,000, rented the Coliseum and promoted a boxing show.

Years later, after Sachs had repaid the loan, Joe was recounting the experience to a friend of his, Chuck Green, at Lindy's restaurant in New York. "A good story," Green conceded, "but I don't believe a word of it."

A few minutes later, Sachs came in. Green called him over and asked him if he knew Joe.

Sachs grinned. "He's the schmuck who gave me ten G's in Chicago!"

Back in 1928, incapacitated, without a job or prospects of ever being able to work again, Joe did not think it was unusual to lend a stranger $10,000 without security or even knowing what he intended to do with the money. After all, it was his fault the man had missed his date.

A footnote to the tale—

In the fall of 1928, Jack Dempsey appeared in a vaudeville act at the Strand Theatre in Long Beach, California. I was a sports writer on the Long Beach *Press-Telegram* and interviewed him. The ex-champion, whose short-lived career as a promoter in Chicago had just ended unexpectedly and unexplained, was disillusioned.

"I quit," he told me in a story that was reprinted throughout the country, "because I was being used as a front, a promoter in name only. Capone's mob wound up telling me who was going to fight and how much I had to pay them. When they started giving orders who was going to win and who was going to lose—and naming the round—I got out."

Jack's partner was Leonard Sachs and, of course his backer was Joe. Joe Lewis, stone broke, had unknowingly financed Dempsey, a millionaire.

There was a telegram for Joe at the hotel: "COMPARTMENT C, CAR 601, THE CHIEF TONIGHT. JOLIE."

Joe went. There was nowhere else to go. He was tapped out and so was Fogarty. McGurn would have to wait.

It was his first time in Los Angeles and he loved it. He moved into the Ambassador Hotel and loafed for the next nine months, hardly missing a day at the hotel pool or on the golf course. Jolson never made a better investment. Joe's body mended, his mind and speech became clearer. He even forgot about McGurn until he received a call from Frank Gusenberg in Chicago.

"There will be some news about the Gunner in tomorrow morning's paper," Gusenberg told him.

An hour *after* the call, on the evening of March 7th, McGurn narrowly escaped death in an ambush when his car was riddled with machine-gun bullets. Joe's friends on the Moran mob had not forgotten.

It was a time for laughter, Hollywood in 1928.

One Sunday afternoon, Joe flew to Agua Caliente with Jolson, Darryl Zanuck and Jack Warner in a chartered plane. A few minutes after taking off, Jolson, an amateur pilot, went into the cockpit and took the controls for a few minutes.

"Let's have some fun with the boys," the pilot suggested. "I'll walk back and let you fly the ship. Do you think they'll mind?"

"I don't think they'll mind," Jolson replied, "but I will."

At the Cocoanut Grove one evening, a drunk made an improper remark to Ruby Keeler, Jolson's current wife. Al slugged him. The drunk's pal came in swinging and Joe dropped him with a left to the jaw. Ben Lyon, the film star, came over, looked at the fallen gladiators and hoisted Joe's hand and Jolson's.

"The win-nahs!" he announced to the applauding crowd.

One Sunday night, late in the fall, Fatty Arbuckle, then skidding to his tragic nadir as a master of ceremonies at the Plantation in Culver City, spotted Joe in the audience and asked him to come up and do a number. That's life, Joe reflected. Eight years previously, as a boy of eighteen, he had trailed the then famous Arbuckle for hours on the boardwalk at Atlantic City, hoping to meet him and sing for him.

He appreciated the invitation but he was certain that Arbuckle did not expect him to accept it. It was a gesture, he was repaying a favor. A few nights before, Joe had bailed him out of jail on a drunk charge. Liberated from the tank, Arbuckle wrung Joe's hand. "Thanks, Joe . . . By the way, I met an awfully nice fellow in there. Bail him out too, will you?" Arbuckle didn't forget his friends.

"Ladies and gentlemen, that game little comedian from Chicago—Joe Lewis!"

The crowd was applauding him. He stood up at his table and took a bow. "Thanks, Roscoe," he said and sat down.

Someone hollered, "We want Joe Lewis!" and in a moment the Plantation echoed with the cry. He could not understand the clamor. He had not sung a note since his last catastrophic night at the Rendezvous the previous winter.

"We want Lewis!" The cries had swollen to a full chorus. He was grateful. He knew he would have to respect the crowd's wishes and he was glad, he wanted to find out if he *could* sing.

Hollywood had just discovered its voice and Joe attempted to rediscover his with the same song, "Sonny Boy." He did a take-off on Jolson's historic lullaby, not only because he was familiar with Al's mannerisms but because it was a slow number and would not tax his limited capacity.

The club was loaded with Joe's friends, among them Jolson, Dempsey, Tom Mix, Ruth Roland, Lew Cody, Buster Keaton, Buddy Rogers and Ruth Elder, and they gave him a tremendous ovation. Joe's performance was unrehearsed but theirs was not. They had planned this night, conspired with Arbuckle, made sure of Joe's presence and started the "We want Joe Lewis" demonstration.

Joe had forgotten his anniversary but they had not. It was November ninth, one year since McGurn's men had left him for dead.

The Hollywood columnists and wire services had been alerted by Jolson. It was a good human-interest story and Joe was immensely popular in the movie colony. Everyone was eager to give him a break.

"Lewis' voice is better than ever!" one syndicated writer reported. "He is on his way back!" predicted another. They wanted him to sound like Bing Crosby and, to them that night, he did. Actually, he sounded like a welterweight Andy Devine.

Two days later, Joe received an offer of $750 a week for a minimum of four weeks in December at the Parody Club in New York, to follow Clayton, Jackson and Durante.

Joe had no intention of taking it. "It would be suicide to follow those guys," he said, "even if I *had* my voice back."

"Take it," Jolson told him.

"No, Al. I'm scared."

Jolson's face hardened. "Then go back selling haberdashery."

9   *Blood Brothers*

"Hope your opening is bigger than our three noses," Clayton, Jackson and Durante wired him to the Parody Club.

It was not.

After the third disastrous night Joe went to the owner, Johnny Hodges. "I can't take your money," he said. "Let's call it off."

"Are you crazy? Business is good!"

"But I'm not." He was still inarticulate, his voice functioning little better than it had a year previously when he had attempted his first comeback at the Rendezvous.

"You have to be patient, Joe," Hodges told him. "You'll be better every week—wait and see."

Joe stuck out the four weeks, his delivery improved and, two nights before he closed, he received a surprising telegram from Chicago. Danny Cohen was out of the defunct Green Mill and the new combination believed that the best man to resuscitate it was the one who had left it to die. Would Joe come back for $1,000 a week plus a cut of the cover charges and a blank contract to remain as long as he desired?

He would, with pleasure.

He was not as pitiful as he had been the year before but his brain and his speech still were not co-ordinated: he lacked the essential timing that makes the difference between a star and a tenth-rater. The Green Mill did some business but neither it nor Joe could recapture their popularity of 1927. Customers were drawn out of curiosity or pity and few came back.

Bugs Moran furnished him with a car emblazoned with an official shield of Deputy Sheriff and he prowled the South Side constantly in search of McGurn. One day at the Cicero dog track he looked up to see the Gunner blocking his path. A mobman, Charlie Fischetti, was with him.

McGurn motioned him to pass.

Joe did not move. This was the moment he had dreamed about and rehearsed countless times. He had visualized his revenge in every form of violence. The moment to act had come.

"I trusted you once before," he said tonelessly. He had declared himself. By the law of their jungle McGurn had to take the challenge and deny his guilt—or back down.

McGurn's eyes narrowed. Then he walked away. Fischetti followed.

The long jagged scar on Joe's face wrinkled into a smile, contemptuous and triumphant. He had his revenge.

It was a dull night at the Green Mill. The last of the drunks had staggered out, shortly past 4 A.M., and Joe was leaving when Pete and Frank Gusenberg, loaded from a night of swilling, roared in. "Joey! . . . How the hell are you, kid?" They shouted, threw their arms around him and smothered him in affectionate embraces.

"I know you're doing the town," said Joe, struggling free, "but you're not doing it any good."

Pete and Frank bellowed appreciative laughter. "You're a pistol, Joe," Frank gasped. "You're a real pistol!"

Joe moved toward the door but Pete Gusenberg intercepted him. "You can't leave now, Joey! We came to see *you!*"

Al Leonard, one of the new owners of the Green Mill, was pale and apprehensive. "Don't leave me alone, Joe," he begged. "You know how they get when they're plastered."

Joe wearily sat down between the brothers, who were ordering Leonard to start hauling whiskey.

"You know something, kid," said Frank with a hiccough, wrapping one arm around Joe's shoulder and pointing with the other to Leonard, now behind the bar, "there's one sonofabitch I don't like."

"Al's all right," Joe responded. "Since business picked up, he's suffering from clean underwear, that's all."

Pete guffawed but Frank did not think it was funny. "He's a chinchy sonofabitch and I hate his guts," he growled. Suddenly his face lighted with the zealous gleam of an Archimedes. "I got it! I'm going to give that sonofabitch a Mickey."

"Lay off him, Frank," Joe pleaded and, hoping to kid him out of his rancor, added, "If he was alive he'd be a sick man."

"I'm giving him a Mickey." Frank threw him a look of warning as Leonard approached with a tray of bottles.

The four men settled down to serious drinking, Joe entertaining the Gusenbergs with an unbroken chain of stories that soon had Frank laughing as loudly as Pete. "You're a pistol, Joey!" Frank cried, pounding him on the back with such ardor Joe thought his spinal column was severed.

He recovered and continued his quips but, to prevent permanent injury from subsequent approval, he kept one arm on Frank's shoulder and slapped *his* back on every pay-off line.

As Frank became more sodden, the benevolent side of his nature asserted itself. He reached into his pocket and pulled out a thick roll of bills. "Here, Joey," he said and slapped them into his hand.

Joe stared at the money. The smallest denomination was a fifty and their sum was at least $10,000. "I don't need any dough," he said and handed it back.

"Take it, I made a killing today." Frank forced the roll into his hand, turned to Leonard impatiently and pointed to the untouched drink in front of him. "Drink up!" he commanded. Joe took advantage of Frank's distraction to stuff the bills in the hoodlum's coat pocket.

Gusenberg whirled around. "Don't be a sucker, Joey. I can afford it."

"When I need a handout," Joe said, "I'll let you know."

Frank scowled for a moment and then wrapped an arm around him. "You're all right, Joey." He finished another drink. "And you know something, you're the luckiest sonof-abitch in town."

Joe nodded. He was too tired to throw him a gag.

"Bet you don't know why you're lucky . . ."

"Let's go home," Pete interrupted with a yawn.

"If you hadn't opened the door at the Commonwealth that morning," Frank continued, "McGurn was gonna plant a bomb in your room." He hugged Joe. "You're the luckiest sonofabitch in town." Joe was so engrossed trying to extricate himself from his embrace that he did not notice the hoodlum slip some bills in his breast pocket.

While they were preoccupied and Pete napped, Leonard poured a fresh drink for Frank and switched it with his own.

Joe remembered one of Frank's favorite stories and clapped him on the back after the punch-line.

"Don't do that!" There was menace in Frank's voice.

"Don't do what?" Joe was puzzled.

Frank tried to speak but could not. He stared at the glass he had emptied in one gulp and his face turned green. A powerful purgative had just exploded in his intestines. He staggered to his feet and called to Pete, who awakened with a start.

Leonard sidled up to Joe. "Get him out of here," he whispered, "there's going to be trouble."

Joe turned pale. "Let me help you, Frank." He offered his hand.

Frank clutched his abdomen with both hands, pain and venom in his face.

"What's the matter, Frank?" Pete was at his brother's side.

Frank pointed to Joe. "The double-crossin' rat . . ." he gasped. "He gave *me* the Mickey!"

"No, Frank!" Joe was shouting his innocence. "Honest I didn't."

Frank groaned and Pete reached for his gun. Before he could draw, Frank grabbed him. "Get me out of here!"

Pete led him to the door. Frank braced himself in the doorway and glared at Joe. "I'll see you tomorrow, *Lewis*— and I'll remember all them pats on the back. I'll . . ." He was seized by another spasm and he left, pulling Pete with him.

Joe turned to Leonard scornfully. "That was smart, Al . . ."

"Don't worry," Leonard said, picking up the bottles, "he won't remember anything in the morning."

"He'll still be on the can in the morning."

Little of the night was left. He slept only fitfully, awaking every few minutes in a cold sweat. He gave up at 10 A.M.

and shaved, so hurriedly that he cut himself, a nasty gash that took almost ten minutes to stanch. Blood from the scar, it was a bad omen.

In changing from the suit he had worn the previous night he removed the handkerchief from the breast pocket and three fifty-dollar bills fluttered to the floor.

Oh no, he groaned. It was bad enough that Frank Gusenberg thought he had slipped him the Mickey Finn but when he remembered that he had given him $150 . . . Joe shuddered. The Gusenbergs were killers. Twice as tough as McGurn because there were two of them. Two pals who had guarded his life at Columbia Memorial Hospital. Two pals who had tried to kill McGurn for him. And this, they had to think, was the way he showed his gratitude. By slipping Frank a Mickey.

Joe finished dressing quickly. This time he was not waiting for anyone to call. He was going straight to Frank Gusenberg and return the three fifty-dollar bills, he would swear that he had not switched the Mickey and hope to hell he would believe him.

Joe knew where to find Frank. It was a cold wintry day and he looked for a cab. None was in sight and he started walking. There was a cab on the next corner. He started for it but changed his mind. No use hurrying, he reasoned, maybe Gusenberg isn't himself yet. He walked up North Clark Street, passed Number 511—Fogarty's old New Rendezvous with its memories—and suddenly his confidence left him. Why should the Gusenbergs believe him? They were animals, incapable of reason. Why should he be able to dissuade them any more successfully than the three hoodlums who had come to his room? They were blood brothers.

"I'll see you tomorrow, *Lewis* . . ." Frank Gusenberg's threat echoed through his brain as he trudged past the 1900 block on North Clark. They did not bluff. He had learned that—the hard way. Should he appeal to Bugs Moran? No,

"Stay off the streets," Joe warned Vincent (Schemer) Drucci (below left), boss of the North Side mob. Drucci ignored him, died the same night with four bullets in his belly. *International News Photo.*

Frank Gusenberg, hoodlum killer (below center), guarded Joe, later threatened him. "I'll remember all them pats on the back," were his last words. *International News Photo.*

Pete Gusenberg (below right) pulled his gun on Joe. Nobody could give his brother a Mickey Finn and get away with it. Pete didn't know he and Frank had less than six hours to live. *International News Photo.*

The place, 2122 North Clark Street, Chicago. The time, 10:35 A.M., St. Valentine's Day, 1929. The corpses, five members of Bugs Moran's gang (including Frank and Pete Gusenberg) and two "friends," wiped out by Capone, McGurn and Co. If Joe had taken a taxi, he would have been the eighth. *International News Photo.*

that wasn't any good. Bugs had not stopped McGurn and he would not stop the Gusenbergs. This was *their* game. He was the pigeon, a pigeon who looked for hunters.

He stiffened. Sirens were screaming and coming closer. He looked up. There was a road block ahead and a cordon of police was holding back a large, excited crowd. Squad cars and ambulances were converging from all directions.

Joe moved into the throng. Everyone's attention was focused on Number 2122, a garage. This was the place, the S.M.C. Cartage Company, a beer and alcohol drop of the Moran gang. A moment later Joe saw Frank Gusenberg. Being carried out on a stretcher . . .

Twenty minutes earlier, at 10:30 A.M., Frank and Pete had been on duty waiting for a consignment of hijacked liquor. Without warning, two policemen entered the garage and ordered the Gusenbergs and their companions to raise their hands and line up along the side wall. The hoodlums readily complied and made no protest as the cops disarmed them. They were accustomed to routine police raids; they would be hauled down to headquarters, go through the legal mummery of an arrest and be sprung by noon.

But not this time.

The policemen were not ordinary policemen. Only their uniforms were bona fide. And they had no intention of taking these law breakers anywhere. In a moment they were joined by two other men in civilian clothes, armed with sawed-off shotguns, and two others carrying submachine guns.

It was St. Valentine's Day, 1929.

Joe watched the seven corpses being hauled out. Five of them—the Gusenbergs, James Clark, John May and Adam Hyer—had been working members of Moran's mob. The other two—Alfred Weinshank, a mechanic, and Reinhart Schwimmer, an optometrist who had an adolescent's worship for gangsters—had dropped in for social calls. Six of the seven were dead when the authentic police arrived. The dying man was Frank Gusenberg. He quickly joined Pete without leaving any words for posterity.

Joe walked away slowly. He stopped at Fogarty's hotel and slumped in a chair. "How do you figure it, John?" he asked. "If I hadn't cut myself shaving and lost ten minutes, or if I hadn't changed my mind about taking that cab, I would have been the *eighth* patsy in there."

"Don't try to figure it," Fogarty said. "When your number is up, it's up. Not a minute earlier or later."

Joe opened the palm of his moist right hand which had been clutching the three fifty-dollar bills since he left his hotel room. "When I see Frank again," he said matter-of-factly, "I'll give him $150 worth of pari-mutuel tickets."

Machine Gun Jack McGurn was arrested that night, positively identified by eyewitnesses as one of the men who had been seen emerging from the garage after the slaughter.

"He's getting warmer," Joe said with a wry smile.

10   *Two Bits Against $50,000*

It was the summer of 1929, America was enjoying the last clenched ecstasy of the boom. Everyone was rich and getting richer, everyone except Joe. He was finished in Chicago and unwanted in New York. Friends offered him money but not jobs. He was no longer an entertainer but an oddity, like a flagpole sitter or an albino. He was "The Man the Gangsters Couldn't Kill." The curious came to see his scars and the permanent grin they carved, like Victor Hugo's tragic hero, "The Man Who Smiles." He might have found work in a tent but not in a cabaret.

"Might as well go to the ball game," his brother Murray suggested one day after a month of fruitless plodding in New York. "The Cubs are in town."

Joe drove Murray toward the Polo Grounds. "Looks like rain," he said, noting the threatening clouds.

"It won't rain," Murray said confidently.

Five minutes later it was pouring. Joe turned around and headed downtown. He wanted to go somewhere, anywhere. He stopped for a traffic light, looked up and saw a sign, JOE HALL, TRAVEL AGENCY. In the show window beneath were several posters. One of them arrested his attention, the lithograph of a horse in full stride.

"Come on!" Murray shouted. "The light's green."

Joe did not hear him. "I know where I'm going," he said.

Two days later he was aboard the *S.S. Leviathan* bound for England. The horse in Joe Hall's window that had attracted his attention was on a poster announcing the Derby at Epsom Downs.

"Why the hell are you going to the Epsom Derby?" Murray had asked as Joe put down his case money for the trip.

"I've never seen one," Joe replied.

He had a little trouble in London making himself understood. After his cab passed his hotel three times he whacked the driver with the back of his hand. That was his fourth and last day in England. The police advised him to leave. Charged with assault and battery against the cabbie, he asked the magistrate, "How else can you get to your hotel?"

Germany was his next stop. On his first night in Berlin he walked into an obscure café alone. Almost immediately the master of ceremonies, a stranger to him, announced, "We are honored tonight with the presence of one of America's outstanding comedians—the great Joe Lewis!"

He was astounded and flattered that he had been recognized. A moment later his ego was deflated when his friends, Smith and Dale of the Avon Comedy Four, joined him. They had spotted him as he came in and had tipped off the master of ceremonies.

Knowing no German, he had difficulty finding companionship, even on the Friedrichstrasse where hustlers were permitted to operate. At last he hit on the idea of pretending he was drunk and trying to count a handful of marks as he staggered along the *Strasse*. Within a few minutes he was surrounded by frauleins eager to help him, even if it took all night, a gambit that would never fail him the world over.

Joe dabbled in German currency for several days and staggered on to Paris. He planned to remain there a week or two, if his money held out, but an item in the European edition of the New York *Herald Tribune* changed his mind. Jackie Fields of Los Angeles had just been matched with Joe Dundee, the welterweight champion of the world, for a title fight at Detroit.

"Jackie's going to be champ some day," Benny Leonard, the master lightweight, had prophesied when he introduced Joe to Fields two years previously.

"And I'll be there when he wins it," Joe had said.

He left for home on the first ship out of Havre. It was an automatic decision. He had given Jackie Fields his word.

Except for his family, no one was aware he had been gone. It was July, everyone was playing the stock market. Now he had to promote enough money to get to Detroit and put a bet on Fields.

He had no music, no act, no voice. Just a straw hat minus a brim, which was supposed to make people laugh, and a cane that had belonged to Flo Ziegfeld.

Not a club owner in New York would give him an audition. It looked hopeless when the manager of the State Lake Theatre in Chicago said he would take a chance on him.

The last-minute cancellation of an act had given him no alternative.

Joe smiled grimly. He still had curiosity value in Chicago, at least in vaudeville. Vaudeville . . . What can I do in *vaudeville?* he suddenly wondered. He had not been able to make himself heard, let alone understood, in small, intimate rooms like the Green Mill or the Parody. How could his feeble, incoherent voice carry through the huge State Lake Theatre with its thousands of seats?

"I'll take it." He *had* to get to Detroit and, who knows, maybe people who went to vaudeville would laugh at his funny hat.

Joe arrived in Chicago the morning of his opening and, unable to find an available piano player, he appealed to an old friend, Solly Wagner, who played at the Midnight Frolics. Solly came to his rescue but on learning that Joe had no music he became panicky.

"What can we play?" he asked desperately an hour before the curtain.

"You were with me at the Green Mill. Try to remember some of those songs."

Solly's memory was a temporary blank.

Joe cudgeled his brain for a tune. "Ta-*tah*-da . . . ta-*tah*-da . . . You know, Solly."

Solly could not possibly know from Joe's uncertain ta-tah-das.

At last Joe remembered the title. " 'Chicago,' Solly! Play 'Chicago' !"

Solly played it and, from that day, it was his song: from Broadway to the Sunset Strip, the opening bars announced that Joe Lewis was coming on.

"Congratulations on your entry into vaudeville," Van and Schenck, his favorite singing team, wired him. "Hope you knock 'em for a row and become a standard vaudevillian."

The patrons at the opening matinee were not knocked for a row. They were unamused either because they did not understand what he was saying or because they did. It was impossible to tell where one of his jokes ended and the next one began. He pounded the stage with his cane and waved his brimless straw hat but no one laughed.

"You folks are so quiet," he said at last. "I like a respectful audience but you people are being downright reverent."

It was not a line for a vaudeville matinee. Between those who could not comprehend Joe's lisped enunciation of *reverent* and those who did not know the meaning of the word, he lost the whole audience.

"I got an impediment in my speech," he said disconsolately. "I just can't seem to say anything funny."

They did not know whether that was supposed to be a joke and they took no chances. They did not want to laugh at his defect, not knowingly.

He told another joke at desperate speed. After the punchline he pounded his cane and its hollow echo was the only sound in the vast theatre. "Come on, folks," he said. "That was your last chance to laugh. I know the rest of the material."

It was futile and he quit trying. Maybe they would like his songs. He gave Solly the cue for "Far Rockaway." There was no response. He gave it a second time. Not a chord. Joe looked down in the pit. Solly Wagner, who had played at the Midnight Frolics until 6 A.M. and had not yet gone to bed, was asleep at the piano.

Solly was awakened, the show went on and the audience went to sleep.

Joe did not become the "standard vaudevillian" Van and Schenck hoped for him but the engagement served its purpose. It got him to Detroit and he saw Jackie Fields win his championship. He had kept his promise.

Where now? New York was out. All he could do there

was go to the ball games with Murray—in the summertime when it did not rain. Los Angeles was out too. He had been its guest. That left Chicago.

A few loyal friends remained but not enough. The Green Mill put him on for two months. From there he caught on with the Beau Monde, across the street from the darkened Rendezvous. That lasted ten weeks. Then he retraced his steps, back to the South Side, back to the Midnight Frolics where he had started, this time without a voice.

It was Joe's last trip around and he knew it.

He was sitting in the Four Deuces, wondering where he could go, when he felt a tap on his shoulder. "The Big Guy wants you," a hard-faced messenger whispered.

Capone had been away. It was common knowledge he had ordered the St. Valentine's Day massacre but, at the moment Moran's gang was being lined against the wall on North Clark Street, Capone was seated in the office of the District Attorney in Dade County, Florida. He had happened to drop in for a social chat. Notwithstanding, lest remnants of Moran's mob should make any impulsive reprisals, Capone had himself arrested in Philadelphia for carrying a concealed weapon. While he was serving his term, his ambassadors signed peace treaties and consolidated the empire. Al was patient, he was only thirty-two.

Joe was escorted to Capone's headquarters, which occupied the sixth, seventh and eighth floors of the Lexington Hotel.

Capone had not seen Joe since the slashing. The scar that bisected Joe's left jaw fascinated him. He fingered his own knife wound that had given him his nickname and smiled. "Hiya, Scarface," he greeted Joe.

"Hello, Al."

"How are things?"

"Okay!"

Capone's flabby jaw hardened. "You're a stinkin' liar.

You're through at the Frolics. You can't get a job on the North Side *or* the South Side!"

Joe shrugged.

"Why the hell didn't you come to me when you had your trouble?" He pointed to Joe's scar. "I'd have straightened things out."

"It's over now."

Capone opened a desk drawer, took out a bulky envelope and handed it to him.

Joe lifted the open flap. Inside was a sheaf of thousand-dollar bills. "What's the gag?"

"I told you it would be waitin' for you—and Capone always keeps his word. Fifty big ones and if that ain't enough, you can have more."

Joe was bewildered. "I don't know what you're talking about!"

Capone was impatient. "Have you lost your memory *too*? I told you I'd back you—any joint in the Loop you want. Remember?"

Joe remembered now. The night Capone blew into the Midnight Frolics and sweated Ralph Gillette into giving him his first raise. That was almost four years ago. He remembered Capone saying something about staking him to $50,000 if Gillette gave him any trouble but he thought it was just a line to impress Gillette; he had not suspected that Al had been ribbing on the square. He closed the flap and handed the envelope back.

"Thanks, Al—but I can't take it."

Capone was not accustomed to being refused—anything. "The smell bother you? It all comes out of the same barrel, y'know."

"That isn't it."

"Then *what* is it? You're washed up, pal. You're back on the Levee, with your ass coming out of your pants. You got to wind up bummin' canned heat and a flop at the Salvation Army."

"I'll take my chances," Joe said.

"You took 'em with McGurn—and you came out a bad second." Capone pushed the envelope toward him. "You won't have to kiss anybody's keaster for a job. You'll be your own boss." He paused and his voice softened. "Take it, Joe."

Joe hesitated. Time had run out for him. He was bankrupt: he had no voice, no money, no material, no confidence, no work and no prospects. "The customers can't understand you, Joe," the kindest of the club owners had explained to him regretfully. Maybe Capone was right. He had been right about everything else in Chicago. Maybe he would wind up flopping in Skid Row gospels.

"Things are different since the market crashed," Capone went on. "The country's headin' for a depression—a bad one."

"I'm not afraid of a depression," Joe said. "I went broke during the boom."

That made Capone laugh. He stood up, the envelope in his hand. "We'll put up the fanciest joint in the Loop." He wrapped an arm around Joe's shoulders. "We'll be partners but I don't want a dime out of it. It's all yours. In five years you'll be worth a million. I'll see to it."

Joe thought about it. A million. That was better than bumming canned heat—or was it? "You can't miss—with me as your partner." Capone and Lewis, Partners. He remembered Cap Goldberg. "And you said you were an entertainer, not a hoodlum." Who was right, Cap or Capone? Cap represented the official law, but was he right? This was Anarchy, 1929, life at a time when the public considered a Constitutional law illegal and refused to abide by it. Capone law, the law of the lawless, was the actual law, the only law being enforced. Men lived by it and died by it. "I can't change conditions," Capone had said. "I just meet them without backing up." Joe looked again at the envelope with the fifty one-thousand-dollar bills inside. Capone was trying to force them into his coat pocket. Joe's hand was in the way, holding his total assets. Two dimes and a nickel . . . He kept thinking. Capone and Lewis, Partners . . . Goldberg and Lewis, friends . . . Right and wrong . . . Poverty and wealth . . . Expediency and . . .

"No dice," he said firmly, pushing away Capone's hand and the envelope. There was no alternative. He had to gamble his two bits against Capone's $50,000. He was a long-shot player and the odds were right, 200,000 to 1.

"You're a sucker, Joe," said the porcine-faced thug who soon would be a number at Alcatraz prison.

"Good-bye, Al." He might be a washed-up tenth-rater but he was still an entertainer. Nobody could take that away from him, not even the Big Guy. That is all he had ever wanted to do, entertain people.

Joe packed that night. He would not see Chicago again for three years. By then Prohibition and this Chicago would be dead, by then his twenties and Chicago's '20's would be gone.

Who speaks for Chicago's '20's?

Carl Sandburg or Louis Armstrong, Gabby Hartnett or Mayor William Hale Thompson, Ben Hecht or Sam Insull, Sherwood Anderson or King Levinsky, Ernie Byfield or Amos Alonzo Stagg, Edgar Lee Masters or Leopold and Loeb?

Or was it Francis Scott Key Fitzgerald, who sniveled, "Here was a new generation . . . grown up to find all gods dead, all wars fought, all faiths in men shaken"?

They speak for the Nightmare Decade who spoke then . . .

Dion O'Bannion, florist, safe blower, gunman, rum runner and founder of the North Side mob, was a sensitive man, proud of his reputation as an upright fixer, pay-off man and general liaison between the Unione Siciliano and the so-called law agencies. One evening in the lobby of a LaSalle Street theatre he encountered, by chance he claimed, the Brothers Miller, Davie and Maxie, who had questioned his integrity regarding a miscarried bribe.

"Hello, Davie . . . Maxie." O'Bannion greeted them graciously as he gently placed a revolver against the abdomen of each brother and fired. Davie fell dead instantly, his intestines blown to bits. Maxie wore his belt an inch higher and the bullet mushroomed on the buckle.

O'Bannion had not "grown up to find all gods dead, all wars fought . . ." Along with his three guns he carried a rosary and went to Mass regularly at the Holy Name Cathedral, where he had been an altar boy, across the street from his flower shop.

Some time later he was standing midst his roses and orchids, a gun in each pocket and a pruning shears in his hand, when three old friends came in. "Good to see you, Deanie!" the man in the middle said, shaking O'Bannion's hand and *holding* on while his two companions fired six bullets into the florist.

The first extras reporting O'Bannion's liquidation had not yet hit the streets before each Chicago newspaper received a telephone call from an interested party. "This is Louie Altarie—A-L-T-A-R-I-E. Two Gun Altarie," the caller introduced himself. "I want to put an ad in the paper that I'll meet the murderer of my pal Deanie any place they want and shoot it out with 'em."

Two Gun Altarie was a loyal friend. A few months previously, another pal of his, Nails Morgan, while enjoying a morning ride on the bridle path in Lincoln Park, was thrown from his saddle and killed when his horse bolted. Immediately upon hearing of the accident, Altarie rushed to the livery stable and rented the horse, a notorious bucker, on which Nails had taken his last ride. Two Gun galloped the spirited steed to a secluded spot and dismounted. "There!" he shouted vindictively, drew his revolver and shot the horse dead. "Nobody can kill my pal and get away with it."

Not even four-legged animals were excluded from Chicago's concept of jurisprudence, the law of the gun, the bomb and the torch.

Earl (Hymie) Weiss, bequeathed O'Bannion's rosary and command of the North Side, declared war on Capone. He organized a motorcade of thirty cars, each equipped with a submachine gun, invaded the suburb of Cicero, Capone's citadel, and turned it into a shooting gallery. After dispersing the innocent citizens with blank cartridges, they blew out the front of every building owned or occupied by the Big Guy's banditti. One gunsel sprayed the lobby of the Hawthorne Hotel with a hundred bullets, in broad daylight.

Capone, flat on the floor of the Hawthorne restaurant, ignored the raid.

Two months later, Weiss' men kidnapped Tom Ross, Capone's chauffeur. They tortured him and, failing to extort any information from him on the movements of his employer, killed him and tossed his body into an eastern Chicago cistern.

Capone ignored the murder—for two months.

The case of the People versus Joseph Soltis, North Side beer runner, on trial for the murder of a gangster named Mitters Foley, droned on perfidiously to its inevitable acquittal and, in the front row of spectators, Hymie Weiss checked off the names on his list, one by one, as the parade of witnesses for the prosecution, intimidated by Weiss' men, filed through the courtroom leaving a perjured trail of lapsed memories.

The judge, bored with the travesty, called for a recess and Weiss, pleased with the way the case was progressing, left with his retinue to process the next batch of witnesses.

Hymie, flanked by two bodyguards, his attorney and an investigator, reached the corner of the Holy Name Cathedral when they were halted by a hail of lead. Weiss fell dead with twelve slugs in his body, one of his bodyguards was killed and the three others were wounded. A bullet chipped the cornice of the church.

Capone justice had been meted out from an upper-story building at 740 State Street . . .

> *On State Street, that great street,*
> *I just wanna say . . .*

The cartridge cylinder had made a full turn and the round robin of killing had paused, momentarily, where it had begun, on the blood-spattered sidewalk across the street from O'Bannion's Flower Shop, the Sarajevo of their world's war.

They spoke for Chicago's '20's and their words were written in gore on the streets, alleys, parks, hotels, bars, brothels, gambling blinds, newspapers, the City Hall, the state capital and the churches.

A hoodlum named Joe Howard slapped Jake (Greasy Thumb) Guzik when Jake was earning his nickname as a waiter at the Four Deuces. Jake told Capone and Capone cornered Howard at Hymie Jacob's saloon at 2300 South Wabash. "What's the idea picking on Guzik?" he asked.

"Go back to your whores, dago."

Capone's retort was six bullets in Joe Howard's head.

Frank J. Loesch, counsel for the Pennsylvania Railroad, president of the Chicago Crime Commission and a distinguished member of the National Committee on Law Observance and Enforcement, waited humbly, hat in hand, in the anteroom of Capone's headquarters at the Lexington. At last he was ushered into the presence of the Big Guy—to ask him if he would permit the citizens of Chicago to select their own state's attorney in the coming election.

"Sure," Capone smiled. "I'm so strong it don't make any difference which bum is elected." Chicago had an honest election for a change but Capone was right, it made no difference.

When Assistant State's Attorney William A. McSwiggan was mowed down by machine-gun fire near Capone's headquarters in Cicero, Capone released his customary denial of any complicity in the murder and added, "I was no enemy of Mac. I paid him and I paid him plenty."

They spoke for Chicago's '20's . . .

"The only guys you can trust are those you got murder on," Jack Zelig, a Capone Fagin, indoctrinated young disciples. Zelig got murder on many men until the day he vanished in the gun smoke of Red Davison, one he had apparently overlooked.

Alfred (Jake) Lingle, a $65-a-week legman on the Chicago *Tribune,* bet $500 a day at the Washington Park race track. He was Capone's chief of police, he fixed everything from a dog race to an election.

Lingle was entering a subway kiosk, en route to Washington Park, when a blond, hatless man raised his left hand, pressed a .38 caliber Colt revolver to the back of the *Tribune* man's head and dispatched a bullet through his brain. More than 300 persons were within sound of the shot, ten witnessed the killing and the slayer disappeared forever.

Two reliable eyewitnesses swore that they saw Machine Gun Jack McGurn leave the scene of the St. Valentine's Day slaughter with a Thompson gun under his arm.

"That's impossible," a pretty blonde named Louise Rolfe testified. "He was in bed with me."

The Law believed Louise Rolfe, nol-prossed the charge and McGurn lived to shoot another day. He conspired with John Scalise and Albert Anselmi, notorious Unione Siciliano gunmen, to assassinate Capone for $50,000 and, the same day, betrayed them to Capone. Shortly after, he was master of ceremonies at a historic testimonial dinner in honor of Scalise and Anselmi.

Dozens of champagne toasts were hoisted and countless tributes were paid to the long and brilliant careers of Scalise and Anselmi. At last McGurn shook each by the hand and said, emotionally, "Good-bye, John . . . Good-bye, Albert. We're all gonna miss you."

"I'm not goin' nowhere," said Scalise.

"Me neither," said Anselmi.

McGurn and one of his aides nodded sadly, trussed the honored guests to the rafters with baling wire and Capone bludgeoned them to death with a baseball bat. McGurn shot off their fingers and planted bullets in their eyes, his personal tribute to the two pals who, less than three months previously, had stood beside him in the St. Valentine's Day massacre.

They spoke for Chicago's '20's.

They did not analyze, they acted. F. Scott Fitzgerald, Edna St. Vincent Millay, John Dos Passos, Henry L. Mencken and Edmund Wilson did not speak for them and it is possible that they did not speak for the '20's as eloquently as these bootleggers, thieves, prostitutes, pimps, politicians and murderers who lived, loved, hated, dreamed, hoped and died, oblivious that theirs was supposed to be a lost generation.

It was their Renaissance, their golden age of opportunity. The ratification of a Constitutional Amendment that could not be enforced made anarchy inevitable and only they, as anarchists, were prepared to cope with it. They assumed control and made Chicago the capital of lawlessness because, as Nelson Algren said, it was always "a hustlers' town that kept two faces, one for the hunter and one for the prey, a town for bulls and foxes where the lambs wind up head down from a hook." Capone's claim that he was not illegal but that the law was, would be vindicated. Prohibition was repealed and Capone died a free man but it would take thirteen years, ten months and twenty-nine days to prove that blood was as important as whiskey.

In this tragic twilight of morality Joe Lewis walked through a no-man's land between right and wrong, a line as indefinable as a Prohibition agent's loyalty. District attorneys, mayors, governors, congressmen, senators, judges and cabinet members went astray or fell but Joe did not lose his way.

"Here was a new generation . . . grown up to find all gods dead, all wars fought, all faiths in men shaken."

Fitzgerald's generation was not lost, not more than any other that had gone before or would come after. He was lost. It was a time when "every man stood alone with his own symbolic bull and had either his moment of truth or his early death in the afternoon." Joe Lewis, a member in good standing of that generation, was born only four years later than Fitzgerald. He enjoyed drink as much as Fitzgerald did, perhaps more, but he did not blame it on his lost gods, lost faiths, lost dreams, a lost wife or even a few losses Fitzgerald never suffered: a lost face, a lost voice, a lost livelihood.

Scott Fitzgerald and his kind could not take the '20's. They folded, like any patsy who can't take a punch. One belt threw them. It might be an unfaithful wife, a war, a taste of alcohol or a fortieth birthday: any one was enough to make them quit. Fitzgerald could not pick himself off the floor with nothing to hold him back except a bellyful of whiskey. Joe, a speechless cripple, the left side of his face hanging open, his right arm paralyzed, his blood running out, lifted himself off the floor and dragged himself back to life.

Joe made it because he had courage and the will of survival, a strength born of a humble yet overwhelming desire to live so that he could entertain people, so that he could make people laugh.

The voice that was gone forever? The scars? He forgave

his Chicago. She had hurt him and tried to kill him because she had loved him so much. He knew that and he forgave her because she was drunk and didn't know what she was doing.

He could have put in with Capone but he didn't. He had had enough of hoodlums. He was leaving Chicago. And gangdom.

A few months later, Joe's closest friend would be a man named Schultz. Dutch Schultz.

11   *A Bad Pretzel*

The man who had been billed as the "King of Cabaret Entertainers" was now second banana to a comedian named Al Trahan in *The Second Little Show,* a flimsy revue, directed by Monty Wooley, that was staggering through a three-week tryout at the Wilbur Theatre in Boston. And he was providing the only flicker of amusement in the dismal proceedings.

In a skit written by the then unknown Robert E. Sherwood, en route to becoming a distinguished playwright, Joe was cast as Moe, an Indian trader who sells the island of Manhattan for twenty-four dollars and a keg of rum. Joe-Moe is subsequently made the Chief of his tribe as a reward for putting one over on the Dutch, who obviously did not know how valuable a keg of rum was. The theme is something less than belly-shaking in print but as interpreted by Joe, or by contrast to the rest of the material, it was amusing.

"Joe Lewis is the only member of the cast worth seeing," John A. Malloy wrote in the Boston *American,* "but he wasn't on long enough to save the show. If the management had any brains, it would give him the lead."

The notice cemented a long friendship between Joe and Malloy, and alienated Joe from the rest of the cast, particularly Trahan. Instead of his being given additional numbers, one of his specialties was dropped.

"At least let me *prove* it's lousy first," he entreated the producer, Dwight Wiman.

"Sorry, Joe," Wiman told him. "Trahan's agent wants that number out . . . and Trahan has a run-of-the-play contract, you have only two weeks."

"And I'm giving you two weeks' notice right now," Joe countered.

The Second Little Show opened in New York at the Royale Theatre on August 25, 1930, with J. C. Flippen in Joe's spot but he had the last laugh on Trahan. The show did not last two weeks.

Months without work ended with a fast two weeks at the Nut Club in Greenwich Village, followed by a shot at the King's Terrace at two hundred dollars a week. Here, in the closing number of his early show one evening, his voice gave out. He went to his dressing room, gargled desperately with solutions and tried to speak. Beyond a scratchy, hardly audible whisper not a decibel came forth.

He went outside, frantically searching for someone—anyone—to substitute for him in the late show, a pinch hitter to hold the job until his voice returned. He walked several blocks and stopped at many speakeasies on his safari. At last, discouraged almost to quitting, Providence appeared in the persons of two old friends, Harry Miller, a detective in the Chicago Police Department, and at his side Bill Gleason, a quondam baritone.

"Harry," Joe addressed the detective, croaking badly, "what are you doing with poor Bill?"

"Taking him back to Chicago and throwing him in the can, unless his wife drops charges. Poor Bill is having marital troubles."

Joe had an idea. "Do me a favor, Harry."

"Anything within reason."

"I'm in a spot." Joe consulted his watch. "I'm supposed to go on at King's Terrace in thirty minutes but, as you see, I've lost my voice. If you'd let Gleason go on for me . . ."

Miller looked at Joe as if he were unhinged. "I told you he's under arrest."

"But Harry, the King's Terrace is on the way to the station. It's a hot night. What's wrong with stopping in for a drink and—"

"And Gleason singing fifteen or twenty songs."

"Ten songs—twelve maybe . . ."

"And what'll *I* do?" The cop took a tighter grip on Gleason's arm. "Sing harmony?"

"He'll be safe on the stage." Joe looked at the dejected prisoner. "You wouldn't try to escape—would you, Bill?"

Gleason shook his head.

Joe turned to the policeman. "We've known each other for a long time. Would I put you in a jam, Harry? I'll sit with you ringside. You'll be ten feet from him, almost touch him . . . I need this job, pal."

"Okay, Joe." Miller knew what Lewis had gone through, he could not turn him down. "As for you, Gleason . . ." He glared at his prisoner. "One false move and—"

Bill Gleason was introduced and launched his first song, off-key. After sixteen bars of dissonant caterwauling, Joe turned to Officer Miller. "Take him, Harry—*now!*"

It was a year since Wall Street crashed, the fingers of depression were closing around Prohibition's neck. The only places making money were the hardware stores selling padlocks for bankrupt speakeasies. This, Joe decided, was a good time to buy a club. He did not have a quarter, what could he lose?

Joe bought the Chateau Madrid on West Fifty-fourth Street from an old friend, Lou Schwartz, no money down. He leased out the kitchen, hired a six-piece band, established a cover charge of two dollars per head and opened with an impromptu show that included, among the guest masters of ceremonies, Jolson, George Jessel, Jack Benny, Harry Richman, Jack Pearl, Joe Frisco, Ted Healy, J. C. Flippen, a contrite Al Trahan, Clayton, Jackson and Durante. He had friends.

He was in his dressing room, adjusting his tie, when two hoodlums, neither of whom he recognized, entered unannounced.

"Not a seat in the house," one of the visitors scowled. "And a line waiting."

Joe measured the pair and observed the familiar bulges in the specially tailored waist pockets to accommodate .38 caliber Colts. "I'll find you a table, boys," he said.

The spokesman shook his head. "Not *one* table, Lewis."

"How many do you want?"

The hoodlum's face darkened. "Save your jokes for out there. We're cuttin' a piece."

Joe was aware that most of the top-drawer speakeasies in New York, like Chicago, were owned or "protected" by mobmen but he did not intend to be intimidated. "I got a partner," he said.

"You got another."

"Pardon me," Joe said, shouldering past his visitors. "I'm on." The band was playing "Chicago."

"We'll wait," the hoodlum said.

Joe did his show and circulated among the guests for a couple of hours before returning to his dressing room. His prospective partners were waiting for him.

"Give me a break, boys," he pleaded. "I just started. I'm tryin' to get even."

"Everybody's got to make a buck," the hoodlum's voice hardened. "Quit whinin' and start countin'."

"But I told you, I got a partner."

"You're a friggin' liar. Lou Schwartz is out. We checked. You came in on no pair."

They were calling him but he had to try and run the bluff, there was no choice. "I got connections," he said.

"In Chicago maybe. Not here. Quit stallin', Lewis."

He played boldly. "Can't you get it through those thick skulls? You're too *late!*"

The spokesman grabbed Joe by his lapels. "Don't lie to us."

"I'm not lying. I told you I got a partner."

The hoodlum's face almost touched his. "Who is he?"

"He doesn't advertise."

"Who is he?" The hoodlum tightened his hold.

Joe cudgeled his memory for a name. A name came to him, the name in the headline on the front page of the newspaper on his dressing table, "DUTCH SCHULTZ SOUGHT IN MOB KILLING." Why not Schultz? He owned the Embassy Club and half a dozen other traps. Joe lowered his voice. "Schultz . . . but you didn't get it from me."

The hoodlum let go of his collar as if it were charged. "Not the Dutchman."

Joe had nailed him. "There's only one Schultz," he said.

It was the hoodlum's turn to sweat. "Somebody's got his signals crossed," he apologized and offered his hand. "Don't mention this to Dutch—please."

Joe shook his hand. "I won't," he promised. He had no idea what Schultz looked like.

The second hoodlum, who had not said a word, glared at Joe. "Why the hell didn't you tell us this three hours ago instead of wasting our time?"

"Shut up!" his companion barked and insured it with a vicious backhand to his mouth. "Don't you know a square-shooter when you see one?"

Business held up but Joe didn't. Every show was a trial. Some nights his voice was a hoarse, gibbering whisper. The first Sunday night was an exceptionally bad one. He could not make himself heard above the raucous crowd.

Two men at a ringside table particularly disturbed him. Oblivious of him, they did not stop talking during his act, their conversation and laughter mounting in direct ratio to the lulls his material was producing.

A bellow from their table killed the punch-line of one of his favorite gags and he stopped, fixed his eyes on them and lashed, "Would you two bums mind stepping outside for a few years? And wait for a late summer."

The crowd laughed for the first time in the show.

One of the two offenders became aware that they were attracting attention and whispered to his companion. The latter, seated with his back to the stage, turned around. "Louder!" he shouted. "And funnier!"

The crowd had been fighting Joe all night and he wanted to strike back. "Why don't you stick your head out of the window—feet first?" He spoke slowly and fairly distinctly.

The crowd liked the crack. All except the heckler. He hissed.

"You ought to have yourself vulcanized," Joe laughed, "you're losing air."

The crowd gave him a hand. He had not heard that music for a long time. Now they waited to see if the heckler had a comeback.

He did. "Louder!" he repeated. "And funnier!"

Joe was genuinely annoyed now. He did not mind batting back a couple of cracks but this pest was lousing up his act. "One more interruption, sir," he said, "and I'll have the head waiter hit you on top of your head and bend the point."

The crowd howled.

"Incidentally," Joe gave him the other barrel, "if they ever put a price on your head—grab it."

Joe's voice was almost gone. He cued the band leader for a dance number and left the stage, throwing his detractor a withering look as he passed his table.

"Couldn't take it, hey?" the heckler cackled.

Joe stopped. "Screw, bum. If you had any real dough you'd be at Twenty-One."

"Sit down, Lewis." The heckler's voice was hard and commanding.

"We haven't been introduced, nor will we."

The heckler smiled. "That's no way to talk to your partner."

"Partner?"

"My name is Schultz."

Joe was incredulous. This was the great Dutch Schultz, this ordinary-looking man in his twenties? This was the mighty Arthur Flegenheimer, the ruthless murderer who controlled New York?

"Hiya, Dutch . . ." he heard someone greeting the heckler. Of all the names in the directory he had to think of Schultz and claim he was his partner. And of all the loud-mouthed crums in the joint he had to pick out Schultz to insult in front of three or four hundred people. "If they ever put a price on your head, grab it." He winced. He picked his spots: there *was* a price on Schultz's head.

"Hope you enjoyed the show," Joe said airily.

Schultz looked up. "When does it go on?"

The head waiter arrived with two buckets of champagne. "Your wine, Mr. Schultz."

Schultz shook his head. "Mr. Lewis can't stand noise.

I'm afraid them corks would bust his little eardrums."

Joe examined the labels on the bottles. "With the price I charge for Piper-Heidsieck," he said, "you can make a little noise."

After they killed the two bottles, Schultz stood up. "Let's go, partner," he said.

"Where?" Joe asked.

"A ride."

"Am I comin' back?" Joe was serious.

"Let's go."

The first stop was the Cotton Club. They ordered a couple of shots and Joe put a fifty-dollar bill on the bar.

Schultz grabbed the bill, crumpled it angrily and pushed it into Joe's pocket. "Don't *ever* do that to me," he said. "I'm Christ."

Joe stared at him.

"You're lookin' at Christ!" The paranoiac killer thought he was Christ and, to thousands—yes, tens of thousands— he was Christ. He was The Law in the Bronx, all of Harlem and Manhattan above 86th Street.

"I ain't a bad pretzel." Pretzel was his word for German. He went through life wanting people to love him or at least like him. Hardly any did, especially those who were paid to.

After the Cotton Club they went to the Club Abbey and then to the Embassy. Here Dutch introduced him to his partner, Owney Madden, who owned the Cotton Club and pieces of several other leading cabarets, including Texas Guinan's. Owney was the Sullivan to Schultz' Gilbert and if the unknowing wondered why they were immune from the law it was because they did not know that these men, like Capone, could truthfully say in the words of the Sullivan-Gilbertian Lord Chancellor, "But I, my lords, embody the law."

From the Embassy Schultz took Joe through Times Square and pointed out the domain that, he was certain,

soon would be his. "It's Lepke's—for the time being."
There was no question in his mind that he—with a little
help from Owney; Big Bill Dwyer, his vice-president in
charge of breweries; Bill Duffy, a Sing Sing alumnus who
bossed sports enterprises; and James Hines of Tammany
Hall, a judge as corrupt as he was distinguished—soon
would take over the mid-Manhattan sector.

Joe looked at the Dutchman and he saw another Capone.
Schultz was born in the Bronx but he imagined, as the
erstwhile mop-boy did, that he was a Caesar. His father,
who worked in a livery stable or a saloon when he worked,
deserted his mother when Arthur was fourteen. Arthur
would show his mother—and his old man, wherever he
was—he would show them all. He was taking in $10,000 a
day on crooked policy number banks and it was only the
beginning, he was just twenty-seven years old.

From Times Square they went to St. Patrick's Cathedral.
"Here's where I leave you, Dutch," Joe said.

"I'm as kosher as you are," Schultz retorted, clamping a
tighter grip on Joe's arm, "but I'm a Catholic too. I ain't
passin' up nothin'. In our business we need all the good
luck we can get."

The Dutchman became a nightly customer at the Chateau
Madrid. He had performers like Helen Morgan, Morton
Downey and the Yacht Club Boys at his Embassy Club
but Joe's place was his unofficial headquarters. He drank
heavily and not too well. One night he came in with
George McManus, a notorious gambler who had just been
acquitted of the murder of Arnold Rothstein.

Schultz was in a violent mood. "You been holdin' out on
me, Joe."

Joe was nonplused.

"About Danny Cohen."

Joe had not thought about Danny for a long time. He did
not know what had happened to him after he left the

Green Mill nor did he care; Danny was a forgotten scar. "What about him?"

"You didn't tell me he was in town."

"I didn't know he was."

Schultz was skeptical. "You didn't know he had a beer joint out on Long Island with Chuck Green?"

"No, I didn't."

"Now you know. I found out tonight."

Joe shrugged. "It's a big town."

"Not big enough. Not after what he done to you. But don't worry, pally, I'm taking care of him."

"Leave him alone."

Schultz was drunk and emotional. "Any friend of Mc-Gurn is an enemy of mine. Let him talk to the sword." This was his death sentence.

"Promise me, Dutch, you won't touch him."

Dutch reconsidered. "All right, I won't hurt him. Just slap him around a little and run him back to Chicago, with the rest of the rats."

"A beer joint on Long Island. Isn't that punishment enough?"

Schultz' eyes caught a striking blonde at a nearby table and he forgot about Danny Cohen. Dutch was a pushover for blondes.

As the Chateau Madrid was a hangout for mobsters, all reservations had to be approved by telephone in advance. Hoodlum protocol. One night a friend of Joe's, Harry Wallach, called. "I got Vanny Higgins with me and I can't ged rid of him. He wants to come up and catch the show. Okay?"

"No," Joe replied "The Dutchman's in." Schultz and Higgins were building up to a blood bath.

Wallach called back in twenty minutes. "Vanny's coming up."

"You got to stop him!"

"Can't. He just kissed us off and grabbed a cab. He'll be there any minute."

Joe hurried to Schultz' table. "How about going out and getting something to eat?"

"I ain't hungry," said Schultz.

"I am."

Schultz looked at his watch. "After the show."

Joe tried to distract his attention but Schultz spotted Higgins immediately and reached for his pistols.

"What the hell are you doing, Dutch?" Joe sprang between Schultz' guns and Higgins.

"Vannie Higgins just came in." Schultz nodded over Joe's shoulder.

Joe looked and pretended not to see Higgins. "You better stop drinkin', Dutch, that isn't Vannie."

"Move—before you're hurt," the Dutchman ordered.

"I tell you it isn't Vannie Higgins."

Schultz' eyes narrowed. "Whose side you on, Joe?"

Higgins sat down two tables away in a direct line with Schultz.

Joe nervously stood up.

"Sit down, you asshole." Schultz held his two guns below the table cover, ready. He grinned. His luck was running. He had been trying to corner Higgins for more than a year. Now he did not have to move out of his chair. First Higgins, next Bugsy Siegel. Lepke and Luciano would talk business then. On his terms.

Joe sat down. "Look, Dutch," he said, "I don't care if you kill him—but not here. It ain't good for my business."

Schultz did not take his eyes off Higgins. "How would you like to go to Europe for a month or two?"

"Europe?"

"All expenses paid. I'll run the joint."

"As a shooting gallery?"

Schultz put one of the .38's on his lap. With his free

hand he pulled out his wallet and dropped it on the table. "Take out ten G's," he said.

"What for?"

"I'm buying the joint."

"I'm not selling."

Schultz was mystified. "I don't get it. You say I shouldn't knock him off here because it'll hurt business but when I offer to buy the gaff you say no. Is that fair, Joe?"

"I'm not selling. Put 'em away, Dutch."

"I'll give you twelve-five." Schultz stiffened. "He's standing up."

This was Prohibition. A man's life hung in the balance while a hoodlum tried to buy a speakeasy because the owner had a house rule against murder on the premises.

While they were arguing Higgins walked out.

The hoodlums became more difficult to handle, business dropped off and, after nine months, Joe was fed up. He received an offer from the Roman Pools in Miami Beach, opposite the Roney Plaza, and he took it. His brother Al, on a hiatus from the haberdashery business, took over the management of the Chateau Madrid and wired every day for money.

Schultz took a dislike to Al in the belief he was robbing Joe. The truth was that without Joe the Madrid could not survive.

"There are only two customers in the place," Al reported to Joe one night during the third week. "We owe the acts eight hundred and I haven't got eight bucks."

"Where's Dutch?" Joe asked.

"He's one of the two customers."

"Put him on." A moment later Joe was telling Schultz that he needed eight hundred dollars to close the club.

"You should have taken the twelve and a half G's when I offered it to you," said the Dutchman but he lent him the money.

Joe returned to New York. He caught on in a tacky up-stairs speak, the Vanity on Fifty-first Street between Sixth and Seventh avenues, signed a four-weeks contract and did well enough that the owner picked up his option for another four weeks. But Joe asked for a release. His throat was getting worse, he wanted to bake it in California. And George Olson, the band leader, made this possible by offering him a job at the Plantation in Culver City.

The owner of the Vanity was disappointed but understanding. "Good luck to you, Joe." He shook his hand warmly.

Joe waited.

"Oh, yes," the owner said at last, "your money."

"Eight hundred," Joe reminded him. The man had an unretentive memory.

The owner evaded Joe's eyes. "Give me your address," he said, picking up a pencil, "and I'll send it to you."

"I'm leaving for Los Angeles in the morning."

"The pony express delivers mail to Los Angeles now." It was an obvious stall.

"Don't bother," Joe said. "My secretary will pick it up."

The owner beamed. "That will be fine. Any time, Joe."

Joe was halfway down the long flight of stairs when the owner called down. "Joe!" He had remembered a detail without which his integrity might be questioned. "What's your secretary's name?"

Joe stopped. "Dutch Schultz," he called up. He owed the Dutchman eight hundred. Two debts could be canceled with one call.

The owner, sick with fear, ran after Joe and chased him all the way to Dave's Blue Room, begging him to take the money. Joe was enjoying the rib and kept him on the hook for more than an hour.

"Please, Joe," the owner pleaded, "don't send *him* to my place!" Schultz, a mean drunk, was poison to club owners.

A few weeks previously he and Charles (Chink) Sherman had tangled at the Club Abbey. It had started with a joke about Dutch's current blonde and had become serious. Sherman shot Schultz in the shoulder. Schultz clubbed him with a chair, broke his neck and stabbed him seven times with the jagged fragments of a peanut bowl. By morning the Club Abbey was padlocked.

Joe was bored with hoodlums and with being their jester. One year in New York had been the equivalent of his five in Chicago. He was tired of living in a world of violence. Within a year the two biggest mobmen in the United States, Capone and Schultz, had offered him money, partnerships and protection. He did not blame those who had said yes—other entertainers, prize fighters, policemen and politicians—but he wanted to make good on his own.

The Dutchman walked into a Newark, New Jersey, restaurant, the Palace Bar and Chop House, with three bodyguards, Lulu Rosenkrantz, Abe Landau and Abbadabba Berman. They were not enough.

Schultz was in the toilet when Charles (The Bug) Workman, a top torpedo, came in.

Workman pulled the chain.

His belly full of bullets, Schultz raved for two hours in the Newark City Hospital. "I want to pay," he said at last. "Let them leave me alone."

They left him alone.

His body was unclaimed for two days until his widow borrowed the money to take him to the Bronx. The casket was smuggled out of a back door, and he was interred as a Roman Catholic. Mrs. Emma Flegenheimer, his mother, insisted that a Jewish prayer shawl be placed on his coffin. As he always said, he needed all the good luck he could get, now more than ever.

Another king had departed, age thirty-two, the day before he was to kill a special rackets prosecutor, Tom Dewey. Lepke and Luciano wanted Dewey eliminated too but they were fearful of the consequences and tried to dissuade Schultz from his murder plan. The Dutchman told them he did not need their assistance, he would take care of Dewey on his own. Lepke and Luciano chose the lesser of two evils, they thought, and had Schultz killed, to save the life of the man who would send Lepke to the electric chair and Luciano to exile via Dannemora prison.

"If you had your life to live over again," the Dutchman had been asked a few weeks earlier, "what would you do?"

"I'd never take the name of Schultz," he had answered. Out of a lifetime of crime that was his lone regret. "It's short, swell for headlines. You couldn't get Flegenheimer in a headline. If I'd stuck to it, I'd never been in trouble. Nobody'd ever heard of me."

It was immaterial. The next generation never heard of him.

Schultz, Luciano, Lepke, Madden, Colossimo, Torrio, O'Bannion and Capone. They spoke for the '20's.

They were answered by Charles Lindbergh, George Gershwin, Babe Ruth, Ernest Hemingway, Ralph Bunche, Amelia Earhart, John Steinbeck and Ernest O. Lawrence, spokesmen for the America that found the generation Scott Fitzgerald lost.

And arms locked with all, one who would know Roosevelts, Rockefellers, Harrimans, Baruchs and Vanderbilts as intimately as he had the hoodlum aristocracy, was a man named Joe Lewis, a rebel who cherished independence so dearly that he defied death to maintain it. That determination to express himself—the perennial struggle of the individual against conformity—would make him the most unique comedian of his time.

the thirties

JOE'S AND AMERICA'S

*"I wish I'd learned a trade,
then I'd know what kind of work I'm out of."*

JOE E.

12   *Sam, You Made the Pants Too Long*

George Olson's Plantation in Culver City was southern California's leading cabaret in 1931, a dubious distinction in the Gobi of American night life.

"I found a horseshoe," Joe sang on his opening show. "Will it bring good luck to me?" Three years previously, the night he had sung "Sonny Boy" and Jolson had led the cheering section, the room had brought him luck. A start back anyway, even if he had not gone far. Maybe this time . . .

The Plantation folded one month later, on the Fourth of July.

The owner of the building asked Joe to take over and Joe ran the club for ten months. It was a war of attrition. One night the audience was composed of two loyal devotees, Harry Russell, a gambler, and his friend, Jack Lewis. Their applause rattled in the big club.

Joe finished his last number and walked to their table. "You boys must like this place," he said. "I'm giving it to you." He handed them the key, walked out and took the first train to Chicago.

He made the familiar rounds again but jobs were almost nonexistent, his voice was unimproved and his material was pathetic. No longer able to sing seriously, he had replaced his Irish ballads with Jewish dialect comedy.

He sang a love song, "When Nathan Got Married to Rose of Washington Square."

> *Jake sang "Eli Eli" and someone stabbed him with*
>   *a fork.*
> *Levinsky hollered murder because*
> *The fork it smelled from pork . . .*

He sang of Cohen and Goldberg, the kosher Damon and Pythias, the former a borrower, the latter a lender who prescribed with each loan of his worldly goods:

> *Take what you want if you nid it*
> *And do what you wanna do wid it.*
> *But remember, don't use it, don't soil it,*
>   *don't spoil it*
> *And bring it beck when you're through . . .*

—until the day Cohen looked longingly at Goldberg's wife. He impersonated a rabbi and chanted in jive—

> *Come on, you Hebrew people, be in Schule at nine,*
> *'Cause it's Rosh Hashanah time in Dixieland . . .*

He continued to do "Far Rockaway" where—

> *Sadie, Moe and Jakie*
> *All day long play put and takie*
> *Far, far away on the shores of Rockaway.*

He rented a prop fur coat, larded his accent and sang, Oh! Oh! I'm a Yiddisher Eskimo.

It was not anti-Semitic by pre-Hitler criteria, or anti-Eskimo, only anti-entertainment. Joe, a proud Jew, was unaware that he might be disparaging his people. He laughed at their humorous traits without malice or self-consciousness. If he had not already affected a brimless straw hat he probably would have worn an oversized derby.

This was before Jews became sensitive—to gas—before the laughter of native Yiddish comedy was suffocated in the kilns of Germany and in six million Jewish throats.

Joe abandoned the material before that and for a different cause. It was imitation; he was forging, consciously or not, the styles of Smith and Dale, Ben Welch, Fanny Brice, Harry Green, Lou Holtz and Eugene and Willie Howard with none of their distinctions. He did not want to be a counterfeiter. He wanted to be original, unlike any other entertainer who had ever lived, but he had no other material and no money to buy any. He kept shooting blanks.

After a particularly dismal audition at the Midnight Frolics he looked at the owner's pained expression and said, "Don't take this too hard. I get worse."

Nothing sounded funny. He could think as fast as ever but the words clogged and jumbled in his throat. In frustration he hit upon the idea of camouflaging his disability by pretending he was drunk and staggering on the stage as he had as a boy in Atlantic City when he improvised his first bit of stage business while singing, "Stumblin' All Around."

He staggered and no one laughed. Joe could not understand. A drunk was a standard comic. People always had laughed at muddled boozers whose liquor-thickened tongues prevented them from speaking clearly. Why didn't they laugh at him? He did not have to act. Was that it? he wondered. Was it too real? How do you make the real unreal? You compound reality.

Joe took to drinking heavily. He started as soon as he was out of bed, in the early afternoon, and did not stop until he returned to bed, between 6 A.M. and 8 A.M. He drank because he was out of work and out of luck, because he was lonely, because he liked the taste of rye and because, he thought, the constant glass at his lips disguised his facial nerve paralysis and the imbecilic grin it had etched on his face.

At last the customers were convinced that Joe was a drunk. And he was.

One day he awakened more distressed than usual, a stiletto-like pain stabbing his abdomen. News of his misery reached the cauliflower ears of Big Sam, his erstwhile bodyguard.

"Come with me," the hoodlum ordered. "I got a croaker who'll fix you up." Joe was too weak to protest.

The doctor was grave. "Mr. Lewis," he said as he studied the ominous shadows on the x-rays before him, "you are a sick man."

"That isn't news," Joe groaned.

The doctor looked up. "How much whiskey do you drink a day?"

"Any given amount."

The doctor did not smile. "I asked you, how much whiskey do you drink a day?"

There was a note in his voice that precluded further joking. "Two quarts, sometimes more."

"Mr. Lewis, if you don't stop drinking, you'll be dead in less than a year."

Joe looked from the solemn face of the diagnostician to the x-rays. "No booze at all?" he asked, terrified by that prospect more than the death sentence.

"You have ulcers, bad ulcers . . . and a few other things. Either you go on the wagon or you're a goner."

". . . a few other things." Joe was afraid to surmise. He stopped drinking that day and did not touch a drop in the following seven months that he worked at the Vanity Fair, a fourth-rate oasis on the North Side.

They were seven long, dreary months.

He was eating his usual 5 A.M. snack, now milk and toast, in the booth of an all-night restaurant and he suddenly became aware that someone was talking about him.

"So I take Lewis to the croaker last year, and he warns

him that if he don't lay off the booze he's headed for the deep six." It was Big Sam's voice, coming from an adjoining booth. Joe was about to look over the partition and greet him when Big Sam laughed maniacally. "Joe's a great practical joker, y'know. He's pulled a few dillies on me. But wait until he hears this . . ." He lowered his voice and Joe had to strain to hear. "Joe hasn't got ulcers—or anything else wrong with him. The croaker was on the level but the x-rays weren't. They belonged to another gee. I framed it with a dame I know at the clinic. Is that a rib or is that a rib?"

Big Sam transported his listeners into paroxysms of laughter, all except Joe. It did not occur to him to be grateful that he did not have ulcers. He was so furious at Big Sam that, without realizing, he quaffed the full glass of milk.

"Compliments of the man in the light suit, over there," said the waiter, placing a drink in front of Joe and pointing to one of the four customers in the Vanity Fair. "He would like to see you . . ."

"Some other time." Joe acknowledged the drink with a nod and turned away. He was not in a convivial mood. He had received his week's notice and no other jobs were available, at least to him.

A few minutes later the waiter returned. "The man in the light suit, who sent you the last drink—he wonders if—"

"What do you want me to do, have an affair with him?"

"Remember me, Joe?" The man in the light suit had come up behind the waiter.

Joe looked up to see a young man in his middle twenties. "Why?" he asked. He had an aversion to pests who, introduced once, probably with a crowd some 4 A.M. in the semidarkness, would five or ten years later demand to be remembered by their first names.

"You did me a favor," the young man said pleasantly. "And the Big Brothers."

Joe remembered. Back in 1925 he had done a benefit for the Brothers, a Chicago Jewish youth organization, and this young man, then in his teens, had been the master of ceremonies. "Your name is Marovitz."

"Abe Marovitz." He gratefully shook Joe's hand.

"Sit down, Abe." Joe ordered a bottle of rye.

Marovitz looked around the desolate room, "Dice cold, huh?"

"It's the pipes," Joe said hoarsely, pointing to his throat.

Marovitz, a struggling lawyer, knew about his troubles. He had been a prosecutor in the State Attorney's office when Joe was cut up. "Why don't you get yourself fixed up?" he asked.

"I was fixed. I want to get unfixed."

"There's only one place. The Mayo Brothers in Minnesota."

Half a dozen drinks later Joe agreed to go to the Mayo Clinic and Abe said he would accompany him; it was time for his annual checkup.

One of Marovitz' clients, Mike Rand alias Gus Winkler, a Capone gunsel, disapproved. "You can't leave me now," he protested. "I need you."

"Sorry, Gus," Marovitz said, "but I want to help Lewis . . . and see what kind of shape I'm in."

"How about *my* health?" Winkler had had an eye shot out recently during a million-dollar post office robbery and the other was overstrained from his vigilant lookout for the police, who suspected he had engineered the holdup, and his colleagues, who were certain he had not apportioned the loot equitably.

"Keep out of sight, Gus."

Winkler's good eye glistened. "Good idea, Abe. I'll go along wit' you."

They were in their drawing room, Joe and Abe playing cards and Winkler kibitzing. An egomaniac, Gus resented not being in the act but casino was too complicated for him. He patted the gun in his shoulder holster and, for no reason except to hear his own voice, he boasted, "Y'know, I'm the toughest guy in Chicago . . . maybe the toughest guy in the whole country."

Abe took the big ten and, without disturbing the cards in his left hand, crossed a short but devastating right to Winkler's chin, knocking him off his chair and onto the floor. "Your play, Joe," he said, unruffled. Joe's eyes were transfixed on the hoodlum sprawled on the floor.

Winkler came around in a few seconds, ruefully rubbed his chin and tried to clear his befogged brain. "Hey!" Incredulity was mixed with rage. "W-what's d' idea of settin' me on my ass?"

Abe did not deign to turn his head. "That's to show you're not even the toughest guy in this room."

The Mayos could do nothing for Joe that Dr. Orth had not done for him six years previously. "Time can be the only healer," he was told.

A local newspaper reported that a wounded Chicago gangster had come to Mayo with his mouthpiece and his personal jester.

Winkler's tension increased as the train approached Chicago. "I can't go back to my hotel," he said, "and I'm afraid to register in a new one." He turned to Marovitz. "Got any ideas where I can hole in for a while?"

"I have an extra room in the Seneca," Joe said, "bar and everything. Stay there." He gave Winkler the key to 1005, his playroom.

Gus was mowed down by mob shotguns the next day and an eight-column photograph of a key, eight times actual size, was splashed across the front page of a Chicago newspaper.

"THE KEY TO WINKLER'S MURDER AND THE MILLION-DOLLAR POST OFFICE ROBBERY!" screamed the caption. The story explained that the mysterious key was the chief piece of evidence that had been found on Winkler's bullet-riddled body. The police were certain, it went on, that the lock to the door, desk or safe that it fitted would reveal the bulk of the million dollars lost in the holdup.

Joe shuddered. The number 1005 was clearly visible on the key, the key to Room 1005 in the Seneca Hotel.

He met Marovitz at an obscure bar. "They'll trace the key to me by morning, if they haven't already," he said. "It will come out that Gus went with us to Rochester and I'll be dead. Everybody will be positive I had a piece of the holdup. I'm blowing town . . ."

Marovitz was equally disturbed. "I'm in this with you, Joe. I'll go to the D.A. and see—"

As he spoke, a police officer sidled up to Joe and slipped something in his hand. Joe looked down. Exhibit A, his key to Room 1005, was in his palm.

Joe was bewildered. "Thanks—but how did you—"

"You got a break coming, buddy," the cop said and walked away.

Joe and Abe became friends, a relationship in which the shrewd little lawyer, later a member of the State Legislature and a Superior Court Judge, exerted a greater influence on his private life than any other person.

The opening of the Chicago World's Fair in 1933 brought Joe and Sophie Tucker together at the 225 Club on East Superior Street, a small room seating 125, in a version of "Stormy Weather" that even Ethel Waters could not match. They resembled a whale and a minnow, the mighty Sophie standing frontstage, singing with all her heart and voice, and huddled behind her little Joe wearing a yellow raincoat and carrying an umbrella over which a Brobdingnagian fellow in a red fox-hunting coat poured buckets of water supplied him by a gnomelike figure.

The big stooge was the late Paul Small, a three-hundred pound acrobat-comedian who had been Paul Whiteman's double until the King of Jazz went on a diet. Small subsequently became bottom man in a troupe known as the Eight Arabs and, when it broke up, he and the top man, a flyweight named Leo (Spunky) Bartolome, bounced around Chicago until they caught up with Joe and convinced him that he needed them. Joe paid them seventy-five dollars a week when he worked. Small, destined to become one of the most successful theatrical agents in the country, would perform many services for Joe but none as valuable as introducing him, in 1933, to a song writer named Fred Whitehouse. "The guy's got a piece he wants you to hear," Paul said, "a take-off on 'Lord, You Made the Night Too Long.' "

Joe was not interested. "Lord, You Made the Night Too Long" was a hymn and there was no percentage doing parodies on religious songs. "People resent it," he said. But he listened to it, he knew how it felt to be turned down without an audition.

> *You made the coat and vest fit the best,*
> *You even made my lining strong.*
> *But, Sam, you made the pants too long.*

Whitehouse paused. "You know Leo Fox, the tailor?" Joe nodded. "Wish I could afford him."

"He's got a cutter named Sam. I got the idea watching him."

> *I wear a belt and I wear suspenders.*
> *I figure what can I lose?*

> *But what good is a belt and what good are sus-*
> *penders*
> *If my pants hang over my shoes?*

Joe grinned. This was not the kind of humor that had ever been identified with him; it was pure whimsy, the kind of material Frank Fay used, but he liked it.

> *I get the damnedest breeze through my BVD's,*
> *My fly is where my tie belongs.*
> *Sam, you made the pants too long.*

"How much?" Joe asked.

Whitehouse hesitated. "Twenty-five bucks too steep?"

Joe could not afford it but the lyrics appealed to him. Who knows, he conjectured, maybe other people were getting weary of songs about hot love, cold love, old love, new love, dog love, puppy love, lost love and stolen love and might be interested in an indignant yet mournful complaint about a pair of pants whose seat was where the feet belonged.

The twenty-five-dollar song was the beginning of a metamorphosis. It would take ten more years to complete the evolution but gradually the bombastic buffoon with the brimless hat, the cane, the blatant jokes and the crude Yiddish ditties would vanish and in his place would emerge a droll, Rabelaisian wit with the deft touch of a pixie.

"Sam, You Made the Pants Too Long" became his trademark and his talisman. Twenty years later audiences continued to demand it but he sang it only on rare occasions, first donning fur earlaps. "I can't listen to it," he protested but he was jesting, it would always be a part of him, a reminder of his first step in the unconscious search for himself.

A Chicago boxing man named Segal wanted a favor. "I got a new boy starting at Marigold Gardens Fourth of July. Just out of the amateurs but handles himself pretty good. Got a nice right . . ." Segal frowned. "Trouble is, I can't get his name in the paper. Nobody heard of him."

"I know most of the sports writers around town," Joe said. "I'll put in a good word."

"I got a better idea. A picture of you and the kid."

"Me? What good would that do?"

"I forgot to tell you. His name is Joe Louis. Same as yours. Get it?"

"Sounds silly."

"You're a big shot in Chicago, Joe. I know the papers will go for it." Segal was a persuasive man. "I'll bring a photographer around tomorrow."

"Not too early," Joe cautioned.

Segal, a photographer and young Joe Louis arrived at 10 A.M. It was impossible to arouse Lewis. The mighty fists that would put so many men to sleep could not awaken this one. Louis pounded Lewis' door in vain. They left three hours later without the picture.

"What's the difference?" Lewis consoled Segal. "He'll get knocked out and no one will ever hear of him."

Joe Louis was not knocked out. He knocked out one Jack Kracken in one minute of Round One.

"A fluke," Joe Lewis laughed. That was July 4, 1934.

In the next twelve months Joe Louis pulverized Willie Davies twice, Larry Udell, Jack Kranz, Buck Everett, Alex

Borchuk, Adolph Wiater, Art Sykes, Jack O'Dowd, Stanley Poreda, Charley Massera, Lee Ramage twice, Patsy Perroni, Hans Birkie, Red Barry, Natie Brown, Roy Lazer, Biff Benton, Roscoe Toles, Gene Stanton and Primo Carnera—twenty-two consecutive victories.

And Joe Lewis bet against him twenty-two consecutive times. "It can't last," he said confidently.

While Louis was leaving a trail of horizontal victims from Madison Square Garden to Los Angeles, Lewis was leaving a trail of defunct cabarets from North Clark Street to the Levee. He was the only Joe Lewis being knocked out.

"Why be an actor?" Dennis Cooney, the owner of the Frolics, asked him. "An actor is a pimp. Get yourself a roadhouse out of the county where you can gamble. Take my advice."

Joe took Cooney's advice. He acquired a lease on Lincoln Tavern on Demster Road and borrowed several thousand dollars, including a considerable amount from Cooney, to renovate it, hire Ben Pollock's orchestra, put on an expensive show and advertise.

On opening night two deputy sheriffs stationed themselves at the entrance to the gambling room and announced they would padlock the place the instant a roulette wheel turned.

Rains came the second night and the storms continued incessantly for the remaining twenty-nine days and nights in June. There was no gambling, no business and no forecast of clear weather.

The only customers were Joe's personal friends—Fogarty, who was now running a horse book at the 5100 Club; Joe Goldberg, still on the police force; Harry Harris, a promising young song writer, Marovitz—and remnants of the Capone and Bugs Moran mobs.

Milton Berle, already a name in show business, came in

one night and, being Berle, quickly moved into Joe's act from a ringside table.

"I don't know what I'd do without you, Milton," Joe said, "but I'm willing to try."

This only encouraged Berle and Joe invited him to the stage. He wrapped his arm around Milton affectionately. "Berle is a wonderful guy," he introduced him, "and a great comedian—but personally, I can't see him."

Lewis and Berle did not meet on the stage again until 1943 at a War Bond rally in New York City. Before Joe could say hello to the audience, Milton took the microphone out of his hand. "Joe Lewis is a wonderful guy, and a great comedian—but personally, I can't see him."

The crowd roared at Berle's wit.

Uncle Miltie beamed. He might borrow a line but he would always return it, even if it took him eight years.

The other Joe came back to Chicago in the summer of 1935, twenty-one years old and invincible, signed to meet the colorful derelict, King Levinsky, in a mismatch that no one took seriously—except Joe Lewis. He took the short end of the odds, as always.

The King was dead in one round minus.

"You look punchy," Lewis told the Kingfish next day.

"I got that way in the ring," Levinsky came back with the standard retort originally minted by Slapsy Maxie Rosenbloom. "What's your excuse?"

"Betting on you," Lewis snapped.

By Labor Day Joe's third club had gone the way of the Chateau Madrid and the Plantation, he had tapped out as a cabaret owner in New York, Los Angeles and Chicago.

"There's only one way to get even," he told Cooney.

Cooney was holding his head with both hands. "Go 'way, Joe."

"We'll get well this time!"

Cooney finally found the strength to ask, "How?"

"Louis is fighting Max Baer September twenty-fourth. This is the time, Denny! Remember what Baer did to Schmeling?"

Cooney groaned "I can't forget what Braddock did to Baer."

It took Lewis almost four hours to convince Cooney that all their problems would be solved if Dennis would loan him a few thousand to bet on Baer.

It took Louis almost four rounds to make Baer quit. By now he was hurting Lewis more than his opponents.

Joe worked out his debt at Cooney's Club Royale on South Wabash Street. On closing night his pals packed it for the customary wake. "Where to now?" Marovitz asked.

Joe had not thought about the next move. He called Hall's Travel Bureau in New York and told Hall he wanted to make a trip.

"Where, Joe?"

"A slow boat—some place."

"How about France? You'll like the Riviera."

"Let's stick to this country."

"In a boat?"

"Why not?"

"I can put you in a tub going to Los Angeles around the Canal but it'll take twenty days. Is that too long?"

Joe was eager to leave but not in a hurry to get anywhere. He had not gotten anywhere in a long time. "Make a reservation. I'll be in New York tomorrow."

Abe, Harris, Fogarty and the boys were hoisting a few to his future on the Coast when a pall of silence fell over the room. An uninvited guest had arrived.

Coming toward Joe was Machine Gun Jack McGurn.

A dozen years of murder had left no marks on Vincent Gebardi. He was little changed from the handsome, amoral thug who, eight years earlier, had told Joe on Diversey Parkway that he would not live to open the Rendezvous.

He held out his open right hand. "Hear you're leavin', Joe. I came to say good-bye."

Joe looked at his eyes. They told him more than his words. This was McGurn's way of saying he was sorry. "Thanks, Jack." He shook his hand.

"Where you goin', Joe?"

"California."

"California?" McGurn's face darkened. "Will you see George Raft out there?"

"I usually do."

"Do me a favor . . ."

"What?"

"When you see Raft, spit in his eye."

Joe was surprised. "George is a right guy."

"The hell he is," said McGurn vehemently.

"When did you guys split out? You used to play golf together."

McGurn's eyes were hard and mean. "Spit in his eye, Joe —for me."

"But why?"

McGurn glowered. "I went to a movie last night and you know what? Raft was in it—playing a *cop*!"

Joe looked at him. This must be a joke but the Gunner's face reminded him that McGurn never made jokes. "He wasn't a *real* cop, Jack. He was only acting. That's his job— he's an actor."

McGurn was incensed at Joe's affront to his intelligence. "I know Raft's an actor. He could've played a priest, a bookie, a bartender or something respectable like that, couldn't he? He didn't have to be a cop, the sonofabitch." He pointed a foreboding finger. "If you're on my side, Joe," he said, "you'll spit in his eye."

Machine Gun Jack McGurn turned and walked out.

"Take this with you, Joe," Marovitz handed him a small gold mezuzah, the traditional Jewish good-luck symbol, within it a miniature parchment scroll inscribed with texts from the Bible. "It was blessed by the Pope."

Joe did a take. "The Pope?"

Abe nodded. "When I was in Rome last year. He blessed two of them for me." The other dangled from his key chain. "It'll bring you luck . . ."

It was Joe's fifth day at sea. The Lincoln Tavern and Louis-Baer debacles had receded into the spinning wake of the big liner. He was standing at the rail, enjoying the cool spray, lazily twirling his key chain around his left forefinger. He touched the mezuzah Abe had given him and wondered if it would bring him luck.

Also on the chain was a key. Joe stared at it a long time. At last he remembered what it unlocked, he unfastened it and tossed it overboard. It was the key to his car, a Dodge sedan, that he had forgotten in a no-parking zone at Fifty-fourth Street and Seventh Avenue, New York City, when he went into Hall's Travel Bureau to pick up his steamer ticket.

14   *Comic Valentine*

Frank Fay was on stage with his Undiscovered Stars of Hollywood, an opportunity show for untried talent that had made the Trocadero the leading night club on Sunset Strip. The hopeful young amateurs were still undiscovered in the shadows as the suave old professional stood alone in the spot-light and sang a tear-choked threnody to a lost love.

At a back table, Billy Wilkerson's mask of serenity did not deceive Frank Orsatti. As a theatrical agent it was his business to be privy to the emotional fluctuations of Hollywood's haut monde and it was obvious to him that Wilkerson, who published the powerful trade paper, the *Hollywood Reporter,* by day, and operated the Trocadero at night, was troubled.

"What's with him?" Orsatti asked, accurately diagnosing the cause of Wilkerson's distress.

Wilkerson shook his head sadly. "Fay used to be a funny man but since Stanwyck fluffed him he won't do anything but torch songs." He looked around at the restive crowd and the dozens of unoccupied tables. "People got enough troubles of their own without listening to his."

"I got a guy for you, Billy—the funniest comedian in the country."

"Groucho Marx is the funniest comedian in the country."

"Marx is good but he isn't a night club comic."

"Who are you peddling?"

"Joe Lewis . . ." The name did not register. "From Chicago."

Wilkerson's face was still blank. "Who is he?"

"The kid who was slashed, remember? He worked out at the Plantation a couple, three years ago."

Wilkerson nodded vaguely.

"I always level, Billy. Joe is stranded. Can't get work anywhere. It's a question of eating or . . ."

"Bring him around." Wilkerson started to leave. "I don't promise anything, but we'll see . . ." Fay went into the third or fourth reprise of his torchure. Wilkerson winced and turned to Orsatti. "I'll try your boy Sunday."

Joe's opening night was disastrous. The most inept novice he introduced was more effective than he. Nonsense is one of

the most hazardous arts, anything less than a bull's-eye is
silliness. Joe's act was not funny, it was silly. Back in his
dressing room, whipped, he remembered something W. C.
Fields had said. "If at first you don't succeed, try try again.
Then quit. No use being a damn fool about it." He was
through. When you flop as an M.C. in a Los Angeles amateur show . . .

Wilkerson and Orsatti came in. "You were bad, Lewis,"
Wilkerson exploded, "unbelievably bad! You were scared
to death and the crowd knew it. You fidgeted, you didn't
know what to do with your hands, you had no co-ordination,
no confidence . . . and that stooge! What's his name?"

"Spunky Bartolomae."

"Get rid of him."

Joe expected Wilkerson to be provoked but he resented
his order to revise his act. "You can keep your advice—*and*
the one night's pay. No talent—no money. We're even."

"Who said anything about one night's pay? I hired you for
a week and you'll work for a week. That's the way I do business." Wilkerson opened the door. "The reason you flopped
out there is because you *think* you're finished. And if you
don't get hold of yourself, you *will* be finished."

Orsatti followed Wilkerson out. "I'll make this up to you,
Bill," he said when they were out of Joe's hearing.

"Make what up?"

"The deal was for one night."

"All Lewis needs is a chance," said the man reputed to be
one of the hardest dealers in Hollywood. "He starts at three
hundred, not a cent more."

Joe stayed on for another week. And another. And another.

It was impossible, even for Wilkerson's astronomers, to
find enough undiscovered stars seven nights a week and he
was compelled to adopt a policy of Sundays only. He paid
Joe the same amount for the one show that he had for the
full week. Joe earned it on Thursday.

Thursday was audition day, the day on which he had to face a battalion of stage mothers armed with sopranos, tap dancers, impersonators, jugglers, harmonica players, magicians, acrobats and assorted performers they had spawned, not to mention a zooful of animal acts, never less than two snake charmers. They begged, cajoled and abused Joe, they offered anything for an acceptance and threatened everything after a rejection. Most of the moppets were as short of talent as their progenitors were of dignity but, now and then, the one-in-a-million shot came in.

For several weeks he passed over a wide-eyed little girl, accompanied by a mother whose elbows were not as sharp as the others. The little girl continued to come and, one Sunday night, he introduced her at the Trocadero. That night a star named Judy Garland was born.

A tawny girl from Texas told Joe she was desperate, she owed a month's room rent. Joe believed her and wanted to help but he did not like her repertoire. "The Troc won't go for opera," he said. "Jazz up one of those heavy babies and I'll put you on." Mary Martin jazzed up an aria from Verdi and she never worried about room rent again.

Sunday night at the Troc became an institution. By eight o'clock every table was filled. Producers, directors and agents waited in line to greet Joe's discoveries with contracts and he discovered many talents, among them Deanna Durbin, Martha Raye and Tony Martin.

Each Sunday night Joe's voice became stronger and clearer. Each Sunday night his co-ordination was improved. He alone knew of each triumph, the articulation of a syllable or a word he had been unable to enunciate the previous Sunday. His truant confidence was coming back from limbo.

It was good to see a full house again, after almost ten years, and hear the applause, applause without pity. It was like old times except that the cast was changed. The Capones, McGurns, Druccis, Schultzes, Maddens and Lucianos were gone. In their places sat L. B. Mayer, Darryl Zanuck, Joe Schenck, Harry Cohn, Jack Warner and Louella O. Parsons, the rulers of this world. He closed his eyes. The applause sounded the same.

The gods of Tinsel Town are notoriously resentful of anything less than homage but Joe's irreverence delighted them. One night he was talking to Jackie Fields, the ex-welterweight champion now skidding down the familiar chute to obscurity, when the head waiter came up. "Mr. Mayer would like to have you join his table," he informed Joe. "*L. B.* Mayer," he added venerably.

Joe nodded. "As soon as I can."

An hour later a member of the Mayer party, a $7,500-a-week director who could not conceive of God keeping L.B. waiting an hour, approached Joe, who was still with Fields. "Lewis," he raged, "Mr. *Mayer* wants you!"

Joe looked up. "I'm talking to Jackie Fields," he said softly and continued discussing the relative merits of Barney Ross and Jimmy McLarnin. Joe treated kings like peasants and peasants like kings.

He is one of the few men who ever succeeded in making Hollywood laugh at itself and pay a cover charge for the privilege . . .

"I know a beautiful girl who came to Hollywood hoping to break into pictures. She became famous. Producers went crazy about her. All the famous screen lovers—John Barrymore, Tyrone Power, Clark Gable and Don Ameche—they all made love to her. But she still didn't get into pictures."

He was developing a style.

Zanuck, one of his aficionados, put him in two semi-epics at Twentieth Century-Fox Studio. The first was *Holy Terror,* a forgettable fable starring Jane Withers, Joe being cast as one Pelican Beek. This was followed by the evanescent role of Smiley Watson in *Private Number,* an olla-podrida personally produced by Zanuck with a cast that embraced Robert Taylor, Loretta Young and Patsy Kelly.

"So many of my scenes were left on the cutting room floor," Joe recalled fifteen years later, "I still get fan mail from the janitors."

Wilkerson raised his salary to $600 a show. He appeared on the NBC radio network four times as the guest star of Al Jolson's "Shell Chateau." A field of greyhounds competed for the Joe Lewis Trophy at the Hollywood Kennel Club. And a collector for the Internal Revenue Department informed him that his income taxes were $900 in arrears.

Joe had made good.

The Sundays passed swiftly and with increasing success.

Another show at the Troc was over. As he attempted to thread his way through the crowd, friends and strangers on all sides reached out to him, trying to grasp his hand, congratulating him and begging him to have a drink. He acknowledged each with a wave of gratitude and an assurance he would join them in a little while.

"Dice got hot, eh, Joe?" A familiar voice whispered close to his ear. He turned and saw Abe Marovitz, just arrived in California for a vacation.

They were having breakfast the next afternoon when Joe received a call from the Internal Revenue Department. The Treasury Department wanted $900. Joe protested that he had paid it eight or ten months previously. That was possible, the agent admitted, all Joe had to do was produce the receipt.

Joe turned to Abe helplessly. Everything he owned was in his two wardrobe trunks, there was no room in their bulging compartments for receipts.

"Check your bank," Abe said. Joe was bemused. The left side pocket of his trousers was his bank. He had lost confidence in locks some years previously when the owner of a Chicago hotel disappeared with $750 that Joe had placed in the hotel vault for safekeeping. It was safer to carry your money. And simpler, Joe said, you knew instantly how much you had, if any.

"Only it doesn't keep records—or receipts," Abe reminded him.

"Square it, Abe."

Marovitz persuaded him to transfer his account from his pants to a bank and drew a check for $900, on the back of which Joe indignantly scrawled, "PAID UNDER STRONG PROTEST." (The Internal Revenue Department subsequently refunded the full amount with interest on discovering that he had already paid it.)

"Now that you're rolling," Abe told him, "you have to start buying protection."

Joe looked at him suspiciously. "What are you selling, Abe?"

Marovitz ignored the question. "The least you should do is save five thousand a year for ten years—in case of another depression."

Joe thought it over. "Yeah, but what if there isn't another depression? I'd be stuck with fifty G's." He later put the line in his act at Abe's request and it always brought laughs but when he said it the first time he was in earnest. He ultimately agreed to take out an insurance annuity for his mother. It was a start and Abe was pleased.

"I told you my mezuzah would bring good luck!"

Joe nodded. "It sure did. I sent it to my sister Florence in Bridgeport . . . and she finally got married."

It was St. Valentine's Day. Hollywood loved him in 1936 as Chicago had loved him in 1926. And Joe was in love with the world. He had a pocketful of money, a bellyful of booze and a dame waiting for him. This was his world. As long as he had them, and could entertain people, he had everything.

It was dawn when he returned to his hotel. The elevator operator handed him his customary morning paper and Joe handed him his customary dollar bill.

Joe was undressing, now and then glancing at the paper on his dresser, when the headline hit him: "CHICAGO GANGSTER KILLED."

The dead gangster was Machine Gun Jack McGurn.

There was no gratification in Joe's face as he read the story.

Friday, February fourteenth.

A man lies in his bed staring into the darkness. An hour ago he was tired. But sleep had not come. Things were rough. After Capone went to the can he was nothing. The Outfit was making more dough than ever but not with machine guns. They didn't need them. Or him. He was old-fashioned. Now they ran things with smooth talkers like Charlie Fischetti, Jake Guzik, Paul Ricca, Willie Bioff. He hadn't shot anybody in a hell of a long while.

He turns on the light and looks at his watch. It is 11 P.M. He starts dressing.

His wife turns over sleepily. "Where you going?"

"Bowlin'," McGurn answers.

"This time of night?"

"Can't sleep."

His wife turns away from the light.

McGurn, his coat off, is bowling with two other men in the Avenue Recreation Rooms, a second-floor alley on Polk Street. Pins are clattering at the far end of the polished lane.

Two men walk in, one with a submachine gun under his arm. He sprays McGurn with fourteen bullets. McGurn topples like a tenpin but with less noise.

The man who has lived by the Thompson gun has died by

the Thompson gun. The son of Papa Gebardi, the alky cooker, has gone down like his father.

The killer goes to the score pad, rips off the sheet with McGurn's initials and his uncompleted score. Always get a receipt.

Twenty witnesses look on as the killer takes a square card from his pocket and drops it on the bleeding body. It is a ten-cent greeting card with a ten-cent verse:

> You've lost your job,
> You've lost your dough,
> Your jewels and handsome houses.
> But things could be worse, you know.
> You haven't lost your trousers.

A comic valentine, delivered ten minutes late. Ten minutes after the seventh anniversary of the St. Valentine's Day slaughter. Someone had not forgotten.

James Clark, John May, Adam Hyer, Alfred Weinshank, Reinhart Schwimmer, Pete and Frank Gusenberg.

Machine Gun Jack McGurn.

One for seven. It's a bargain unless you arc the one.

Mrs. Louise Rolfe McGurn, now twenty-eight, had saved her husband many times. When he made a whore out of her and was subsequently convicted of white slavery and sentenced to Leavenworth prison on three counts of violating the Mann Act, she, as the prosecutrix, suddenly forgave him, married him and set him free. When, as already accounted, he was identified as one of the machine-gunners seen leaving the scene of the St. Valentine's Day massacre, she swore under oath that he at the time had been in bed with her.

Louise does not save her man this St. Valentine's Day. While he lies in a pool of blood in a Skid Row bowling alley she is in a bar drinking cognac with Marjorie Swift, the nineteen-year-old daughter of a former mayor of Chicago and a member of one of the city's most illustrious families.

Louise McGurn lost no time after the Gunner went bowling.

His three brothers carry his remains to the grave. His mother sobs, "I want my Jimmy." From the island of Alcatraz his old boss orders a six-foot pillar of white rosebuds to be placed at the head of his coffin, "From Al," and Mrs. Theresa Capone, Al's mother, is among the mourners. The dead man had been good to her son.

"Why should anyone in the world want to kill Jack?" Louise cries out when a corps of newspapermen presses her for a statement.

"He was in a hard business," one of the writers says.

"I don't know what Jack's business was," says the little blonde girl who had lived with him almost ten years. "He never told me and I never asked him. All I know is that he was perfect." She bursts into tears. "Why did they take him away? He was mine! Nothing else counted . . . He was always doing little things . . . always remembering me. Jack was too fine. He never did anything to anybody."

"He never did anything to anybody . . ."

Joe's forefinger unconsciously traced the scar on his face. He resumed undressing, lost in thought. Wonder who got him? He recalled the long nights that he, with a gun in his pocket, went looking for McGurn. But for the grace of God or that anonymous cop who picked him up, he could have been McGurn's killer, hiding in some hole now as the man who got him was.

It was a sense of relief, not pleasure, that Joe felt. Vengeance had vanished with his twenties. He had learned that the best way to get even is to forget it. He had turned the *other* cheek.

McGurn had sworn to kill him and, in a way, he had. He had killed him for eight years. Eight years, three months and five days.

Now McGurn was dead and he was alive. The score was settled.

And he was one up. He had not spat in George Raft's eye. He never had taken orders from McGurn.

He remained at the Trocadero for a record run of fifty-nine consecutive weeks. Wilkerson wanted him to stay indefinitely but Joe was restless. California had been good to him. Six years previously it had given him back his strength. Now it had restored his confidence. He was grateful but he had to move on.

It was not Hollywood he wanted to show, but Chicago. And New York.

15   *E Stands for Eclipse*

He wanted this to be his greatest performance and he hoped that his best would be good enough. His mother would be watching, for the first time. Joe had never invited her before because he did not wish her to see his act. He catered to lads and loreleis who liked their humor a bit gamy. Now he was at Loew's State Theatre in a vaudeville revue produced by Louis Sobol, the Broadway columnist. With Sobol as a monitor it would be safe for Mama to listen.

There was another reason he had never permitted her to see him work. The scar. "She mustn't ever know," he had charged Al in the hospital, "it would only hurt her." It was the family's best-kept secret. He visited her regularly but he always sat on her left and he kept his bad cheek turned away from her.

He would slap on an extra coat of greasepaint and ask the electrician to keep the lights down. And keep his left cheek turned away from her side of the house. Maybe he could get by. At seventy-eight Mama's eyes were a little dim.

He sat in his dressing room, waiting to go on. There was a tap on the door and a beautiful girl walked in, a newspaper clutched in her hand. "You don't know me, Mr. Lewis," she said, "but I had to come in. I had to say good-bye to somebody. I haven't anybody . . ." Tears choked her voice.

"Where you going?" Joe asked.

"I'm going to commit suicide."

Her face was slightly familiar. "Sit down." He poured half a tumbler of whiskey and handed it to her.

She opened her newspaper. "We were going to be married . . . next Sunday." She pointed to the photograph of a prominent aviator who had been killed in a crash the day before. "I haven't anything to live for now."

"Sure you want to knock yourself off?"

She nodded.

"Then drink your drink . . . it'll make it easier."

She gulped the whiskey and Joe gave her a refill. And another and another. She finished the bottle and there was a zealous gleam in her eyes. She began undressing.

"Hey!" Joe cried as her skirt dropped to the floor. "What *is* this?"

"You helped me, lover," she said, "and I'm going to help you."

"Not here." All he needed was Louie Sobol to walk in.

She unbuttoned her blouse. "I won't disappoint you, Joey."

He grabbed her and closed her open blouse. "Are you nuts? I've got to go on in a couple minutes."

"I know," she said. "I'm going on with you."

"On the *stage!*"

"Of course. We'll make a great team, Joey. You'll sing

and I'll do my act." With a flick she was out of her blouse.

He suddenly recognized the deft movement and the magnificent body. She was one of the most famous strip-teasers in the country. And lush, in every meaning of the word. Joe thought of his mother and all the other mothers waiting in the big theatre. He thought of this crazy peeler out there, with or without a G-string.

"Okay," he said, "but I need a drink first."

"Me too."

He dug out an extra bottle he saved for emergencies and filled her glass. She emptied it in two throws and he continued pouring. "What about him?" he asked, pointing to the photograph of the aviator in the newspaper. "Don't you have to go to the funeral or something?"

"Whose funeral?"

"His." He held the paper close to her face. "The fellow you were going to marry."

At last her bleary eyes focused on the photograph. There was no reaction. "Never saw him before in my life," she said truthfully, hoisted her glass once more and passed out.

He looked at his mother questioningly, afraid to ask her how she had liked the show.

"It was nice, Joey," she glowed. "Very nice." She was proud of all her children and loved them equally but she understood Joe the least. She worried about him and lived for his calls, to hear his voice and know that he was all right. "How are you, darling?" he always began and she always replied, "By me everything is jake." He was close to her then. Yet, when he came home on his infrequent visits, he acted as if he were a stranger, as if he did not belong there. She did not know that her Joey would never feel that he belonged in any home, even his own; the only home he knew was a hotel room.

He would occasionally bring a few friends, like Harry

Harris and Abe Marovitz. Harry would go straight to the ice box, Joe never. "Your son," Harry would sigh with affectionate disgust, nibbling a chicken leg. "I got to warm up his own home for him. Mama, in show business do you know what it means to warm up a house?"

Mama Klewan nodded. "I know." Joe loved her deeply. She could feel it. He had showed it in many ways but not when he was near her. It was as if he were a boy of sixteen again, embarrassed more than angered because she had found out he was rehearsing with a burlesque show. He was affectionate and good to her, he made her laugh and they had fun singing "Rosie O'Grady" together, but there was a bridge between them that had never been crossed. He sent her a generous money order every week, much too much money, but she shared it with the synagogue, to protect him from harm. She did not fully understand him but she knew him. She had always known that he was the loneliest and the most sensitive of her eight children. That was why he had run away. He wanted to be with people. He wanted to entertain the whole world and hear everyone laugh, every day, so he would be less lonely. Please God, she prayed, help him pick out a nice Jewish girl and settle down . . .

The roué who boasted in song and story of his conquests was, off the stage, a painfully shy and amazingly chaste man. He would not fall in love until he was forty years old, nor marry until he was forty-four, nor ever settle down. "I never was much of a dame-man," he told me one night.

And he wanted to be.

He had played the Trocadero fifty-nine straight weeks but to the New Yorker, as George M. Cohan put it succinctly, everything west of Broadway was Bridgeport. In New York Joe was a $200 comic. He worked at the Frolics on Broadway at Fiftieth and at a succession of transient deadfalls whose names disappeared almost before the paint was dry.

The other Joe was never out of the headlines. Their names were constantly confused, to Lewis' disadvantage, and worst of all, Louis seemed indestructible. After he finished off Max Baer, he annihilated Paulino Uzcudun and Charley Retzlaff, the latter in his favorite round, the first.

Now Lewis faced a quandary. The other Joe was matched against Max Schmeling.

"You can't bet on the Kraut," Jolson told him.

"I've bet against Louis twenty-seven times running. I can't switch now."

Jolson's face hardened. "A Yom Kippur Jew. You bet on that Nazi bastard and we're through. *Through*, you understand?"

He understood Jolie's fury. Joe had a stranglehold on his own conscience. He was an orthodox Jew and proud of his heritage. He had never worked on Yom Kippur and, wherever he was, he went to the synagogue on that day to beg for atonement. He went other times too, with Marovitz, and he had never missed a memorial service for his father. He knew where he stood. Hitler's purge of the Jews had begun and Schmeling was on Hitler's side.

"Give me five C's," Jolson demanded. He was taking no chances, Joe was going to be on the winner this time.

Joe reluctantly handed him five hundred-dollar notes. He had bet on his namesake for the first time, the only time Louis would be knocked out in more than seventeen years.

To Joe the knockout was anticlimactic. Ten days before, another right-hand punch had flattened Johnny Black forever and a part of Joe died out in Ohio in front of a neon sign flashing "Dardanella." He had picked that one. He had told Johnny he was one to three to die in the gutter and he wished that he had been wrong.

"Sorry about the five hundred," Jolson said.

"It was worth five hundred to get rid of him."

He was not quite rid of him. After the Schmeling debacle

a vindictive Louis made a spectacular comeback to demolish the former champion, Jack Sharkey, Al Ettore, Jorge Brescia, Eddie Simms, Stanley Ketchell, Bob Pastor and Natie Brown—with Lewis betting against Louis every time.

The public was clamoring for a showdown between young Joe Louis and old Jim Braddock, still the heavyweight champion by reason of his sound judgment in not defending the title since removing it from Baer. The match was ultimately made.

"JOE LEWIS VS. JIM BRADDOCK!" read the huge neon letters on the marquee of an Atlantic City theatre. The management hoped, with justifiable confidence, that the public would confuse Joe Lewis with Joe Louis and buy tickets in the belief they would see the Brown Bomber square off against Braddock on the stage. Queues wound around the block.

Braddock received $2,500 for the week and Lewis five hundred, a small dividend on the tens of thousands of dollars he had invested on the other Joe.

It was a one-shot act and he was out of work again, but not for long. His new agent, Abe Lastfogel of the William Morris office, had landed him the part of a labor agitator in a musical, *Right This Way*. (This was in the long ago of 1937 when a labor agitator was a standard comic character.)

Desperately as he needed a job Joe was reluctant to take it. Seven years had failed to erase the bitter memory of *The Second Little Show*.

"This can't miss," Lastfogel assured him. "Irving Kahal, Sammy Fain and Brad Greene have written a great score. Tamara—you know, the sexy Russian girl who introduced 'Smoke Gets in Your Eyes' in *Roberta*, she's in it. So is Blanche Ring, one of the best comediennes in the business." Lastfogel leaned over confidentially. "And that isn't all. They got an angel who's good for at least a hundred thousand, a stage-struck blonde named Alice Alexander. Money is no object. They're going to try out the show in Cleveland and Boston before they bring it to New York. It can't miss . . . And you're getting five hundred a week, not bad for a starter."

Joe sat in his dressing room at the Hanna Theatre in Cleveland, a portable radio at his side. He was listening hopefully when it happened . . .

". . . eight . . . nine . . . ten—and *out!* The winner—and the new Heavyweight Champion of the World—JOE LOUIS!"

Joe mournfully turned the knob. He had bet against Louis thirty-five times. He had hexed him into the title.

The door opened and Monte Proser, the publicity agent for *Right This Way,* came in. He knew, by the expression on Joe's face, that he had heard the news.

"It isn't a joke any more," said Proser. "Every time I put your name in a story, some lamebrain on the copy desk changes it to L-O-U-I-S and hangs on a headline that the fighter is in our show. You got to *do* something."

Joe looked at him helplessly. "What can I do? Fight him?"

"You got to change your name. There's no other way out."

"Sure there is. He can change his name."

"Don't be ridiculous, Joe. He's champion of the world now!"

"Makes no difference . . . His real name isn't Louis, anyway. It's Barrow."

"And yours is Klewan."

Joe smiled. *"That's* it! We'll both go back to our real names."

"Be serious, Joe. It's tough enough getting mixed up with *Ted* Lewis."

"I *am* serious." Joe had appropriated Lewis as a stage name fifteen years previously in Philadelphia because a press agent had been unable to spell Klewan. "I can't change names every time I change press agents," he said.

"Then do something with it." Proser was desperate. At last he had an idea. "What's your middle name?"

"Never had one."

"Then we'll make up one."

Joe shook his head. "John Charles Thomas can get away with it. I can't."

Proser pleaded vainly. "At least a middle initial. Please, Joe!"

Joe thought it over. "All right," he compromised. "K . . . Joe K. Lewis. How's that?"

Proser shook his head. "It doesn't fit." He tested the other twenty-five letters. "I like E," he announced at last. "Joe E. Lewis . . . Joey Lewis. That's *it!*"

Joe shrugged.

"Don't you get it? Joe E. Lots of people call you Joey . . . Hey!" Monte's face lighted up. "That's what they call a clown! A Joey. After the great Joe Grimaldi . . ."

Proser left and Joe picked up a pencil. He had an idea for a song. He scribbled the key words. Soon he would be singing it, a zany lament in the mood of "Sam, You Made the Pants Too Long."

> *Everybody steals my name—*
> *Sinclair Lewis, who's a writer,*
> *Joe Louis, who's a fighter.*
> *I recall Ted Lewis when he used the name of*
> *   Schneider*
> *And Clare Booth Lewis too.*
> *I met a guy while fishin'*
> *Who made this frank admission,*
> *If he hadn't used my name,*
> *It would have been the Lapidus and Clark*
> *   Expedition.*
>
> *Why don't they steal a name like Sitting Bull?*
> *Charley Retzlaff, Howard Hughes?*

> *George Washington, Spike Jones or a name like*
> *Newport News?*
> *Why don't they use their own instead of stealing*
> *names of others?*
> *Maybe it's because these people never had*
> *fathers or mothers.*
> *But there's a certain clown who makes me wear*
> *a frown.*
> *He even stole my first name.*
> *He calls himself Joe E. Brown.*

Right This Way opened in Cleveland with Tamara, Blanche Ring, Guy Robertson and Joe E. Lewis. Joe E. saved it from being a total disaster.

"Lewis doesn't seem to have much to do with the play," William F. McDermott, drama critic of the Cleveland *Plain Dealer,* wrote, "but he is an adroit entertainer, an unusually likeable jack pudding with a disarming way about him. The audience was devoted to him and his was the particular triumph of the evening."

The week's run drew a miserable $3,200.

The New York opening, at the 46th Street Theatre, was a nightmare. Joe was alone on the stage in the middle of a comedy routine when a statuesque blonde, wrapped in a long, white ermine cape, appeared unannounced from the wings. It was obvious, to the audience, that she was one of Joe's stooges.

Joe had never seen her before.

She walked to the center of the stage and, oblivious of Joe, who was speechless, she made a speech. "I want to thank Mr. Brad Greene, who wrote the score," she began, "I want to thank Mr. Irving Kahal and Sammy Fain, who wrote special songs. I want to thank Marianne Brown Waters, who wrote the book. I want to thank Miss Tamara, Miss Blanche Ring, Mr. Guy Robertson and Mr. Joe E. Lewis. I want to thank . . ." She wanted to thank every member of the cast, backstage crew and theatre staff—and she did. At last she finished thanking the orchestra, the patrons, the critics and the ushers, and returned to the wings.

Alice Alexander, the stage-struck blonde, had made theatrical history: she had delivered the first curtain speech ever made before the curtain fell on the first act, a distinction that would cost her $100,000.

"She must have been afraid the show wouldn't last the first act," Joe E. commented wryly and resumed his routine where he had been interrupted.

Harris, who had come to New York at Joe's request to write some songs, sat up with him to wait for the notices. The critics unanimously lauded Joe.

"The evening was Lewis'," the New York *Times* reported. "The show is at its best when there is Mr. Lewis to do the mugging."

"It is only when Lewis runs through his well-known monologues," Howard Barnes wrote in the *Herald Tribune,* "that the show makes you sit up and take notice. He is extremely funny."

"I'm glad for you, Joe," Harry said as they walked back to the Warwick Hotel but Joe detected a false note in his voice.

"What's the matter, Harry?"

Harris was embarrassed. "You and I are pretty close." He realized its absurdity the moment he said it. He was closer to Joe than Joe's three brothers. From the day he had met him rehearsing with Johnny Black at Ager, Yellen and Bernstein's Music House on Clark Street they had shared everything—except Joe's dames. Joe could have a million phone numbers and he wouldn't give you one. But that was his blind spot; it didn't bother Harry, he got enough on his own. Money? What can you say about a guy who has only twenty bucks in his kick and gives you ten? Joe did that in 1925 when he split up with Black. What can you say about a guy who draws forty bucks a week and gives you the whole forty? Joe did that when he was dying in the Lincoln Tavern. What can you say about a guy who goes two weeks without giving you a dime and then slips you five hundred when you expected only two?

"You want new songs the year around, don't you?"

"Of course."

"And you want me to keep writing them?"

"You know I do."

"I was thinkin', Joe . . ."

"Quit vamping, Harry, let's have the melody."

He wished he could retreat but it was too late. "Why don't you give me a set amount every week, not in chunks?" It was out. Joe had no system about paying. A man had to know what was coming in, didn't he? He had to have some security, didn't he? But he was afraid to look, he knew the expression that would be on Joe's face. "So I'll know I have a regular income . . ."

Joe looked at his friend. Had Harry gone daft? Who had a regular income in their business except Tucker and Richman? "It'll have to be my way, Harry." He did not mean to be arbitrary and he did not think he was chinchy, but it was the only thing he could say. He could not conscientiously promise Harry a set amount every week; he did not know if he would have it.

Nothing more was said. Harry went back to Chicago without saying good-bye. Joe was saddened but he had more immediate troubles. The show was not going well . . .

The turkey went into its fourth dismal week. Three doors from the theatre, at Dinty Moore's Restaurant, Joe was eating with Lastfogel, who was going to catch his performance that evening.

Joe looked at his watch. It was 8:10, time to change. "I'll pick you up in fifteen minutes," he said and left.

Five minutes later, Lastfogel saw Joe coming back. The Napoleon of agents, worried that he was late, started wolfing his food.

"You don't have to eat so fast, Abe," said Joe, "the show just folded."

Right This Way died but a part of it would live as long as lovers the world over sang or hummed or whistled "I'll Be Seeing You," a hauntingly beautiful song that was lost because Tamara Drasin, unfortunately cast as a Boston debutante, had sung it in a guttural Volga accent. A few years later, flying across the Atlantic to entertain the armed forces overseas, she would plummet to her death in a crash that her friend and fellow entertainer, Jane Froman, miraculously survived.

Tragic Tamara sank beneath the plane-strewn waters off Lisbon as a lost song was being discovered.

I'll be seeing you . . .

The forgotten song was remembered on the war fronts, a song of hope salvaged from a hopeless flop, a song that would forever remind Joe of one of the two great loves of his life.

16   *Thirty*

It was a sultry Sunday afternoon in June, Chicago was boiling. The phone rang and the operator said New York was calling Mr. Mack.

"This is Joe Lewis," a grating voice came on. "You said if I ever needed a piano player . . ."

Austin Mack smiled. He had said it one night as they sat around the Four Deuces but that was in 1926, this was 1938.

"I need one now," the strident voice continued. "I've got a week at the Earl Theatre in Philly."

The spindling, baldish man, deceptively owlish-looking in his horn-rimmed glasses, waited for Lewis to say how much.

"I know we can get along," Joe said.

Austin Mack weighed the offer. He had just finished two years at Harry's Bar and had no immediate prospects of employment. But one lousy week at the Earl! And he had to go from Chicago to New York to Philadelphia to get it. And Lewis had not said how much. It was not very alluring, any way you looked at it . . . but it was a week's work and he remembered Joe Lewis as a stand-up guy. "You got a piano player," he replied, unaware that he was making a lifetime contract.

Austin had no roots, no base, no goal beyond living one day at a time, simply and tranquilly, with his wife Cassie. He had come out of Brunswick, New Jersey, and had gone to war with the 77th Division. He was supposed to have been assigned to the 308th Infantry Band and had played a short while for Elsie Janis, "The Sweetheart of the A.E.F.," but he wound up as a stretcher bearer in France. One night, after six months in the front lines, he was carrying in a wounded man when a barrage hurled him to the ground. The wounded man was killed and Austin was hit in his left knee.

In the twenty years that followed he and Cassie had been nomads, from Perry's Place on Coney Island to his brother Roy's show at the Midnight Frolics in Chicago to playing for Eddie Leonard, the great minstrel man, to a long run with Texas Guinan.

Miss Guinan, holding forth at the Royal Club in New York, had become displeased with a member of her band, a vocalist who sang too stiffly because of a recurrent boil on his neck. "Get rid of the guy with the boil," she ordered her manager. The next day, after satisfying Miss Guinan that he was not susceptible to cysts, Austin had replaced the unfortunate fellow, Don Ameche, who, once rid of his infection, had gone on to the higher arts in Hollywood.

They got along, as Joe said they would. The week in Philadelphia was followed by two weeks at the 500 Club in Atlantic City and when Marovitz wired Joe that he had promoted a week's work in Chicago, Joe automatically made reservations for three. The team was formed: Joe, Austin and Cassie, a spirited, selfless woman who would dedicate the rest of her life to being the balance wheel, nurse, guardian and avenging angel for two characters out of *Alice in Wonderland*.

"By the way, you're playing the Chez Paree," Abe said offhandedly as if he were referring to a two-buck nautch-house instead of Chicago's top cabaret, a glittering showcase for the great names of show business.

Joe looked at the spacious room on the site of the old Chez Pierre where he had made his start in Chicago with Johnny Black. "How did you do it, Abe?" he asked, overwhelmed.

"Fritzel is a client of mine. He owes me a favor." Mike Fritzel and Joe Jacobson, who had opened the Chez Paree in the early '30's, ran a game room in the back with the benediction of the police and in violation of the statutes of the State of Illinois. It was Abe's function, as their attorney, to maintain an entente cordiale between them and the antithetic agents of the law.

Joe was fearful. It was a long way from the dives he had been playing—the Vanity Fair, the Frolics, the Nut Club and the Club Royale—to the Chez Paree. Was he ready? Would his voice carry over the immense room and its five hundred seats? Had Abe overmatched him?

"In a couple years you'll be making two thousand a week," Marovitz predicted.

Joe shook his head. "I could never make that kind of money. I don't have the act."

He was a hit and Fritzel held him over. One night, the au-

dience was cold and did not immediately respond to his
japery. "I'm not Joe Louis, the boxer," he snapped, "so stop
fighting me already." That loosened the crowd. "Anyway,"
he went on, "I'm getting rave notices." He took a clipping
from his pocket and began reading, " 'The Chez Paree has a
great show, thanks to the lovely chanteuse, Gertrude Niesen
—and despite an unfunny comedian, Joe E. Lewis . . .' "

The crowd howled as Joe solemnly read a succession of
scathing comments about his performance. One fellow in particular was almost convulsive. At last Joe finished. "I have
been reading from the latest issue of *Billboard,* the theatrical
weekly," he said and took the clipping into the crowd to
prove its authenticity.

"You look like a man who would know a *Billboard* notice
if he saw one," he said to the hysterical customer who was
having difficulty remaining on his chair. "Is this bona fide
and does it say I'm unfunny?"

The man, Jack Benny, wiped the tears from his eyes,
looked at the clipping and went into another paroxysm of
laughter.

"Jack is a sentimental man," Joe remarked to the crowd.
"He cries when Roy Rogers falls off his horse." The crowd
roared. "Jack Benny," he went on, "is the man who in one
year was responsible for the sale of two million radios. I
know I sold mine and my brother Al sold his."

The favor Fritzel had done for Marovitz proved a bigger
favor to himself. He wanted to keep Joe indefinitely but
Marovitz pulled him out at the end of four weeks. "Is this a
way to treat a client?" Fritzel protested.

"I have other clients," Abe replied. Among them was Lou
Falkenstein, owner of the High Hat Club on Rush Street, one
of the many cafés Joe had emptied in the past month. Falkenstein was desperate. "You got to get me Lewis," he had
told Abe.

"He's yours. Twelve hundred a week."

"You mean for two weeks."

"I mean for one week, Lou."

"But he's a $600 act. That's all Fritzel paid him. I know!"

Abe turned to leave. Falkenstein stopped him. A moment later he was studying a contract Marovitz had already prepared, at $1,200 a week. "Is this a way to treat a client?" he asked.

"Lewis is a client of mine too . . . Sign here, Lou."

Falkenstein signed.

Joe was over the hump, past the thousand-dollar limit for the first time in eleven years. "How did you do it, Abe?" he asked.

"The first thing they taught me in law school," Marovitz said, "was to make your fee before the client's eyes dry . . . Sign this too, Joe."

"What is it?"

"Another annuity."

"Make it out to Henrietta." His oldest sister would be provided for.

Austin did not and never would have an agreement with Joe, written or verbal, but the following week his pay was doubled too.

"Remember your first raise at the old Midnight Frolics?" Austin recalled.

Joe nodded. "I bought a pair of spats."

Austin smiled. "And put 'em on the wrong feet. You had 'em buttoned on the inside instead of the outside!"

Business at the High Hat increased in inverse ratio to that of the Chez Paree. In his first ten days Joe drew more customers than the famed Howard Brothers, Willie and Eugene, had in two weeks.

The Chez Paree was dying. "I've got to have him back, Abe," Fritzel pleaded.

"You've got him," Marovitz said, adding softly, "at seventeen-fifty a week."

Fritzel glared at his lawyer. "I expected to pay him twice as much as I did last month but not *three* times. It's robbery!"

"It's a bargain, Mike. Six months from now you'll wish you could buy Lewis for $1,750 a week."

Fritzel paid.

"How do you do it, Abe?" Joe was unable to comprehend what was happening to him.

"Sign this," Abe ordered. It was another insurance annuity. "That takes care of Ida." Another sister was provided for.

He had been gangland's favorite jester, his songs and quips echoing across the Levee and up on the North Side. Now he was playing to the society set from Lake Shore Drive and they were laughing as loudly as the hoodlums and their harlots had, often at the same jokes. He had learned that humor knows no caste system, it transcends all barriers: social, economical, geographical, moral. There were not two kinds of audiences but two kinds of material: funny and not funny.

He had proved he was a funny man in Hollywood and Chicago but it was still Bridgeport. In New York he was just another comic who had been in a flop musical and had played third-rate joints for ten years without getting close to the Versailles, the Riviera or any other class cabaret except as a customer.

It was the night after Joe closed at the Chez Paree and, as was his custom, he came back to give his successor a sendoff. As he was leaving with Marovitz he came face to face with Harry Harris. They had not seen each other or spoken since the night they had talked money in New York.

Joe grabbed Harry's arm. "What did I ever do to you?"

Harris laughed nervously. "Forget it."

Joe whipped him around as if he were a wrestler's stooge and hurled him into the elevator.

"Leave him alone, Joe," Marovitz shouted.

"Stay out of it, Abe." Joe pressed the button and the elevator doors slammed shut.

He unloosened his stranglehold and looked at his old friend with great hurt. "I finally make the Chez Paree . . . and where were you? You didn't come once—did you?" He hoped Harry had sneaked in to catch his show.

"No, I didn't."

Joe's face tightened, dejection fighting rage. "But you come the night after I close. You come to see Romo Vincent."

"I wrote his songs, Joe."

Joe said nothing. For the first time in the years Harry had known him he saw tears in his eyes.

"I'm opening at the Continental in Miami Tuesday," Joe said. "Be there." He slipped a bill into Harry's hand, a thousand-dollar note.

"I don't like Jorge Sanchez because he is rich," he told the opening-night crowd at the Club Continental in Miami Beach. "I like him because he is *very* rich."

Jorge Sanchez, sugar planter, playboy, multimillionaire and one of the hundred leading challengers for the title of Joe Lewis' Best Friend, sat at a ringside table and roared. With him was a party of fifty guests, including his private rumba band. Café society's most fabulous spender, he had come by his profligacy honorably. His father once imported the seventy-five-piece Metropolitan Opera orchestra from New York to serenade a guest at his plantation in Cuba. The guest, Elizabeth Laurent, a Philadelphia socialite, was impressed and soon became Mrs. Sanchez.

Joe had met Sanchez on his first trip to Florida in 1928 and they had become friends. Every year Jorge and his wife Brownie had begged him to come to Havana for a visit and each time Joe had stalled him.

"No more reprieves," Sanchez said with finality when the show was over. "Brownie says I can't come home without you." Joe protested for another stay but Sanchez would not listen. "Wait till you see the dames I got lined up," he whispered.

"First I'll show you our girlie houses," Sanchez announced as they began their tour of Havana.

Joe looked at his watch. It was 1 P.M. "Isn't it a bit early for that sort of thing?"

Sanchez smiled and, a little while later, he was ringing the bell of an old hacienda. "Youngest girls in the whole world work in this one."

The door opened. In the doorway stood a woman holding an infant in her arms.

Joe stared at the baby and turned to Sanchez. "She's a little *too* young for me."

Sanchez recounted the story to Winston Churchill a few weeks later and it became one of the Prime Minister's favorite anecdotes.

An event of far-reaching effect happened that summer of 1939. Charles (Gabby) Hartnett, the husky catcher whose dramatic home run on the last day of the season would beat the front-running Pittsburgh Pirates for the National League pennant, was named to succeed Charley Grimm as manager of the Chicago Cubs.

"That's gratitude," Joe stormed. "Grimm wins two flags, two seconds and two thirds in six years and they fire him."

A few days later he chanced to meet Mrs. P. K. Wrigley, whose husband owned the Cubs, among other things. "I've been a loyal Cubs fan for thirteen years," Joe told her. "I've hardly missed a home game when I've been in Chicago. But I'll never set foot in Wrigley Field again as long as I live. Please tell your husband that." He opened a package of Beech-Nut chewing gum and offered Mrs. Wrigley a stick.

Joe's self-imposed exile from Wrigley Field left him homeless in the afternoons. One day, out of ennui, he went to the Arlington Park race track for the first time.

That day a horse player was born.

The firing of Grimm has cost Joe well over a million dollars.

The other Joe continued to fare well. Since winning the title he had beaten Tommy Farr, Nathan Mann and Harry Thomas—Lewis, out of habit, always taking the odds against him. Now the Bomber was rematched with Schmeling and Joe E. was distressed. He could not bet on Louis—once, against the same Schmeling, had been enough—and he would not bet on a Nazi paratrooper.

Worse, far worse to a gambling man than betting on a loser, is not being able to bet at all. It was just as well, Louis nailed the German in one round minus.

Following this came Joe E.'s dream match: Lewis versus Louis. His bona fide namesake, John Henry Lewis, light-heavyweight champion of the world, was signed to avenge the House of Lewis.

He didn't. The Brown Bomber required less than one round to knock out *two* Lewises.

Paul Small, his erstwhile stooge, who had become a theatrical agent for William Morris, visited him in New Orleans.

"I think I can move you into the number one spot in New York," Small told him as they sat in the steam room at the Athletic Club.

"What's the opening date?"

"I'm putting together a package for Ben Marden's Riviera . . ."

As they talked, a husky Southerner kept interrupting with

unsolicited opinions, mostly unfavorable, about people in show business. Joe asked him to find another steam pipe but the pest remained and continued to intrude.

"I can go along with a joke," Joe snapped, "but you're ridiculous."

The boor roared and moved closer.

"You're bigger than I am, Paul," Joe told Small at last. "Belt him."

Small belted the stranger. The stranger belted him back. It was a rugged melee and each was knocked down several times but Paul landed a lucky one and scored the last knockdown.

One of the astonished onlookers whispered in Paul's ear.

Small turned chalky. "Let's get out of here," he shouted to Joe and made for the door, "before he comes to."

"Why?" Joe asked.

Small pointed a trembling finger at the prostrate gladiator. "He's the A.A.U. heavyweight champion of Louisiana!"

Small had promised to give Ben Marden the greatest night club show in America for $6,500 a week and he delivered Sophie Tucker, Harry Richman and Joe Lewis on the same bill.

It was a happy reunion. They recounted Joe's war with McGurn, and Richman added a personal footnote to the gangster era of show business: "I was playing the Palace Theatre in Chicago and had just been paid. On my way to the hotel a stickup man poked a gun in my ribs and cleaned me. I had friends around town and the next day I received word that Capone wanted to see me at the Metropole Hotel. My wallet was waiting for me, not a cent missing. 'After this,' Capone told me, handing me a slip of paper, 'keep this on you wherever you go. If anyone bothers you, flash it.' "

Richman pulled out a worn, creased slip of paper. It read:

"To whom it may concern: Harry Richman is a very good friend of mine.

(signed) Al Capone."

Small's masterstroke was the division of the loot. The supporting acts cost $500 a week. "That leaves $6,000," he told Sophie. He paused, summoning courage for the big question that had been disturbing him since he had put the deal together. Sophie's volcanic disposition and her justifiable pride were legendary. "What do you think," he asked apprehensively, "about splitting it even?"

Sophie Tucker, the greatest drawing card in cabaret business, glared at him. "Was there any question about *not* splitting it even?"

Joe Lewis, three months ago a $600 comic when he was lucky to find work, now had an established salary of $2,000 a week. He was Big Time.

The '30's, Joe's and America's, were ending. For him, as for his country, they had been an interim, a prelude, a time for restoration. It was a decade without character of its own, an interlude of ambivalence, dosing its hangover of the '20's, douching its corruption and simultaneously scenting itself for its hoped-for lover in the '40's.

And it had been a time to pay. The lords of Prohibition were in cemeteries, penitentiaries and exile. A new order was rising, Joe's second generation of gangsters. This time he would know how to take care of himself.

Joe would live his forties as riotously as his twenties, achieving his sweetest victories and suffering his mightiest defeats. In them he would discover the truth of Hilaire Belloc's words, that nothing is worth the wear of winning save the laughter and the love of a few friends.

the forties

JOE'S AND THE WORLD'S

*"Money isn't everything,
it just quiets the nerves a little."*

JOE E.

> *It doesn't take much money*
> *To tie that wedding noose.*
> *It only costs two bucks, a measly deuce.*
> *Without that license I can get the same*
> *So what's the use?*
> *I'd rather be a bachelor on the loose!*

Joe was leering like a puckish satyr and the elegant opening-
night crowd at the Versailles was laughing. All except
Letty.

> *A honeymoon is lovely, I've often heard it said,*
> *That breakfast served in bed is worth a deuce . . .*
> *Until you find next morning you can't lift*
> *Your orange juice.*
> *I'd rather be a bachelor on the loose!*

Letty was young, beautiful, cultured, popular and immensely wealthy. She had everything she wanted except Joe.

> *If I should share my bed and board*
> *I might be bored in bed.*
> *I need it like a hatrack needs a moose . . .*
> *I'd rather be a bachelor on the loose!*

It was a lie. Joe was the loneliest man she had ever known.
The Lewis the crowd saw and laughed with, even the Joe E.
his friends knew, was not the man she loved. She had seen
behind the mask. He needed her, as she needed him. She
was certain of it.

The first show was over and, at last, he made his way back to their table.

"That's your one song I don't like," she said.

"It gets more laughs than 'Lohengrin.'"

"In the act."

What was the act?

"There are lots more important things than money," he said on the stage. "The only thing is, they all cost money."

Was it a gag or his philosophy?

"I always say liquor improves with age," he said on the stage. "The older you get the more you like it."

Was it a jest or an admission?

"Being a comedian is just a hobby with me," he said on the stage. "Horse racing is my real business. I just work as a comedian so I can make money to put back in my business."

Was it a joke or a fact?

"Money can't buy love," he said on the stage. "Let me have it and I'll do my own shopping."

Was it a line or his belief?

After studying Joe at close range for ten years, I believed that in his search for a stage personality he had discovered his true self, a shadow that had found its owner. After knowing him a few years longer, I realized that the theory was fallacious, no more than a half-truth because Joe and his alter ego were interchangeable, on stage and off. His nature, like his humor, cannot be explained so simply.

He drank hard, he gambled heavily, he made love promiscuously—he *was* a vagabond, a gay, gregarious, carefree Villon who lived without restraint, leaping from bar to bookie to boudoir—but for long stretches of time he lived like a monk, withdrawn from the world, shy, molelike, an alien to society, conditioned not to require love, not even to desire it.

Except C.O.D.

Letty was not a one-night stand.

"We could be happy." She reached for his hand.

Must she press? he thought. Nothing is going to happen. She's society, educated in Europe, got more rocks than I'll ever see. Who's kiddin' who? I'm just a bum from Jefferson and Cherry streets who got lucky. But not *that* lucky. I'm not overly bright but I know when I'm out of my class. He bet on blood lines.

"Drink up," he said.

She drank up, wondering why he got loaded every night. Was it the scar? She never noticed it except when he self-consciously turned his left cheek away from her. Didn't he know he was an attractive man? She had told him often enough and had meant it. The first time she had seen him he reminded her of an illustration out of the *Pickwick Papers* but as she came to know his soft brown eyes, his over-sized tilted nose and his strong mouth, he became handsome. Was it his voice? He joked about it on the stage but that was a cover-up, he was sensitive about it. Didn't he realize that its peculiar hoarseness was a distinction, another mark that set him apart?

"I nearly forgot." She handed him a diamond-studded cigarette case, engraved to him with all her love.

"What's this for?"

"Opening night!"

"But I've had a thousand opening nights!"

"This is my first."

"Thanks . . ." He stared at the case and she felt him pulling away from her. "I have to go over some lyrics." He stood up. "I'm introducing a new number on the late show."

"Good luck, darling." A moment later she turned to call him back. Instead, she put the cigarette case back in her purse. She would slip it in his pocket later.

The wedding hall was very spacious,
The bride was very sweet and gracious,

But where, oh where, was the groom?
The crowd was quickly growing,
By now the hall was overflowing,
And with all those people there,
There wasn't an inch to spare.
The groom couldn't get in.

The audience became restless. Joe had never kept them waiting this long for a laugh.

The butcher got in, the baker got in,
His uncle who plays horses in Jamaica got in.
But no room for the groom.

A few smirking smiles appeared. The initiated got it, or thought they did. The out-of-town buyers were bored.

The groom couldn't get in.
His brother-in-law from Toledo got in.
A guy with a rented tuxedo got in.
But no room for the groom.

There was a ripple of laughter. Joe continued the doleful tune.

He'd often been in the place before
And this was his contention:
He always thought the place was large enough
To hold a Democratic Convention.
But the groom couldn't get in.
A farmer got in, his dairy got in.
I know a guy from Buffalo who was a fairy got in
But no room for the groom!

The crowd was applauding and would not let him leave until he had given them another chorus.

But the thing that made the groom get mad
After he waited hours,
Was when a Western Union boy got in
With a big bouquet of flowers.
But the groom couldn't get in.
A tenor got in, a soprano got in,
Even Vincent Lopez and his goddamn piano got in—
But no room for the groom!

Letty's immobile face reflected her disapproval. "I'm not a prude, Joe, but . . ."

"It's a clean song, Letty."

She nodded. "Who wrote it—Carrie Jacobs Bond?"

"Show me one blue line!" His indignation, real or feigned, was convincing. "Maybe it isn't the song . . . but the audience."

"Could be I'm prejudiced," she said. "Seems to me your groom didn't *want* to get in."

She laid it on the line. That bothered him. He was addicted to dames who wanted to go to bed with him for dough or a job in the line or a line in Winchell's column. Inexperienced with any other kind of women, he rationalized that the semi-professionals were the best. It fitted into his code of ethics. It seemed simpler and more honest to give a dame fifty bucks or a hundred than to romance her with foolish lies and rubber promises, gambits he parodied in his act. He could not satirize himself. Why call it love when it was only a lay? Letty was different. She didn't need or want money, a job or publicity. She talked like someone who had gotten the message, she said she wanted him period. And he could not believe it. His humility would not permit him to believe that any woman—least of all, a young, rich and brainy socialite—would want him. There had to be a catch, a switch at the finish. He wasn't rising to the bait, not even on diamond-studded hooks.

What does she want me for, he wondered, and what would she do with me if I was ever sucker enough to marry her? He knew her set. It had become *de rigueur* to be banged by prize fighters, criminals, night club operators and affiliated studs who constituted the new aristocracy of café society. What kind of a wife could she make him? How long could she take his brand of life, getting up at 2 P.M. and going to bed at 6 A.M., sitting around crowded, smoke-choked traps drinking, always drinking, and listening to his same jokes and songs every night seven nights a week, fifty-two weeks a year—or else *not* being with him and, sooner or later, going to sleep earlier and with someone else? He was an expert on infidelity, accustomed to seeing men play musical beds with other men's wives. Sometimes a man cannot help being unfaithful to himself, but being unfaithful to another . . . no, that was unnecessary. Let them cheat who must; he wanted no part of that misery, giving or taking.

"It wouldn't work," he said. "I belong in bars. You don't. I can't do you any good—and you can't do me any good."

She winced. Must he hurt? He did not want to hurt, she was sure. He knew how it felt.

"You're not a gambler, Joe. That's the act."

Joe smiled wryly. He had blown fifteen hundred at Belmont Park that afternoon.

"You bet on long shots," she said, "but not the longest."

"I don't bet on fillies."

"I'll bet on anything . . . even myself. I'm going to divorce Tom."

"Do what you want, Letty, but remember, "I'm a bachelor on the loose—and I'm staying that way."

"I'm not asking for insurance. I don't copper *my* bets."

Joe looked at her and, for the first time in his life, he knew he was in love.

He was playing the Continental Club in Miami Beach and Harris was with him to work on the fall show.

"You're going on the wagon," Joe ordered.

Harry was nonplused. "Don't you like the songs?"

"Who's talking about songs? It's you. Every time you have two drinks you get that look in your eyes. What's with you and that little singer?"

"Velma Israels?" Harry laughed. "Don't worry about her. She's just a nice kid."

Joe scowled. "They're all nice kids. And they all want to put nice halters on some chump when his guard is down. Give me your word you'll stop drinking."

"Isn't that silly, Joe? You've known me almost twenty years."

"The pledge, Harry."

"But I'm forty years old! If I haven't weakened by now . . ."

Joe was unimpressed. He was only a year younger than Harry and, though he had been certain that he was invulnerable to marriage, he was no longer sure.

"Not a drop, Harry. Promise." He needed his moral support.

"If it'll make you feel better." Harry gripped his hand.

His next engagement was at Ciro's, Billy Wilkerson's new club in Hollywood. Joe intended to keep as far away from Letty as he could.

"Dear Joe," L. B. Mayer wired him. "Regret it is impossible for me to be at your opening. Wish you best of luck, will be seeing you soon."

"Would be there but am in the hospital," Harry Cohn, boss of Columbia Pictures, wired from Cedars of Lebanon. "Know you will knock 'em dead."

Zanuck wired his disappointment that the press of a conference precluded his being at the opening but, with the exception of these three penitent heads of major studios, Hollywood's Who's In was in full attendance.

They loved his "No Room for the Groom" as much as "Sam, You Made The Pants Too Long," but most of all they enjoyed his sallies directed at Hollywood.

"This is the only place where they marry to legalize separations," he gagged. "I know a couple that was remarried four times. People kept introducing them."

One night he introduced an Academy Award winner and announced that the distinguished actor had just signed a contract with Paramount that allowed him to make one extra wife a year.

He recalled his own career in the studios. "People ask me, 'Joe, why don't you make pictures?' That's like asking me, 'Joe, why don't you starve?' But it wasn't always like this. A few years ago I made two pictures. The first one grossed— oh, seven hundred dollars. The second one flopped but that's the way it goes, you can't hit all the time. Law of averages.

"I still like Hollywood. I like the weather. No matter how hot it gets in the daytime, there's nothing to do at night."

Gossip columnists linked his name with Jane Frazee of the Frazee Sisters, a song-and-dance team he had brought from Florida. He wanted Letty to read the items and yet he hoped she wouldn't. Like the most tormented torch-bearer who came to see his act, hopeful of forgetting his woman, Joe wanted to remember and simultaneously forget.

"STILL ON WAGON," Harry wired from Miami Beach two weeks later. "MARRIED VELMA THIS AFTERNOON."

Joe kept dating Jane, and gambling heavily. He needed antidotes.

They were at the Clover Club, an illicit house of chance, early one morning. The casino was packed with the movie colony's high-rollers when the manager rushed in. "Raid!" he shouted. "It's a raid!"

The room was in instant panic as croupiers scooped up fistfuls of chips and currency, as screaming stars, directors and producers scurried for the exits and as the door splintered under the pounding of axes, iron bars and fists.

One head remained cool. Joe made no move to leave.

"Let's go, Joe!" Jane cried.

"What's the excitement? They're just making retakes on *Drums Along the Mohawk.*"

He kept moving: the Chez Paree, the Mounds Club in Cleveland, the Colonial Inn in Miami Beach. At last, at the insistence of Lastfogel, he returned to New York in the fall of 1941.

"What saloon, Abe?" he asked his agent.

"Joe, I'm putting you in a show."

"What saloon, Abe?"

"Hear me out before you say anything. You know the great English musical comedy star, Jessie Matthews . . ."

"What saloon, Abe?"

"It's called *The Lady Comes Across* and you're going to co-star with her and Mischa Auer."

Joe's eyes brightened. "A movie?"

Lastfogel shook his head. "Legitimate. Rehearsals start next week and . . ."

"Good-bye, Abe."

Lastfogel held his arm. "This can't miss, Joe."

"That's what you said about *Right This Way.*" Four years had passed but the scars were unhealed, as raw as his eleven-year-old but still fresh wounds from *The Second Little Show.*

"This has a wonderful score and a great book," Lastfogel argued.

"Not for me. Until theatres let actors make up their lines as they go along, I'll stick to saloons."

"Quit gagging, Joe."

"I'm leveling."

Lastfogel appealed to his reason. "I can always put you in a night club. A big musical doesn't come along every year . . ."

"Thank goodness."

"If I muffed the chance to put you in a Broadway hit, you would fire me—and I would have it coming. So I shouldn't have said it can't miss. Anything can miss—and anything can *hit*. You pay me a lot of money for my advice. I say take it."

Joe respected Lastfogel's judgment as much as his integrity, but Abe did not know him as well as he knew himself. He would not attempt to convince Abe that it was not courage he lacked but desire. He did not enjoy shouting across footlights so that no one in the balcony would miss a word. This destroyed the illusion, at least for him, and with it his pleasure. Lastfogel was a sober, respectable man. He could not understand that doing a musical, with two matinees a week, disrupted his way of life. A normal day for him began at 2 P.M. or 3 P.M. when he arose and called room service for his four freedoms: breakfast, newspapers, mail and a scratch sheet. No musical was worth that sacrifice. Yet, he did not want Lastfogel to think he was an unreasonable client and, who could tell, maybe Abe had gotten lucky and caught another *Show Boat*. At worst, he could use it to try out some new songs.

The show opened in New Haven and Joe stopped it with his first song. It had been on his mind almost a year, since the day in Miami Beach Austin had torn a sheet off their calendar, the month of February.

Joe had stared at the crumpled page. "February is over,"

he sighed. "The big money is over for another year." He
picked up the sheet. "It was such a short season . . ." He
had brooded about it and one day the team of Lester Lee,
Danny Shapiro and Jerry Seelen, who had written "No
Room for the Groom," put his grief to music.

> *Poor little February, I know how you feel.*
> *You must feel exactly like a dog.*
> *Why should there be thirty days in Sept*
> *And thirty-one days in Aug?*
> *Poor little Feb, what a dirty deal.*
>
> *Fate just took a look at you and mocked.*
> *Why should there be thirty days in Nov*
> *And thirty-one days in Oct?*
> *They know you're not as happy as June, July or May*
> *So every four years they do you a favor,*
> *They slip you an extra day.*
> *Poor little Feb, go fight City Hall.*

The crowd at New Haven loved it.

"We're in trouble," he called Lastfogel after the performance. "I sing, dance and *look* better than Jessie Matthews."

"Everything will be all right in Boston," Lastfogel assured
him.

Everything was not all right in Boston, or anywhere else.
The same day that the critics bayoneted the show, the Japs
attacked Pearl Harbor.

"I'm enlisting," Joe told Lastfogel. For him it was 1917
again and he was fifteen, only this time his sister Henrietta
could not stop him.

"You'll get your chance. Meanwhile, the show opens in
New York January tenth, as scheduled."

"I'm going in the service, Abe—*now*."

"The only service you can perform is to entertain. And everyone is going to need entertainment, more than ever."

Joe read him the devastating notices the show had received in Boston. "*This* is entertainment?" His face hardened. "Book me out."

Lastfogel was puzzled.

"Get me a job in a saloon—or I'll get someone who will."

"Happy New Year, darling."

He could think of nothing happy this new year might bring but when he saw Letty and felt her warm lips, he was happy.

"How do I look?" She lifted her left hand to her face so that he could not help but notice she no longer wore a wedding band.

He wanted her but he could not afford her. Marovitz took first count on his money to pay for the insurance annuities that could not be touched for twenty years. Horses, dice and booze took what was left. He had a hard time paying his hotel bill. And the prospects were not good. Lastfogel had not come up with a saloon job of any kind. *The Lady Comes Across* was certain to flop *if* it opened on January tenth, which he doubted. Two days later he would be forty years old. Too old for the war, a war going badly, a war in which he was unwanted. He had insisted on taking a physical examination and the Army had insisted on rejecting him. He could not lift a cup of coffee, let alone a Garand rifle, with his right hand. And he had an aluminum plug in his skull. How could he, a 4-F physically and financially, conceive of marrying a youngster like Letty?

"I missed you, darling," she said.

He did not tell her how much he had missed her. He did not think he had the right.

Joe continued loving her, admitting it to no one, least of

Joe and his favorite casino player, Mrs. Pauline Klewan, his mother, now in her ninety-seventh year. This is a rare photograph of Joe, the cork is in the bottle.

Spencer Tracy, John Barrymore and George Jessel (l. to r.) sit one out with "the funniest man in the world" in 1936 as he sets a record of starring 59 consecutive weeks at the Trocadero in Hollywood.

Ex-Mayor Jimmy Walker (left) and former Postmaster General James A. Farley award Joe the New York *Mirror* Gold Medal for being named "the outstanding night club performer of 1942." *Copacabana Photo.*

all to her, and concealing it from everyone except Austin and Cassie. He chose to suffer alone, drinking, gambling and working, his infallible therapies against the ills of mankind.

"Topical songs, that's what they want now," he told Shapiro, Seelen and Lee, and they came up with the "H. V. Kaltenborn Blues."

> *I try to be fair when Winchell's on the air,*
> *I always try to digest his views.*
> *I try to be brave but I'm just a slave,*
> *I've got those H. V. Kaltenborn blues.*

> *My ears try to cling to Raymond Gram Swing*
> *But my head tells my ears to refuse,*
> *I can't be a traitor to my commentator,*
> *I got those H. V. Kaltenborn blues.*

George Wood of the William Morris office had news. "You open at the Copacabana January ninth."

Joe chortled. "So the musical is off?"

Wood shook his head. "It opens January tenth."

Had Wood and Lastfogel blown their tops? How could he be on a West Forty-fourth Street stage from 8:30 P.M. to 11:15 and do a supper show at the same time in a club on East Sixtieth Street?

"It isn't as tough as it sounds," Wood explained. "You're doing only one show at the Copa, around midnight. You can make it . . . if you don't take too many curtain calls. The Copa's dying but there aren't any good jobs available. I had to *make* this one. Lastfogel's orders. Proser has never used name acts. I had to sell him on changing his policy."

"I thought you said he was dying." Monte Proser, his press agent five years ago, was now hiring *him*. Big-hearted Monte, who had given him the E in his name.

"He can't afford a name act. That's how I got him to double you, by cutting your price. He wanted to put you on for a week. I made him book you for three."

The Copacabana wasn't Ben Marden's Riviera or the Versailles, it lacked class and customers, but Joe had ordered Abe to come up with a saloon job and he had to take it.

If he could bring in this parlay, he might . . . no, that was expecting too much. Letty was beyond his reach.

Watching him, Letty wondered what more she had to do. She had gotten a divorce, happily. She had waited a year to make sure that she loved Joe and wanted his way of life, to the exclusion of all others. She did.

It has to be, she kept hoping.

Joe went into the Copacabana and, the following night, opened in *The Lady Comes Across*.

"Why don't you stay out of my racket?" Danny Kaye wired. "But as long as you're in it, good luck."

Luck, talent and material he had. Lustily, he sang—

I can't get the merchandise, it's tough to get stuff!
Who can think of a family? Who can think of romance?
What good is having a family? I'd rather have a shipment
Of pants—with zippers.
Can't get deliveries, it's tough to get stuff.
Can't get commodities, the going is tough.
You can't have children unless you get Henderson's okay,
So call up Mr. Henderson before you go to sleep,
'Cause you can't get the merchandise,
It's tough to get stuff!

New York's first-nighters, already feeling the pinch of wartime rationing and shortages, laughed for the first time

at their plight. The audience belonged to Joe. He could sing
or say nothing unfunny.

Life to me is melancholy
The only thing that keeps me alive
Is hoping, praying for Monday, Wednesday, Friday
    at 8:45.
Ted Husing's all right and Bill Stern is bright
But I don't care for sports when I'm in my shorts,
I've got those H. V. Kaltenborn blues.

Whenever he's on, my cares are quickly gone
He thrills me right down to my shoes.
I'm really sincere, it's got me right here—
            (touching his heart)
I've got those H. V. Kaltenborn blues . . .
Or maybe heartburn.
Those H. V. Kaltenborn blues.

It was past 11:30. The curtain fell and Joe and Austin took
off in a waiting car for the Copacabana, followed by half
the audience, who wanted more. It was almost 4 A.M. before
he left the Copa for a snack and the morning papers.

Letty was with him in his room at the Warwick when the
verdict came in.

"Listen to this!" She shrieked, clutching the New York,
News. "Burns Mantle says quote Joe E. Lewis is a *genius* at
entertaining unquote."

"He must have been drunk," Joe responded.

She nervously opened the *Herald Tribune.* " 'Lewis, one
of the *great* men of the night clubs, sings some characteristic
songs with his customary magnificence.' Richard Watts, Jr.!"

"What did he say about the show?"

"He didn't . . ." She opened the *Times* to Brooks Atkinson's review. "Quote Mr. Lewis is the only performer who

has a chance to show what he can do. On three occasions he steps out of the plot to sing droll songs in a style that belongs in a musical show unquote."

Joe was puzzled. "Didn't anyone *mention* the show?"

Telegrams were pouring in. "What do you mean you can't get the merchandise?" Eddie Cantor wired. "You're delivering it, you damn fool."

Joe glanced at the papers. The toughest critics in New York had become a cheering section, his.

"I give the show two days," he said disconsolately.

"With such notices? You'll run two years, at least."

"Two days."

Letty was beaming at a paper. "Listen to this! 'Every now and then you can reach into the show and pull out a plum. The plum usually turns out to be Joe E. Lewis, who gets riper as he goes along.'"

"Time to go home." He gathered the papers from the bed.

"I'm staying here, Joe. I'm free now." She smiled hopefully. "Don't say no, darling, when the Lady Comes Across."

"I got a matinee tomorrow—on the stage." He led her to her suite across the corridor.

She was angry and disappointed. "You're right about one thing, darling," she said as he kissed her. "It sure *is* tough to get stuff!"

She waited for a caustic reply but there was none.

The greatest ad-libber in the world did not know how to say I love you.

The Lady Who Came Across Somewhat on Forty-fourth Street did no better than the one at the Warwick and, as Joe prophesied, barely lasted two nights.

"It wasn't a bad show," he said. "It was a bad theatre. The seats faced the stage."

Nevertheless, Lastfogel's long shot paid off. The nectarean notices by such respected drama critics as Burns Mantle, Brooks Atkinson, John Mason Brown, Richard Watts, Jr., Dick Lockridge, John Anderson, et alii, created a star. He was a star without a play or a theatre but he had an audience, and the only proscenium he would ever need: a square foot of space.

Joe's three-weeks contract at the Copacabana expired January 29th. He was held over, not for one midnight performance but three shows a night, for an unprecedented run of thirty-eight weeks until October 2nd, including five weeks at the Piping Rock Café in Saratoga Springs, operated by the same management while the Copa, lacking air conditioning, was closed.

In those nine months a legend was born and Mayor Jimmy Walker awarded him the New York *Mirror* Gold Medal for being named, out of sixty-one nominees, "the outstanding night club performer of the year." Joe was pleased but he had no illusions. Anyone could get up there. The trick was to stay.

"Lewis has no competitors," Damon Runyon wrote of his favorite comedian and gin-rummy companion.

"And if Runyon knew how to break up his kings," Joe cracked, "he wouldn't have to write for a living."

Franklin D. Roosevelt, Jr., stopped at Joe's table one night and, fascinated by Letty, showed no disposition to leave. "The least you could do, Joe," he said, "is to introduce me to the young lady."

"Letty," said Joe, "meet Mr. Liebowitz of Philadelphia. A nice lad but . . ." He tapped his temple sadly. "He thinks he's the President's son."

Letty smiled tolerantly and humored Junior as he attempted to prove he was a Hyde Park Roosevelt and not a Philadelphia Liebowitz.

The story reached the White House and, on young Franklin's first visit, his father greeted him, "Hiya, Lieb." The President personally thanked Joe and expressed the hope that he would "continue to protect Franklin, Jr., from your lady friends."

Winthrop Rockefeller dropped in one evening and Joe promised to do the town with him. Rockefeller was hesitant, he had to make an early train to Los Angeles.

"I'll cut one show," Joe told him. He started his middle show a little late and telescoped it with his last show. The crowd would not let him leave and he had to come back for repeated requests until he was on longer than if he had done two regular shows. He had performed for two hours and thirty minutes.

When he returned to his table, Rockefeller was gone. "By the time you get off the floor," he had left a note, "I'll be in California."

One night his friend, Laurette Taylor, introduced an unassuming young man who was writing a play for her. "Remember the name," she said, "Tennessee Williams."

Joe shook his hand. "I write too. My pen name is Mississippi Mud."

The horsy set was waiting for him at Saratoga. Jock Whitney gave him a gold money clip with an encased dollar bill, engraved "So You'll Never Be Broke"; Herbert Bayard Swope wired him, "I'd rather listen to you than beat the last race—well, almost," and the Vanderbilts, Woodwards, Wrights and Riddles vied for his favor.

He was in Sam Riddle's box and the veteran turfman, owner of a long line of champions, the mighty Man O'War and War Admiral among them, was admiring his latest challenger, Lord Kitchener. "He'll beat Whirlaway," Riddle prophesied.

"Maybe," Joe hedged, remembering Whirlaway's runaway of the Kentucky Derby, Preakness and Belmont Stakes the previous year.

"I spent $20,000 on Kitchener," Riddle told him. "Tell me the truth, Joe, isn't he gorgeous?"

Joe looked at the sleek thoroughbred. "Sam," he said, "if you spent twenty G's on me, I'd be gorgeous too."

A Calumet four-year-old won a handicap and Joe was chosen to crown the victor. "Say something, Joe," Warren Wright, the squire of Calumet Farm, requested.

Joe, one arm around the horse's neck, sighed, "This is the closest I've been to a winner all week."

The Copacabana wanted to extend his stay indefinitely but he was restless, he wanted to see his pals in Miami, Chicago, Hollywood and, most of all, those who had gone to war.

"I have to get overseas," he told Lastfogel.

Abe promised to do his best. Meanwhile, Joe had to fulfill a contract at the Chez Paree that had been deferred almost a year during his record run at the Copa.

The Chez had a problem. It had been raided a few days previously, during one of Mayor Ed (Boss) Kelly's periodic waves of reform, and though the owners had been assured by co-operative police officers that the ban on gambling would be lifted in a day or two, it was still in effect. Without the wheels spinning, they did not need Joe to attract players and, even more important, they could not pay his salary.

"You know Mayor Kelly," one of the owners pleaded with Joe the night before his opening. "Be a pal and go see him."

"I always drop in on Kelly to say hello."

"Tell him unless he lets us open, we can't pay the nut!"

The Mayor was delighted to see him. After a couple of laughs Kelly became solemn. "I know why you came, Joe." He lowered his voice. "And it's only because we *are* good friends that I'm doing this favor . . ."

"I didn't come for any favor, Mayor."

"You're getting it, anyway." Boss Kelly's face was hard. "I know the Chez Paree has been pulling all kinds of wires to make me open up gambling." The Mayor winked at Joe and grinned. "You got nothing to worry about."

"I told you, I didn't come for that purpose."

"It makes no difference whether you did or didn't." The Mayor extended his hand. "Here's my hand on it."

Joe reluctantly gripped Kelly's hand.

"As long as I'm Mayor of Chicago," Kelly pledged solemnly, "and as long as you play there I will *never* permit gambling at the Chez. Tell them bastards that!" Kelly was vindictive. "I saw you blow five G's there in less than an hour one night."

Joe was speechless.

"Don't thank me, Joe," said the Mayor. "What the hell are friends for?"

He was singing his ode to H. V. Kaltenborn when the head waiter slipped a note to Austin, who handed it to Joe. He glanced at the slip of paper and stopped the show.

"There is an impostor in this room wearing a Navy officer's uniform," he announced. "Lights!"

The house lights went on and the crowd, heavy with tension, craned to examine every Navy officer present.

"His name is Rosenthal," Joe continued, "and he is posing as a relative of the President."

"Get him!" Angry shouts went up, boos and catcalls echoed through the club.

"There he is!" someone screamed. There was a hubbub in the back of the room and, a moment later, a terrified young man in a Navy uniform was led through the aroused crowd.

"Stop!" Joe held up his hands. "I guess it is Franklin D. Roosevelt, Jr." He brought the President's son to the stage and, grateful that Joe had stopped the gag before he was lynched, he joined Lewis in his elegy to Poor Little Feb—

> *Poor little February, only twenty-eight days,*
> *Twenty-eight reasons just to grieve,*
> *No Xmas, no Thanksgiving, no Fourth of July,*
> *No daily double; no, not even a New Year's Eve.*
>
> *My tender heart just aches to see you pine,*
> *I guess there's just one thing left for you to do,*
> *Drop Eleanor Roosevelt a line.*
> *If March gave you a present,*
> *Would it be so absurd?*
> *Would it make any difference if the first of **March***
> *Began on March the third?*
>
> *Poor little Feb, hang your head up high,*
> *You were born 'neath an unlucky star.*
> *But one consolation you will always have,*
> *At least you're a month with an R . . .*
> *Please pass the oysters . . .*
> *Take a letter to F.D.R.*

Becoming an intimate of the famous did not change Joe's sights. His loyalty to his old cronies never lessened.

When the War Rationing Board informed Toots Shor that

he had been a mite careless, an indiscretion of a few hundred thousand points that would preclude his serving any meat for the duration, it seemed that one of New York's favorite restaurants was doomed.

Toots was ready to padlock the place when Joe appeared. "I'd rather be standing outside Toots Shor's starving," he announced, "than sitting inside the Colony belching."

The clarion had sounded. Joe E. led the faithful into the fold and continued his non-meat diet at Shor's until V-J Day. Toots' business trebled.

Every offer he could not consider because of other commitments he sought for B. S. Pully, a struggling comedian. "You won't regret it," he assured club owners. It was not out of generosity or sentiment that many hired Pully but because it was good business: Joe steered well-heeled friends to Pully's club and personally built up enough checks to underwrite his salary. That Pully, on his own, was a first-rate comedian, as he subsequently proved in *Guys and Dolls,* did not enter consideration.

Champagne had flowed all evening at the Copa and everyone at Joe's table was giddy and gay, all except Pully. A few days previously he had had a beef with a cab driver and he had been arrested for assault and battery. His case came up in the morning.

Jack Entratter, manager of the Copa, Hal Conrad, a Broadway columnist, and a couple other pals of Joe needled Pully on the probable sentence he would pull until Joe called a halt. "Leave Pully alone," he ordered, wrapping his arm around his friend, "and let's have a few laughs."

Pully gratefully thanked his St. Francis.

Joe's mischievous eyes narrowed on a solid, middle-aged citizen seated at an adjoining table, his wallet sticking invitingly out of his right rump pocket. "Lay you twenty to ten you can't lift it," he whispered to Pully.

Pully shuddered. "Isn't it enough I'm going up the river for assault and battery?"

"It's just a gag," Joe said. "I'll give it right back to him."

Pully shook his head.

"Fifty to twenty."

Pully needed the fifty but he was afraid. "What if I get caught?"

"Isn't that silly?" With them at the table was an old friend, a police captain.

Pully was still hesitant. "I haven't got the nerve, Joe . . ."

"A hundred to forty."

Pully wet his lips nervously. "Bet." He reached over and deftly plucked the wallet from the customer's hip as if he had been a pickpocket all his life. "Here." He gingerly handed the wallet to Joe. "Get it back to him." Pully tossed down a drink and wiped his perspiring brow.

"Let's cut it up," Conrad suggested.

Joe looked sternly at the newspaperman. "Lad, you're a cheater."

Pully had regained his composure. "Maybe Hal's right. How much is in it?"

Joe opened the wallet and inspected its contents. "By the way, Pully," he said, "whose court you coming up in?"

"Judge McConrey in Brooklyn—and he can't be fixed. I tried."

"Better get it back," Joe said, handing the wallet to Pully. "How?"

"The way you got it." Joe stood up. "I don't know about you guys," he said sotto voce, "but I'm getting out of here."

"Wait for me!" Pully pleaded.

"You got work to do." Joe led the exodus from the table. Entratter sidled up. "What's the gag?"

"It's no gag," said Joe. "Y'know whose pocket Pully picked? Judge McConrey's of Brooklyn!"

Joe's gags, sallies and parodies echoed throughout the town, quoted by columnists and unquoted by plagiarists.

One night in Lindy's, Joe openly charged a celebrated comedian with lifting his material. "It isn't true, Joe," the hijacker swore. "I take an oath on my brother's wife."

"Your brother is in California," Joe snapped. "Your mother is right here in New York. Why stretch it?"

Joe walked into a Greenwich Village club one night and the crowd roared, "The Groom! The Groom!" He was flattered upon being recognized instantly until he became aware that no one was looking at him.

"Give us the Groom!" the crowd was demanding of a comedian on the stage, who was doing one of Joe's routines.

The counterfeit spotted Joe, blanched and tried to make an exit.

"We want the Groom!" The crowd was stamping and shouting and the loudest voice was Joe E.'s. At his side was an old friend, the owner of the club.

"The Groom!" the owner bellowed to his larcenous comic, who had no alternative but to sing "No Room for the Groom."

On an early morning a few weeks later, Joe was with a luscious new doll when, after one champagne too many, she confessed that she was related to the comedian who had stolen his best song.

"The Groom?" Joe asked.

She nodded. "My husband."

The imitator continued to duck Joe until he cornered him one night at the Stork Club.

"Forgive me, Joe," he begged, offering his hand.

"For what?" Joe took his hand. "We're even."

He did a skit with Parkyakarkus, a comedian, for a benefit and subsequently Parkyakarkus made a short for Columbia

Pictures with Don Wilson, the radio announcer, in which he sang "I Love a Commercial," a number owned and copyrighted by Lewis.

"Sue Columbia," Joe instructed Marovitz. "That's my material."

A Columbia executive, Jack Cohn, brother of Harry, the president, wired: "DEAR PAL JOE: WE'VE BEEN FRIENDS SO MANY YEARS. YOUR FRIEND JACK."

Joe replied: "DEAR JACK: YOU HAVE A FINE SATIRE ON FRIENDSHIP."

Orson Welles, feeling his ego a trifle more than usual, came in one night and kept gabbling during the show.

Joe stopped in the middle of a song. "I could louse you up very good too, Orson," he stilettoed, "but I'm too late."

No one could hit against him. He had the greatest change of pace in the business. That was the trick, he had learned. Keep ahead of 'em. When they expect the hard, fast one, throw 'em a curve. Don't watch your money, watch your material. Keep it fresh. Keep switching. Keep 'em off balance. Feint and spar like a boxer. This is a battle. Outfox 'em or you lose 'em. Know what you are going to do but don't have a definite pattern. There must always be an element of surprise. And be yourself. The minute you're not yourself you're in trouble.

Ashton Stevens, the dean of Chicago drama critics, analyzed him best. "Lewis unfailingly expresses nobody but himself," he wrote. "His restricted hymns are calculated to color the cheeks of a Marine but he is a clean guy whose heart is pure even when his lyrics aren't. His genius permits him to get away with mass murder."

There were no dissenters. Long queues lined up every night wherever he played. It took a top rating by Dun and Bradstreet and a yearly retainer to the head waiter to get your name on the waiting list.

The Copa, the Colonial Inn in Miami Beach, the Beverly
Club in New Orleans, the Mounds in Cleveland, the Chez
Paree in Chicago, Ciro's in Hollywood . . . To him they
were not night clubs, they were his homes. The only kind of
a home he had known or wanted since he was sixteen years
old. Lavishly furnished rooms where he could sit around
with his friends, gossip, drink with them, tell them a few
jokes, sing a few songs and gamble with them if there was a
room in the back or upstairs. It wasn't an act, it was a
private party. He could not invite his friends to his hotel
room, not as many friends as he had. Fortunately, he had
made the acquaintance of benign bonifaces from Broadway
to Sunset Boulevard who charged him no rental for their
rooms. They were so thankful for what meager cover charges,
minimums, maximums and gratuities Joe's friends cared to
contribute, without the necessity of anesthesia or prosecution, that they insisted on giving him a few thousand dollars
a week to tide him against perfidious roulette wheels, re-
calcitrant dice, neurotic thoroughbreds and old age, if any.

The middle-aged Puck was the hottest comedian in the
country, and the unhappiest. He was still the wrong Joe
Lewis. The heavyweight champion was doing his fighting in
the U. S. Army.

"You got to get me overseas, Abe," he told his agent,
"or . . ."

"Or you'll get someone who will?" Lastfogel smiled. "That
will take a little doing, Joe. I've just been named head of the
U.S.O."

"Then you can do it!"

"I think I can get you to the Caribbean in two or three
months."

"No ferry-boat rides."

"All right, I'll arrange a trip to England."

Joe shook his head. "I want to entertain the kids who
aren't getting shows."

"They're all getting some shows."

"In the South Pacific?"

"Of course."

"Prisoners of war?"

Lastfogel stared at him. "Prisoners of war? Wake up! They're buried in Jap prisons, behind Jap guns, Jap mines, Jap barbed wire. *Nobody* can get to 'em!"

"The Red Cross could make the contact. I'll pick up a consumptive pianist I know up in Saranac. They can drop us by parachutes over Tokyo." Joe was serious.

"Don't you understand? They're *prisoners!* Haven't you heard about Jap atrocities?"

"The Japs wouldn't hurt me." Joe smiled gently. "I was always nice to opening acts."

20   *Late Show*

Saturday night, March 18, 1943.

The room was darkened save for a single beam, the band broke into a clamorous chorus of "Chicago" and Joe trotted into the disk of light. "Good evening, ladies and gentlemen," he greeted the audience after the applause subsided, "and welcome to Chez Paree." The crowd awaited expectantly, it did not want to miss his first gag.

"You might as well face it," he ended the silence, "*that* was my opening line."

"For my first number . . . Oh yes, I want you to meet . . ." He turned to Austin at the piano. "My pianist: The Late George Apley." Austin rose solemnly and bowed. "Mr.

Austin Mack," Joe announced seriously. Austin stood up again and took another bow. "Austin plays a pretty good piano. I think it's a Steinway." He sidled over to the piano, picked up a Scotch highball awaiting him on the folded top and held it aloft. "Post time!" he called out and took a long swallow.

The show was off and running.

"Some people say I drink too much. And I resent it." A note of irritation entered his voice. "I don't deny it. I just resent it." He took another gulp, put down the glass and returned to the microphone. "My doctor says not to drink, it cuts down your years. Maybe . . . but looking around, I see more old drunks than old doctors."

That loosened the customers. Austin was unobtrusively trying to cue him into a song. "Voom! Voom!" Joe's voice rang out raucously as he cleared his throat and seemed to search for the key if not the melody. "Voom! Voom!" he croaked. "Arrangements. Everything's arrangements." Austin continued his medley. "The title of my first song: 'Since I Lost My Glasses, I Wonder Who's Kissing Me Now?' It's one of those songs if you want to go to the john and miss it, you won't have to shoot yourself."

He paused and listened as Austin kept leading him. "Austin is really indispensable," he said. "When I get out here with a little load, and I'm searching for a number to sing, he just gives me one cue and I'm completely lost."

He ultimately went into a song, a parody on George Gershwin's "It Ain't Necessarily So," in which he plaintively described his plight on being confronted by a strange young lad who paraphrased Porgy's vow to Bess and informed him, "Joe, You is My Pappy Now."

"It ain't necessarily Joe," he protested with an unfeigned charm that never failed to transform a risqué phrase into a droll, inoffensive line.

My doctor says he ought to know, he told me I'm no
  Romeo.
He lifted my tunic and said, "Look, a eunuch,"
But it ain't necessarily so.
I'm too antiseptic, that's why I'm a skeptic.
If that kid's my moxie I got him by proxie,
It ain't necessarily Joe.

Austin went into the next number. Joe hummed a few
bars of "Tea for Two." "My next song hasn't any humorous
words but the music is very funny. Jeanette MacDonald falls
in love with a Southeast Mounted. It's usually a Northwest
Mounted but Nelson Eddy got on the horse backwards." He
hummed four more bars. "You people will have to take my
songs with a grain of Nembutal."

It didn't get the laugh he anticipated. "One more joke
like that can lift me right out of the big money," he commented. "Not that you have to laugh. My gags are insured
by Lloyd's of London—and after tonight Lloyd's will have to
leave London." He was ahead of them, whether they
laughed or not, and they loved it.

"Everybody's breeding things. I crossed a rooster with a
rooster—and got a very cross rooster." Now he was a Mad
Hatter out of another Lewis, Lewis Carroll. "A friend of
mine crossed a chicken with a racing form—and got a hen
that lays odds." He reached into his pocket and pulled out a
fistful of pari-mutuel tickets. "I'm a great horse-follower—
and the horses I follow follow horses." He tossed the worth-
less pasteboards into the air and watched them flutter to
the floor. "A thousand bucks a day for props," he sighed.

He needed a drink now. Leaving the microphone, he
selected a ringside table at random and picked up a highball
in front of a customer. "I drink to be sociable," he remarked, "and I'm the biggest Socialist in town." He saluted

his host with the glass. "There is an old Norwegian saying, *'Svensky in Potorsky Grebin Novoja.'* " He paused and the sucker leaped to the bait, asking what it meant. "How the hell should I know?" Joe retorted. "I read it on a can of sardines. It must mean something." He pulled up a chair. "Mind if I do this sitting down? I hate to stand up while the room is in motion."

Joe settled back, drained the glass and, looking around, noticed a customer at the next table dozing. He reached over and tapped him on the shoulder. "I don't mind when you fall asleep," he told the startled party when he awakened, "but it hurts me when you don't say good night."

A moment later he was back at the mike. "My next number is Seagram's Movement from Beethoven's Unfinished Fifth." He hummed a few bars from "Chattanooga Choo-Choo" and jigged friskily about the microphone, almost tripping on the extension cord. "I want to have fun now, not when I'm old and wrinkled," he chortled, "but now, when I'm young and wrinkled." He flexed his biceps. "I'm in great shape. Every artery is hard as a rock."

The crowd was in continuous laughter now. "Please, not so loud," he held up his hands, "it upsets the pizza which are cooking in an Italian restaurant upstairs."

Austin was valiantly trying to cue him into a song but Joe's sensitive ear caught sweeter music, the dissonant challenge of a drunken heckler. He glared in the direction of his detractor and turned to the crowd. "What can I do?" he asked helplessly. "I can't insult him until he pays his bill." He thrust out his jaw defiantly and recited:

> *It's easy to grin when your ship comes in*
> *And you've got the stock market beat.*
> *But the lad worthwhile is the man who can smile*
> *When his shorts are too tight in the seat.*

Disciples of zany humor let out a roar of approval. "Any-one who takes me for a damn fool," he said, "makes no mistake."

"You can say that again!" bellowed the heckler.

"One more interruption," Joe threatened, "and I'll be forced to continue."

"Me too," retorted the heckler, encouraged by the atten-tion he was attracting.

"You are not obliged to entertain me," Joe gave him the stinger, "and I may say neither are you equipped."

The pest retreated for more ammunition and Joe waved to several friends in the crowd. "Hiya, Abe!" He spotted Marovitz with a party. "My old pal, Judge Abe Marovitz." Abe took a self-conscious bow. "The most valuable thing in the world is friendship," Joe said nostalgically, "and the richest man in the world is the one with the most money." Abe's laugh led the others. "Show me a man who has very little money," Joe added, "and I'll show you a bum."

Austin was making music again. "The title of my next song is, 'It's Better to Have Eaten Oysters Than Never to Have Loved at All.' It was written by one of my oldest friends, Harry Harris, a Chicago boy. Harry isn't here to-night, he's recovering from a terrifying nightmare. Last night he dreamed that Tschaikowsky was alive and had a good lawyer."

The applause didn't reach his standard and he frowned. "These jokes may not sound like much to you but your laughs don't sound like much to me either, so we're even. And may I quote the great French philosopher, La Roche-foucauld. Or was it Leo Durocher? Some shortstop, anyway. He said, '*Cherchez la femme.*' That means, share the broad." The audience was howling again. "At my age all women look alike: Good." Austin's persistent cuing failed to interrupt the cataract of free association. "Isn't it amazing?

Every corner where they drill for a service station they find gas. And while I'm on the subject, I don't deny Paul Revere gave his horse a good ride but he did take her wide at Lexington."

This was the Joe E. they loved: Rabelaisian, ludicrous, capricious. "I want to introduce my banker, Mr. Morgan." Everyone turned. The night before he had given them a Roosevelt and the night before that a Rockefeller.

Joe directed the spotlight to an elderly, distinguished-looking gentleman at ringside, his goateed chin resting on a gold-headed cane. "Take a bow, Swifty."

The old grifter bowed with dignity.

"Mr. Morgan is my banker. A banker is a man who will loan you money if you can prove that you don't need it."

Joe grinned. He had fooled them again. A line like that was expected from a cracker-barrel philosopher, not a saloon folk-singer. There was a nodding of heads and respectful applause. Now he was a Socrates in cap and bells, a drunken Aesop revealing the wisdom of the ages in logical lunacy. What was wisdom and what was nonsense? Solomon, who was accounted the wisest man of his time, had inscribed inside his ring, "All is nonsense."

Austin was playing "I Love Louisa." Joe took another pull from the glass on the piano. "And now, a song about a fellow and a girl." He paused, an artless look on his face. "Which is as it should be, because if it was about a fellow and a fellow I couldn't sing it. She was the kind of a girl you wouldn't take home to Mother unless Mother weren't home. In college she was the girl voted most likely to. A wonderful girl. Never drinks, smokes or takes a bath. Well, this fellow is supposed to put up a ladder against her window on the second floor but the ladder was too long, so he eloped with the girl on the third floor." Again, with the deft inflections and indefinable magic that ever condoned the ribald, he sang "The Drama Critic's Honeymoon."

The setting was ideal,
There was nothing that it lacked.
The hero had appeal, the heroine was stacked.
A perfect situation but in the final act
The bride gave a very poor performance.
To her "l'amour toujours" was just a saying.
In the second act she tried,
But the critic had implied,
She didn't even know the egg she was laying.

He stopped suddenly. Austin had hit a clinker. "Both hands tonight, Austin. No knuckles, please." Austin continued the melody contritely and Joe's face softened. "I may kid Austin about his artistry but seriously, when Vladimir Horowitz came here last week and heard him play, he stood up and shouted—'Waiter, my check!'"

At last he returned to his love song—

The hero played his part
But his bow, it was too late.
It was all a floperoo,
Thanks to her he didn't rate.
And he couldn't understand it,
At rehearsals she was great.
Once again the critic fell asleep on opening night
Because the bride gave a very poor performance.

He finished the number and fixed a prankish eye on a party of three, a beautiful young woman and two men, seated in the shadows halfway back.

"He spotted you, Jack," one of the men chuckled.

"He spotted me *before* the number," Jack Malloy, Executive Editor of the Chicago *Herald-American*, replied. His companions—Bill Curley, publisher of the New York *Jour-*

nal-American, and his wife Mary—looked at him questioningly. "Don't you remember, Bill?" Malloy asked sheepishly. "I used to be a drama critic."

Curley nodded. "Boston—that's right." He paused. "Was that before or after Joe E. got it?"

"After . . ." There was a faraway expression in Malloy's face as he watched the little man with the laughing eyes continue his act. "I've seen them all," he said. "He's the funniest man in the world."

"I agree with you," said Curley, "but we're prejudiced."

"Everyone's prejudiced who knows him."

After another half hour of impish parodies and maxims on the only arts he considers lively—wenching, wagering and wassailing—Joe introduced the leader of the chorus line, "This kid kicks the back of her head forty times. That's what's the matter with her."

The chorus came on and Joe trotted off to a chorus of "Chicago." The applause was deafening and he came back for a bow. "The management just gave me some good news," he announced. "I'm being held over until tomorrow night!"

He threaded through the affectionate crowd until he reached Malloy's table. He embraced his old friend and greeted the Curleys.

"Great show!" Curley enthused, his wife and Malloy echoing.

"And you publish a first-class tip sheet," Joe responded and promised to rejoin them for a few drinks as soon as he changed his shirt.

"Another night, Joe," Malloy begged off, "we have a busy day tomorrow."

Joe looked at Malloy as if he had kicked him in the groin. Jack knew better. Even the uninitiated did not leave before the last show. As for a crony like Malloy, it was treason.

"All right." Malloy realized his mistake without Joe saying a word. "On one condition. You have to do your take-off on that movie—you know, the one with Ingrid Bergman and Humphrey Bogart."

Mrs. Curley beamed. *"Casablanca?"*

"That's the one." Malloy's eyes begged Joe for forgiveness.

Joe nodded and left for his dressing room, still perplexed. Jack Malloy even thinking of going before the last show? What was happening to the world?

An hour later he trotted back into the spotlight.

"It's my financial pleasure to be here tonight," he began, "through the courtesy of the Arlington Park race track." He swayed a little and accidentally caught his foot in the microphone cord. "I'm not used to working under these conditions. I'm usually drunk."

The customers, uncertain whether he was serious, were diffident about applauding.

"That's what I like about my act," he said. "No hemming and hawing. No excuses. I just come right out and lay an egg . . . But I'm warning you, you'll have to laugh soon. I may not be with you long. They're drafting everybody."

There was a ripple of applause. "No matter what they said about my first show," he said defiantly, "they couldn't say I was funny." He crossed over to the piano and picked up a fresh drink. "I woke up at the crack of ice and I've been cold drunk all day." He took a long swallow. "Even so, I've cut my drinking in half. I don't take chasers any more."

Austin was playing a Stephen Foster medley. "And now a song about a Southern girl. You know the difference between a Northern girl and a Southern girl. In the North a girl says, 'You may' and in the South she says, 'You-all may.'" Joe turned to Austin. "Austin Mack, the Elmo Lincoln of the Keyboard. What a piano player! It isn't what he forgot about piano playing—it's what he remembers that's so lousy."

The laugh was not as spontaneous as he anticipated. "Will

one of the waiters kill himself?" he called out. "I don't want
to die alone." The crowd, dulled by drink, was slow in
warming up. "That's why I like to tell jokes," he remarked.
"I seem to have a knack of taking a joke that can't possibly
get a laugh—and proving it." This aroused a few titters.
"You'll notice I'm doing a very fast show. I'm cutting out all
the laughs."

Self-disparagement invariably broke them up. The applause was loud and sustaining but Joe had not forgiven
them. "I'm not going to get a hernia with this audience." The
customers roared and continued clapping, begging for a re-
prieve. "I'm sorry that happened," he said. "I got a laugh
and spoiled everything. Just when you were beginning to
hate me." He took another drink. "And now a song about
the Big Lie, 'Oh, How I Danced on the Night We Were
Wed.'" This reminded him of a quatrain:

> *The biggest thrill of a honeymoon,*
> *And I say this without invective,*
> *Is the thrill of thumbing your nose*
> *At the house detective.*

The audience took it in stride. "You probably won't like
my music," he said, "but the lyrics are terrible."

"You can say that again!" The heckler had awakened.

"With all the empty manholes in town, why did I have to
be so fortunate as to have you fall in here?"

"Ha, ha, big joke!"

Joe searched the crowd and found his man. "The last time
I saw a mouth like that," he said, "it had a hook in it."

The show continued. "My next song is about a 95-year-old
man, stone deaf, who goes to a concert with a hearing ear
dog . . ."

In his delivery there was always a suggestion of confusion,
as if he was uncertain how a sentence would end. Unhinged

reasoning, idiotic jingles and incongruous aphorisms tum-
bled down a stream of zany association.

"Tonight I'm living dangerously. I'm using my own material . . . I'm different from most people in show business.
I wasn't born in a trunk. I was born in a hospital. It wasn't
until after my father saw me that he put me in a trunk."

Suddenly he spotted Sanchez, who had come in late.
"Hello, Jorge! That's my friend Sanchez. He's a financial
genius. A financial genius is a man who can make money
faster than his friends can borrow it. He's set to make another fortune on a new type of dandruff. It absolutely pre-
vents falling Vaseline . . . Money talks, all right. Mine says
good-bye."

The crowd applauded. "There's one thing about me you
must admit," he said. "I may not say much, but when I do it
means nothing. It improves as it goes along, though. It goes
from worse to bad.

"And now, a song dedicated to Victor Hugo, who wrote
Les Miserables. Which means the wrong broad, I think."
Austin, playing "Tea for Two" in the background, hit a
flat note that did not pass unnoticed. "Tea for two, Austin,"
Joe remonstrated. "No lemon, please."

Joe looked around the room. "Chicago . . ." he said feel-
ingly. "I started out in this town when gangsters came in and
took a shot at you. That's playing 'Stop the Music' the hard
'way . . . And then there were the wonderful shows I
worked with Sophie Tucker. We did an adagio during the
World's Fair. One night I threw her up in the air and
missed. Luckily, the floor broke her fall."

"Ain't funny, McGee!" The heckler had come up for air.

Joe drew a bead on his critic and turned to the crowd.
"His body looks as if it had been under water for six days.
Seriously, he's not well. He has a game head." He turned
back to the heckler. "If I said anything to offend you, sir,
please believe me."

He resumed the show without interruption. "I just read that a man age seventy-six became a father. Goes to show you what some guys will do to beat the draft." He tested his voice with a "Voom! Voom!" "I can sing as well as Tallulah," he said. "And no matter what anyone says, Tallulah's voice is all it's cracked up to be. Speaking of voices, you ought to hear Austin's wife. Cassie has a cold and is so hoarse she can hardly drive above a whisper. I have no problems with cars. Mine doesn't run well but boy, does it park." He coughed. "Seems everyone has a cold. It wasn't like that in Miami. The weather down there is great. No rain, no cold, no snow—just hurricanes."

Austin, making excellent progress through Cole Porter's album, struck a false note. Joe glared at him. "Austin, pull yourself together." Austin nodded and continued playing. "On second thought," Joe added, "you look better pulled out."

Forty-five minutes later he was still rocking the room and Austin was trying to cue him into the hit love song from *Casablanca,* "As Time Goes By."

Joe caught it on the fourth chorus. "I am doing my next song," he announced seriously, "by special request—from my old pal, Jack Malloy. 'As Time Goes By' . . . It's from a picture called *For Whom the Bell Tolls,* with Gary Cooper and Ingrid Bergman. Gary Cooper was so confused. He had a sleeping bag in one hand and a hunk of dynamite in the other. He didn't know what to do—blow up the bridge or get the broad in the sack . . ."

He stopped. "I beg your pardon, it was another picture— *Casablanca,* I think, with Alan Mowbray and Bessie Love. The theme song was written by a fellow named Herman Hupfield when he was broke. Not that he wasn't a good writer, he was very Jamaica-minded. Herman was a horse player and owed money to his bookmaker—or shall we call him a commission man for the nonce?—and the bookmaker told him to write a song to pay his bill. So Herman locked himself up in a hotel room and, after five days, he came up with his first line, 'As Time Goes By' . . . I will now analyze the song—

> *You must remember this, a kiss is just a kiss,*
> *A sigh is just a sigh . . ."*

Joe stopped. "The man's a genius. He calls a spade a spade.

> *The fundamental things apply . . .*

"Now there's a word you don't hear Frank Sinatra use when he sings. 'Come to Me, My Fundamental Baby.'

> *Moonlight and love songs, never out of date . . .*

"How does he know what's going on? He's been locked in his hotel room for eight weeks. They've stopped the room service on him and the waiters are afraid to come up to his room. Herman has been alone too long."

Joe's keen ears picked up an alien sound, like the falling of a chair, a table or a drunk. He was tempted to make a flippant remark but was fearful of losing the continuity.

> *Hearts full of passion . . .*

"This is getting serious." He was referring to the lyrics but many thought it was a protest against the continuing noise. He peered through the smoky haze, trying to locate the disturbance, but it was too far back. It was not uncommon for squabbles to erupt at this hour over the computation of checks, the allotment of girls or the solution to the White Sox. Joe, convinced that the customers were eager to fold or carry on to more intimate entertainment, hurried to the finish.

"And that ends our little nonsense," he signed off. "I don't want applause, just a ten-yard start. Seriously, ladies and gentlemen, I want to thank you for coming. God bless you and when you drive home, be sure you have a car."

He struggled against the departing crowd to explain to Malloy why he had galloped through his request.

Jack was on the floor, and waiters were trying to revive him. That was the thud, and the distracting noise, Joe had heard in the middle of the song. Malloy had dropped dead of a heart attack.

The comedian went to his dressing room, locked the door and opened a bottle of Scotch. For the next two hours, alone in the dismal cubicle, he drank himself sober.

The chairs were stacked on the tables. A large blinding globe was the only illumination. A porter was cleaning up.

"You're late tonight, Mr. Lewis."

"Saturday night, Charley."

"Big night, hey?"

"Big night."

He walked through the deserted cabaret and there was not a sound except the echo of his own footsteps and the rhythmic movement of the porter's mop. The Chez Paree, full of lust and laughter a little while ago, now lay like a naked, exhausted whore reeking of stale beer and love-sweat.

It was only a short walk from the club to where he wanted to go. A few minutes later, he was in front of a darkened building on East Erie Street.

"CARROLL HOME FOR FUNERALS," the sign read. He rang the bell. There was no response. He knocked. Unable to rouse anyone, he went to the rear entrance and pounded on the door.

A few minutes later, a sleepy-eyed night watchman appeared. "Sorry, sir," he said, "we're not open."

"I have to see a friend of mine."

The watchman shook his head. "No visitors are allowed until 9 A.M."

"I have to see him now." Joe pulled out a roll of bills, peeled off a twenty and slipped it into the watchman's hand. "Jack Malloy."

"He's over there," the watchman pointed and softly closed the door.

The odd-looking man in a dinner jacket, a wilted red carnation in his lapel, walked to the lonely slab in a corner of the room.

"You asked me to sing 'As Time Goes By' and you left before I finished it." The comedian's face darkened and a reproachful note entered his voice. "It wasn't polite, Jack," he reprimanded the dead man. "You never did it to me before. Not even in the tough days when I could hardly croak a note . . ." He unconsciously fingered his scar.

"Remember the first notice you ever gave me? It must have been 1931." He prodded his memory. "No, 1930. We were in Boston breaking in *The Second Little Show*. Remember? What a turkey! Every newspaper murdered us—except the *Advertiser*. You said I was the only good act in the show . . . Thanks, Jack. I needed that notice. It was the first good one—after I got cut." He faltered a moment. "And thanks for the fourteen years since then, every one . . ."

Joe paused. "I had just finished the line, 'Hearts full of passion,' when you left." He repeated the chorus from that line and finishing with—

> *It's still the same old story,*
> *A fight for love and glory,*
> *A case of do or die . . .*

He stopped. "Who ever heard of a case of **Do** or **Die**? I haven't—and I drink everything.

> *The world will always welcome lovers . . .*

"I leave it to you," he interpolated. "If the world always welcomes lovers, why in hell do they have house detectives?"

Joe had sung in many places for almost thirty years but he never punched a number with more fervor than he now did in Carroll's Funeral Parlor as he stood alone, without an accompaniment, singing for the last time to an old friend.

As time goes by . . .

He ended the song and the small room was still again. "This reminds me of lots of joints I've played," he said. He grasped Malloy's right hand and held it for a moment.

"I'll be seeing you, Jack."

The clock in the Tribune Tower was tolling six when Joe came out. It was time to go to war. He was heading for Washington, to find out how much weight he carried with the Roosevelts.

21   *Owney*

He was in Hot Springs, Arkansas, sweating out booze.

"Where did you say you're goin'?" asked the scrawny little man steaming in the next tub.

"New Guinea," Joe replied.

"Where's that?"

"That way." Joe pointed in the general direction of Texas.

"Where's it near?"

"Y'know Australia, where Phar Lap came from?"

"Phar Lap. Yeh."

"It's near there."

"Pulled the short straw, huh?"

"I asked for it."

"And they didn't throw you in the loony bin?"

"They said, 'Go with our blessings. We can't get anybody to go out there. Between the Japs and the mosquitoes . . .'"

The little man looked at him with new respect. "I'm proud of you, Joe."

Joe did not hear him. "I want to see that Owen Stanley . . ." His eyes glistened.

"Who's he?"

"Don't you read the papers? Owen Stanley is a mountain in New Guinea, the one the Japs can't get over."

"You're kiddin'."

"How can you kid a mountain?"

"Owen Stanley . . ." He repeated the name. "Joe . . ."

"What?"

"I'd like to go along."

"You serious?"

"'Course I'm serious!"

"Maybe I can swing it."

"*Maybe?* Your man runs the show, doesn't he?"

"We'll see." He called Lastfogel in New York and asked him if there would be room for one more. "What can he do?" Lastfogel inquired.

Joe looked at his friend, now putting on his clothes. "Can you sing or dance?"

"Me *sing?*" The little man was horrified. "You know better than that!"

Joe sighed. "I might as well level with you, Abe. It's Owney Madden."

There was a silence.

"Abe, I said Owney Madden wants to go along."

Lastfogel responded at last. "*The* Owney Madden?"

"The only Owney Madden I know in Hot Springs. Maybe he could do an imitation of Annie Oakley."

Madden crowded the phone. "Tell him I'll be your body-guard out there."

Lastfogel heard him. "Tell Madden we have baby-faced Marines out there who are ten times tougher than he ever thought he was."

Madden angrily grabbed for the phone but Joe pulled it out of his reach. The old hoodlum sank in a chair, his eyes glassy as if staring inside his skull . . .

He *was* tough. Ask anyone—who is still alive. He had been ambushed on the balcony of the Arbor Dance Hall on Fifty-eighth Street in New York and had been left for dead with five bullets in his guts. He had been arrested fifty-seven times before he was twenty years old. He had gone to Sing Sing for killing a cop. He had run New York, and had cleared twenty thousand bucks a *week* on beer, not counting night clubs, taxis, coal, the cleaning and laundry rackets, boxing. He had had eight world champs. He had made 'em and he had un-made 'em. Max Schmeling, Jack Sharkey, Primo Carnera, Jim Braddock, Jack Delaney, Bob Olin, Phil Rosenberg and Sixto Escobar. His front-men had taken the bows, he had pulled the strings.

He wasn't tough, huh? He patted his abdomen, encircled with a wide leather belt, and he felt the seven bumps on his insides. Seven bullets. Not the ones he had stopped at the Arbor Dance Hall when he was twenty years old. These had been fired by professionals. They had pumped more than a hundred slugs at him, but a hundred had not been enough. They had gotten Legs Diamond, Vincent Coll, Dutch Schultz, Abe Reles, and all the others, but they could not kill him. He was Owney the Killer. He would show them how tough he was.

No, he wouldn't. He had not been tough enough to go to war in his middle twenties, for his native England or for his adopted country, and he was not tough enough now. He was

Arthur Flegenheimer (above left), alias Dutch Schultz. "I'm Christ!" he told Joe, offered him $12,500 for the Chateau Madrid so he could murder a rival hoodlum in peace. *Free Lance Photographers Guild.*

Owney (The Killer) Madden (above right), ex-mobster, wasn't afraid of bullets. He stopped fourteen, begged to go to New Guinea as Joe's bodyguard—but Abe Lastfogel said no, he wasn't tough enough. *International News Photo.*

(above) Joe arrives at Port Moresby, New Guinea, June, 1943, to entertain armed forces.

(right) Joe rolls his own—cigarettes, dice, all the same.

not Owney the Killer any more. He was Owney the Fifty-Year-Old. Madden was a war too late.

"I didn't like your friend's crack," he said.

"Don't mess around Abe Lastfogel," Joe said. "He's the toughest five-foot agent in show business."

The train was pulling out, two hours later.

"Good luck, Joe." Madden held on to his hand as long as he could. "And take a good look at that Owney Stanley for me . . ."

Joe had heard many stories about Owney Madden. He did not know if any of them were true or if all of them were true, and it did not matter. He had not changed from his Chicago days, he took a man as he found him, and he had found Madden to be a kind, gentle, and pleasant man who had lived quietly and respectably for many years in Hot Springs with his wife, the daughter of the postmaster, and a wonderful woman.

There was a story that Owney could not leave Hot Springs as long as he lived and, when he died, that he had to be buried within the city limits. That was the deal that had been made after he had survived the last attempted assassination, so the story went. He had agreed to stay "dead" and be buried in some small town, under a penalty of actual death if he ever left it. He had chosen Hot Springs for his exile.

Exile. Owney had been a kind of Napoleon. Now he was just a lonely little gee running out his string in Arkansas. They said he went to the railroad station every day to meet the train from New York. To get his New York paper, and to see if anyone had come in that he knew. It was a nice walk from his home to the station. And . . . he liked to meet the train. The train had been in New York the night before, or that morning. His New York. The New York he would never see again, so they said.

Why couldn't Owney go back? There were many answers,

and Vincent Coll was a part of most of them. They had called Coll the "Mad Dog." He was a hophead and a maniac. He had kidnapped Owney's closest friend, Frenchy LeMange, and had made Madden pay fifty thousand dollars for his return, when Madden was Number One and owned the City Hall. Owney had forgiven him, or had said that he did, the kid was a hophead. One day Coll shot at a man he did not like. The bullet missed its target, hit a baby carriage, and the infant inside died. That was serious. A man who could not shoot straight had no business on the streets of New York City. A couple of days later, Coll received a telephone call. It was a very important call, a reply to his frantic SOS, otherwise he would not have come out of his hole and gone to the booth at the corner drug store. As he picked up the receiver and said hello, a man walked in and stitched a perfect square on the glass panel of the booth, head high to knee low, with a Thompson submachine gun. He did not nick the wood once. The voice on the other end of the phone call, according to some people in the know, belonged to Madden. If it was true, many believed Owney should have been given a medal. Not long after he received a twenty-one-gun salute, in the belly.

Joe looked out of the window and waved.

Owney returned the wave, dejectedly. The forlorn little man who had once had everything except peace now had nothing but peace. He remained in the shadows and leaned against the ancient depot, out of habit; no one would ever get behind him again if he could help it. But it was only an illusion of his pride. No one wanted to get behind him. Owney the Killer was dead. The only thing he could kill was time.

Joe's trip was postponed three times by previous bookings, not his but the Japs. They occupied all of New Guinea except the southern tip and threatened to overrun that as well as Australia and any other land between it and California.

He was playing at Ciro's when the orders came through to report to the Army Presidio in San Francisco where transportation would be provided to "an advanced base of the Fifth Air Force, somewhere in New Guinea." Bases were subject to change without notice, depending on how the war went that morning.

Joe and Austin proceeded north—Austin by train—and the next morning they were given inoculations, uniforms and instructions.

"Can't believe it," Joe said to Austin in the Army Dispensary. "In a day or two we'll be on our way to New Guinea."

"That's what you think!" interrupted Lew Parker, an entertainer on another U.S.O. tour. "I've been waiting almost a month for a ride to Honolulu. Book yourself in the Bal Tabarin, Joe. You're here for the summer and maybe the winter."

"We'll be out of here in forty-eight hours."

Parker laughed and pointed to his latest inoculation. "I've been here so long I'm getting booster shots."

Joe picked up the phone and called General Harold George, head of the Allied Transportation Command, in Washington.

"Almost everything we have is out there fighting," the General explained, "but I'll see what I can do."

Within an hour Joe received a call from an A.T.C. captain in San Francisco. "Report to Hamilton Field with all your gear at fourteen hundred. Two o'clock this afternoon. You'll have to hurry, Mr. Lewis."

"Oh, *no*, Captain!" Joe became pale. "I told General George I wanted to get out fast—but not *that* fast. I have a . . . an important . . ."

"Is she more important than the war?"

"Look, Cap . . ."

"I was only kidding, Mr. Lewis." The Captain laughed. "You're to report tomorrow at fourteen hundred. General George said you would have a dame coming out."

Letty came in a few hours later.

They had cocktails at the St. Francis, dinner at the Fairmont and wound up at the Bal Tabarin. All military traffic to the Pacific was funneled through San Francisco and the town seemed to be filled with Joe's friends, coming or going. They were lined up at Joe's table to say hellos and good-byes, to have a few drinks and a few laughs. The owner of the Bal, his old friend Tom Gerun, hovered over him protectively.

"Let's dance, Joe," Letty pleaded and pulled him toward the crowded dance floor. "That's the only place we can be alone."

The band was playing a nostalgic love song.

"Will I, Joe?"

"Will you what?"

She held on to him tightly, her face against his. "The song, darling . . ."

"The song?"

"Listen . . ."

A pretty girl was on the stage singing.

I'll be seeing you . . .

Joe looked at the vocalist and Letty caught the faraway expression in his eyes.

"Remind you of someone?" she asked.

"Yes . . ."

"What happened?"

Joe smiled sadly. "I hardly knew her. She worked in a show I played. *Right This Way*. Kid named Tamara . . ."

"The girl who was killed a few months ago?"

"She introduced that song—and it died. Now she's dead and the song is number one on the Hit Parade."

She clutched him desperately. Tamara had been on a U.S.O. tour enroute to the armed forces overseas when her plane crashed. Tomorrow Joe would be crossing the Pacific on his U.S.O. tour, and they were saying good-bye to Tamara's song. Was it a coincidence? A premonition?

No, she reasoned, this was baseless imagined fear, the desperate groping of her own insecurity. How can you lose what you never had? This *might* be their last night. Any night can be the last one. Or the first one. The wheel stops when it wills and no one can rig it. Like the night she met Joe. She hadn't wanted to go to Ben Marden's Riviera. It was too big and brassy. Her husband had insisted. They met old friends there and someone brought Joe to their table. She had thought she was married for life. She had not been aware that she was unhappy or searching for something. Joe smiled at her, said something crazy and she was aware. That was how it had begun. Was this the way it would end? She pressed her face against his until she felt the ridge of his scar.

"Joe, marry me."

The song ended and they were caught in the chattering crowd leaving the dance floor.

"Just *say* you will," she pleaded. "Please."

He wanted to marry her but he was afraid. You cannot

marry a girl the night before you take off for New Guinea. It wouldn't be fair to her.

"We'll talk about it . . . when I come back."

"You'll never talk about it. There will always be a reason." She let go of his hand. The year before he had been insecure and had not felt that he was her equal. Now he was in the top money, a tremendous success, a favorite from Park Avenue to Wall Street to the White House. And he was still stalling.

There was nothing he could say short of what she wanted him to say, and he could not bring himself to say that. She would have to be patient a little longer, she would have to wait until he came back. It would not be long, he reasoned, and she knew there was no one else.

Gerun and two colonels were waiting impatiently.

"To Joe E.!" Gerun was pouring his best grape.

They touched glasses, Joe and Letty, and their eyes met. This was the way it would be always. She was certain of it now. They would have a few fleeting moments together, a few words at a time, between shows, between drinks, between gags, between pals. No woman could possess Joe because he belonged to his friends. They felt that he did and they had made him believe it. A woman had to be satisfied with a part-time Joe, the lesser part. Love? It was all love. Joe loved to entertain people. He loved to hear them laugh. He loved to know they loved him. He loved being Joe E., a character he had invented. He loved her too, but this was a single love and he did not have any experience loving one woman or being loved by one woman. He would rather love anonymously or by groups. He was generous with what he did not want. He would give you everything he had except of his emotion. With that he was a miser.

"Come back . . ." she said prayerfully. It took all of her strength to hold back the words, ". . . to me." She had no claim on him. He had warned her, before she had made up her mind to get a divorce, that he was—she smiled grimly at the memory—a bachelor on the loose. He had never promised her anything. She had forced the affair from the beginning.

"Come back." She would not ask God for too much. She would settle for his safe return.

The next morning he kissed her for the last time. "We'll talk about it . . . when I come back," he said as if they were still on the dance floor and she had just asked him to marry her.

"Of course, darling." She knew he had said it only because he wanted to make her feel better, and she was grateful for that. He meant it, she was sure he meant it for now, and that was enough. It had to be enough. There are no guarantees on tomorrow, especially with a man like Joe. You hope for the best and wait for the dice to roll.

Joe closed the door to her room and slowly walked away. Unconsciously he began humming, "I'll be seeing you . . ."

23   *Into the Great Blue Yonder*

"I ain't feelin' so good." Austin shook his head mournfully.

"What's the matter?"

"All them shots. I wanna die."

"As soon as we get through with this briefing, I'll get you something . . . maybe a shot to take away the effect of the shots."

"No!"

An Air Force lieutenant entered the room. "Gentlemen," he addressed his audience of Joe and Austin, "all passengers on overseas flights are required to receive the following instructions—in case of ditching."

"What's that?" Austin asked feebly.

"In case the plane is forced down in the sea," the Lieutenant replied.

"Oh, my God," Austin groaned.

"You'll have to forgive my piano player," Joe said. "He has never been in a plane."

"There is nothing to fear," the officer reassured them. "Chances are you will have a perfect flight."

Austin snorted. "Eddie Rickenbacker crashes into the Pacific—and I'm goin' to have a perfect flight."

"Captain Rickenbacker was saved by the identical equipment I am now going to demonstrate." The Lieutenant pointed to a huge rubber raft on the floor. "There are two of these aboard your plane, the same as Rickenbacker's."

"Let's forget Rickenbacker already," Austin growled.

"And here," the Lieutenant put on a rubber vest, "is your Mae West. To inflate it, you pull these two cords—like so. Take your time—but not *too* much time. Remember, you have only *three minutes* to get out of the plane before it sinks. All right, you're out of the plane now . . ."

The expression on Mack's chlorine-shaded face indicated that *he* was not out of the plane.

"You inflate your Mae West—like so—climb aboard the raft and check your emergency kits. They are in water-tight compartments inside the . . ."

"Oh . . ." Austin's teeth were chattering. He could feel the cold water closing over his eyes.

The Lieutenant opened a sample kit and pulled out several objects, including a hunting knife. "This is your knife," he said.

Austin stared at the blade. "Lieutenant, can I ask a question?"

"Of course."

"If we're forced down, it might be by Jap planes, no?"

"It's possible."

"And there might be Jap submarines around, no?"

"It's possible."

"Tell me, Lieutenant, if Jap planes are strafing us and Jap subs are firing torpedoes at us, what good is that dinky hunting knife?"

"To fight the sharks."

Joe dropped his two bags on the scales.

The transportation officer shook his head. "Forty pounds limit, sir. You'll have to leave one."

Joe left the one containing his clothes. The other was full of whiskey.

"You could have taken half your clothes and half the booze," Austin chided.

Joe disagreed. "Never cut good whiskey, Austin." He nervously checked the freight being put aboard. His search ended at a packing case on which was stenciled, THEATRICAL PROPS—JOE E. LEWIS. He sighed with relief. General George had come through again. The props consisted of three cases of whiskey.

Two hours after the take-off, an engine conked out. The ship lurched and went into a sickening dive. Austin was paralyzed save for his praying lips.

Joe looked up calmly from their gin-rummy game. "New rule, Austin. You can knock with anything in your hand. Thirty-two—twenty-nine—anything."

After Pearl Harbor, their first stop was Canton Island, a coral atoll used solely for refueling, the tiny Island X that Rickenbacker's navigator had overshot. While the plane was being checked, Joe staged an impromptu show under the island's one palm tree, Austin accompanying him on an accordion he had brought along in lieu of a piano.

That was his first violation.

"You were not authorized to give a performance at Canton Island," an officious major in Special Services reprimanded him in Brisbane, Australia upon his arrival at General MacArthur's Headquarters.

"Don't be a damn fool, Major," Joe said lightly.

The Major's hackles rose. "This is a theatre of *war,* Mr. Lewis. We appreciate your coming but must remind you that you are under the supervision of Special Services; you are subject to the Articles of War and you will perform *only* where you are authorized to perform. Is that clear?"

"I came to entertain the men." The tone of his voice said, you've said your piece, boy, now back away and let a man go to work.

The Major consulted a sheet of paper. "Your first show, Mr. Lewis, will be at the Officers Club in . . ."

"I am supposed to entertain as many men as possible in twelve weeks," Joe interrupted. "If there are more officers than enlisted men down here, I'll be glad to start with your . . ."

"Enlisted men *always* come first." The Major scowled at the paper. "I am sure this is a typographical error. There will be a new schedule in the morning."

"Don't get me wrong, Major, some of my best friends are officers."

The Major would answer that in his own way, by billeting him in a fourth-rate fleabag instead of the Queens Hotel. "We're short of accommodations, Mr. Lewis, and I may have to put you up for a few nights at . . ."

"Don't bother, Major, I have a *friend* in town."

The friend was Tom Winterbottom, an Australian, who

managed the Queens. Joe gave him two bottles of whiskey and Winterbottom installed him in the suite originally intended for General MacArthur.

Joe and Winterbottom had finished one bottle when Austin came in, deeply agitated. "That Major!" he bellowed in one of the few rages Joe had ever witnessed.

"*The* Major?"

Austin nodded. "I'm worried sick because I haven't heard from Cassie. So I go to the Major and ask him how can I get word to her where I am. 'You can't,' he says. I asked him why. 'Security,' he says. I argue with him half an hour and then he throws me out of his office. 'Security!' Wait until Cassie hears about it. As if she were a Jap spy or something."

Joe took another drink. "He's gone too far, Austin."

"I'll say he has! I got to cable Cassie, Joe. This is the first time since we've been married that she doesn't know *exactly* where I am!"

Joe nodded. "He's gone too far." He looked at Winterbottom. "What do you think about it, Tom?"

Tom refilled their glasses. "I hate majors on general principles."

Joe telephoned the Major. "Why be irritating, buddy, he asked, "when with a little effort you could be repulsive?" He did not wait for a reply.

Winterbottom pacified Joe. "Don't judge things by the Battle of Brisbane," he said. "The real war is up north."

The following day Joe and Austin left for Townsville, the jump-off spot in northern Australia. There they were herded with six soldiers in a room intended for two. In the morning they reported sleepy-eyed to the Captain in charge of Special Services.

"I trust you had a good night's rest." The Captain made no attempt to mask his sarcasm.

Joe held his temper.

The Captain threw him a taunting smile. "Brisbane sig-
naled us to give you *first*-class treatment."

"I figured that." Joe realized he had made a mistake tak-
ing on the Major in Brisbane when he had been drinking.
But he had an ace left. "Major, do you mind if I live with
General Bertrandius?"

"Who?"

Joe had difficulty pronouncing the name. "Bertrandius.
General Victor Bertrandius."

The Captain bristled. "You'll live where I tell you."

Joe relayed the Captain's injunction to Bertrandius, who
promptly called the Captain and informed him to transfer
Joe's gear to the General's quarters. "Also, Captain, Mr.
Lewis will require transportation while he is with us. I am
assigning you to drive him."

That night, over a bottle of Scotch, Joe persuaded Bertrandius to revoke his order. "Get me a buck private who
knows his way around."

"I guess it would be unfair to the Captain," the General
conceded.

"Unfair to the Captain?" Joe looked aghast. "It would be
unfair to me, Vic! I couldn't stand his company."

The phone rang and the General answered it. "Your
theatrical props just arrived," he relayed the message, "and
they're leaking like hell."

The only war in Townsville was over liquor, women, hotel
accommodations and plane priorities. Joe didn't have to leave
Broadway for this and, after one day of it, he headed for
New Guinea.

In New Guinea, that spring of 1943, General George
Kenney's pathetic little air force of young flyers and old
planes acted as if it were fighting the entire war in the Pacific
alone and, for many months, it was. The survivors of each

raid went up again the next morning and it was a good strike when they could get twenty-five heavies off the ground, a big one when they could throw forty. Twenty-five to forty planes at a time when a thousand and more bombers were pounding Germany every day.

As a war correspondent, I lived with these dedicated men. I ate with them, drank with them, gambled with them, went on missions with them and kept score of the arms, legs, eyes and lives they lost.

It was not the kind of war I had expected, nor the kind Joe had expected. Guys like us, who had called our own numbers instead of waiting for our draft boards to become desperate, had gone to war out of curiosity, ennui and guilt as much as pride. A man runs the way he is gaited and we were accustomed to being at ringside. This was the main event of our generation, at least we thought it was, and we wanted to see it first-hand, not through Ernie Pyle's column or an Errol Flynn movie. Our kind smelled all the flowers, we did not know if we were coming this way again. We would learn that war is waste, boredom, time blacked out, organized murder, and we would come to loathe it as the inhuman crime that it has always been, but back in the United States it had been a challenge, an adventure that had beckoned to us in headlines, posters, movies, newsreels, pin-ups, radio news bulletins, and the smart uniforms and rows of battle ribbons on other men: *la guerre* then had been the most voluptuous bitch in the world and we had to get in her. Telling jokes and writing sports had not been disagreeable occupations, not at the kind of money Joe and I had been drawing, but the first team had been out there and we had not liked the idea of playing to the scrubs. As a friend of mine, Jack Singer, had said the night he left sports writing to go west and be blown to pieces aboard the *U.S.S. Wasp,* covering baseball or football during a war was like peddling peanuts during the Gettysburg Address.

Now we were in it. Out there was out here. I had Singer's job with International News Service, and Joe could hear the Jap guns without sticking his head outside.

Two decades of sport—watching Jack Dempsey, Babe Ruth, Earl Sande, Red Grange, Bill Tilden, Bobby Jones, Jesse Owens, Joe Louis and countless other athletic conquerors in their finest moments—have dimmed, while the deeds of the brave men I knew in New Guinea, now gone a dozen years, grow greener in memory.

They were champions.

Joe saw more than two thousand of them sitting on the ground, covering every inch of the rolling hillside. He had never faced a throng as large as this one, and he was nervous.

It seemed strange working in sun-tans instead of a tux, with only Austin's accordion behind him, under a starry sky instead of a dimly lighted cabaret. His material was intended for the minks who laughed easily because they were hopped-up or manic. Before him was a host of healthy young men, at least ninety per cent of whom had never heard of him let alone seen him, grim desperate men who were going up to fight Japs in a few hours with the price never better than eight to five they would come back.

What could be funny to them?

24   *The Vow*

"Fellow airmen," he began. "I *am* a flyer, y'know. A test pilot for Seagram's." He won them with his first line.

"When I look at you guys I know I'm an old man. An old man is any man who can't take yes for an answer. All I can do is dream. Last night I dreamed I was making love to Lana Turner, Betty Grable and Rita Hayworth. When I dream I don't fool around."

He was making them laugh at their loneliness.

Austin tried to cue him into a song. "My first number is the theme of a hit movie that just came out. A psychological Western. The horse cracks up." Joe cleared his throat with a "Voom! Voom!" and a lyric Richard Rodgers would recognize and disown.

> *I'm beguiled again, now I'm wild again*
> *I'm in a whirl, I got my girl*
> *With child again.*
> *Bewitched, bothered and bewildered . . .*

The G.I.'s were roaring.

"As an encore I'll do a love song, 'Darling, If I Can Have a Honeymoon Tonight We'll Get Married Tomorrow . . .' Voom! Voom! I think I'll sing the 'Wiffenpoof Song' the hard way—with real sheep. The critics say my voice has a dramatic quality. A gripping voice—sort of a half-Nelson Eddy. Voom! Voom! By the way, if any of you guys think I'm crazy, I'll take half the bet."

They gave him thunderous applause and he gave them his favorite songs, from "Sam" to the "Groom" to "Kaltenborn" to "Poor Feb," with an occasional poem.

> *If her bosom heaves like the tide of the ocean,*
> *And she sighs like she's torn by great emotion—*
> *If she breathes like she can hardly catch her breath,*
> *Let's face it: this broad has asthma.*

Their laughter rang through the jungle, laughter he would treasure more than any other honors he would ever receive.

One night he was a double feature. After his performance came a movie, *Private Buckaroo,* a dreadful little charade he had made the previous year with the Andrews Sisters and Harry James. The name of the character Joe played, J. Lancelot Pringle McBiff, was longer than his part.

He gave as many as eight or ten shows a day, from morning until past midnight, in mud and rain, at times without a stage or a microphone, wherever he could find men who would listen to him—in mess halls, jungle clearings, airstrips, hospitals, within sound of Jap guns—and only once did he fail to get laughs.

"This is it," said the truck driver, braking to a stop on a deserted road.

Joe looked around. "Where's the audience?"

The driver pointed to a truck pulled up on the side. Some forty Negro soldiers were aboard.

Joe beamed. "Austin, we're on!"

The opening line did not get a laugh, not even a giggle. Neither did the second or the third or the fourth. He looked at the dour-faced G.I.'s. "I would say something funny here —but I don't want to break the mood."

Not a grin appeared.

"I wonder what I'd do without material? Probably get laughs."

Nothing happened.

He was desperate. "Is this an audience or an oil painting?"

Never before had he gone this long without a chuckle.

"Everybody talks about my drinking. I don't drink anything stronger than pop—and pop drinks anything. People say liquor is harmful. Ridiculous. I had an uncle who drank two quarts a day. He lived to be twenty-four."

The soldiers stood in funereal silence.

"If any of you listened to that last joke, I want you to

know you're in the middle of a losing streak. Talk about luck, I made nine passes last night and the dame still said no dice."

He vainly searched their faces for a smile.

"There was an Italian general in Tunisia," he punched, wearily and grimly. "The Americans were only a thousand miles away. 'Men,' said the General after his men were assembled, 'we are hopelessly outnumbered but we can go down like gallant soldiers. Remember Thermopylae!'

"As he spoke he walked before his men, favoring a slight limp in one leg. 'I want an orderly retreat. Synchronize your watches, men. Seven-ten. The retreat will begin in exactly one hour. But remember, orderly and gallantly. I have a bad limp . . . I'm leaving now.' "

Joe limped off the truck. No laughs. He could not quit now, he had to break them down. He kept firing his best gags and the songs that had never failed. Even "Sam, You Made the Pants Too Long" made their faces longer.

During the chorus of "No Room for the Groom," a large rat scampered across the makeshift stage in front of him. Joe stopped. "Hey, bud," he scowled at the scene-stealer, "I'm doing a single."

The rat stopped a moment and shuffled off.

"Lot of real talent out here," Joe commented, "but he shouldn't have upstaged me."

Even that failed to draw a titter.

He stopped in the middle of the "Kaltenborn Blues." "This song isn't going anywhere," he said, "but at least it has pace. It's not going anywhere fast."

A moment later he gave up, crushed and bewildered. "What happened?" he asked Austin.

Austin shook his head. Nothing like this had ever occurred before.

They were about to leave when the Commanding Officer of

the G.I.'s came up. "Mr. Lewis," he said solemnly, "I want to thank you in behalf of our men. They enjoyed your performance very much."

Joe thought it was a rib. "I would have done a tap dance too but I didn't want to drown out the laughs."

The officer shook his head. "Mr. Lewis, you're the greatest comedian we've ever seen."

"Who are you kidding?" Joe was hurt and angry. "I didn't get *one* laugh from you or your men!"

"Of course you didn't," the glum-faced officer replied. "We all have the mumps."

Joe and I came to know each other in New Guinea. We jeeped from one village to another, looking. I did not know what he was looking for and he did not know what I was looking for. It is possible that neither of us knew what we were looking for.

What did we find?

One day we went to a native village that was half a day's ride from Port Moresby. I had made friends with Enoch, the Chief of the tribe. He gave me stories and I gave him tobacco.

Enoch could not understand the war being waged around him and his people. It had been different in his youth when he was a warrior. Their fighting had begun at sunrise and had ended at sunset; when the first man was wounded the war was over. They believed that downing one man proved as much, or as little, as downing a million men, but it must be borne in mind that they were benighted savages and this was before the white man brought civilization to New Guinea.

A Papuan girl, stripped to the waist and beautifully formed, passed us.

"She has a nice necklace," Joe remarked.

I pointed to the necklace and asked Enoch how much he wanted for it.

The Chief, mistaking my request, called the girl. "Take her, my son," he said. "She will make you a good wife."

"Not girl—necklace," I said.

Enoch removed the strand of shells from her neck and handed it to me. The girl ran away weeping. "Pay no attention to her," Enoch said. "That will be two cartons of Chesterfields."

When we returned to camp and showed our souvenir, an ANGAU man, an Australian who dealt with the natives, examined it and whistled.

"Mates," he said, "you have one of the rarest native possessions. This is a virgin necklace and may be worn only by girls who have never been married. On their wedding night the husband consummates the union by tearing the necklace from his bride."

Joe looked at his necklace again. "It's not *too* rare," he said. "Look."

He held it up to the light. It had been mended in five places.

Another day, in a secluded part of the jungle, we saw a long queue of native women and girls—all ages, shades and sizes of bosoms—waiting expectantly in front of an Army tent. Obviously something was being rationed. We investigated.

Inside, a perspiring young corporal was massaging the undraped breasts of ten Papuan ladies simultaneously, sustaining the mass titillation with the dexterity of a brilliant xylophonist. The rapturous sighs, delirious panting and moans of pleasure provided symphonic testimony of his virtuosity.

"Can I give you a hand?" Joe inquired.

"No, thanks, I can handle it," the corporal replied without missing a beat. "Lots of business today."

"Corporal," I asked, "precisely how is this helping the war effort?"

"We have to keep the natives happy," he said. "It's *their* island, y'know."

I nodded. "But aren't you biting off a little more than you can chew?"

"I'm doing my best, sir." At last he finished with the ten ladies and dismissed them. Their ecstatic expressions reflected their gratitude.

The corporal mopped his brow with his sleeve. "Hard work," he said, "especially in this heat."

"*C'est la guerre,*" said Joe.

Ten fresh ones bounced in, thrust out their bosoms and the corporal sprayed their pectoral muscles in one burst as if they were on an assembly line. "It makes their men wild, even for the worst of these dogs. Out here it's the world's greatest aphro—aphro—"

"Aphrodisiac," I helped him. A corporal who did not know how to pronounce aphrodisiac let alone spell it was stroking a hundred firm, passionate breasts an hour and, from the length of the line winding into the distance, he was certain to run out of strength before knockers. He had the best job in the Army, if he wasn't busted.

"Son," Joe said, "you'll make a fortune with this stuff when you get back to the States."

The soldier shook his head sadly. "I don't think our dames will go for it." He held an open bottle under our noses. "Take a whiff."

It had a horrible odor. "What is it?" I asked.

The corporal lowered his voice. "G.I. insect repellent."

I took Joe to a press conference, held each noon for correspondents representing the United States, England and Australia. The daily communiques of Colonel LeGrande A. Diller, Chief of Public Relations at General MacArthur's

Headquarters, were classics in jabberwocky. On land, sea and air we were still losing the war in the Pacific but we won every battle in Colonel Diller's daily proclamations.

Reporting one of these triumphs of semantics, I had cabled my dispach, "By Hans Christian Andersen."

It wasn't the military censorship that revolted the correspondents, it was the political censorship imposed by MacArthur's advisers who were running him for President while he was supposed to be running a war, and it was the general nonsensorship of his terrified incense-swingers. One of them had three baskets on his desk marked Secret, Top Secret and Tiptop Secret.

After one of my dispatches had been turned into confetti, I confronted Colonel Bernard Tormey, a giant of a soldier from Oregon, the Chief Military Censor. "Colonel," I asked, "what is your criterion of censorship?"

"My criterion of censorship," Tormey replied, "is my goddamn neck."

I looked at his bull-like neck and asked, "Size 19 or 20?"

Colonel Tormey measured me. I, like Joe, had been a marked man since my first day in Brisbane . . .

"Did you file this? The U.S. Army censor handed me a copy of my first cable, a personal message to a friend in California. "Happy Birthday, Sweetheart," it read, with an order to a florist for two dozen yellow roses.

I nodded. It was hardly a notable dispatch with which to launch a career as a war correspondent but I was fighting on several fronts.

"It was changed to 'Greetings of the day, darling' and one dozen red carnations." The censor pointed a finger of warning at me. "And don't try any more funny stuff. We're hep to *all* codes."

Codes? Red carnations for yellow roses? I was dumbfounded. "But why Darling instead of Sweetheart?" I asked.

"Security, mister, security."

Colonel Diller faced his greatest crisis when a village in New Guinea named Fuk-fuk was captured. No one missed the press conference that day.

Diller cleared his throat and began reading the communique, "Allied forces have taken a village that is spelled F-U-K, F-U-K—which, henceforth, shall be given the Anglicized pronunciation of Fak-fak."

There was a silence, at last broken by the weary, cynical voice of Alan Dawes, portly correspondent for a Sydney, Australia, newspaper. "That's what happens to all the 'faks' around here."

There was room for two deadheads on a reconnaissance flight the following day. I wangled one of them and Carl Thusgaard, a photographer from Acme Photos, drew the other.

"You're lucky, Carl," I told him. He had arrived from the United States only two days previously. Sometimes you waited weeks for a mission.

"Lucky?" He did not think so. "I was hoping to go on a combat mission . . . but I'll take it. I can test my aerial camera."

We were instructed to be up by 6 A.M. and ready to be checked out at seven.

Six A.M. came. So did Thusgaard. We shared a tent with two young pilots. He lifted the mosquito bar and shook me. I tried to get up but my head seemed to be nailed to the cot. A few of us had been celebrating in the Officers Club until 4:30 A.M.

"I can't make it," I groaned.

"You have to." He tossed a canteen of water in my face. I needed the Coral Sea. Thusgaard gave up at 6:45.

The Japs didn't bother them over the target. They took their pictures and headed home. Halfway back they ran into a squadron of Jap fighters returning from a mission. It was one of those million-to-one shots that was always coming up. The one recon didn't have a chance against thirty Zekes.

That night I wrote Carl's obituary and, within the next month, the two pilots in my tent followed Thusgaard. Three out of four. Why, I wondered, had I survived? I could not have fouled up my life half as well had I done it deliberately. It had taken me twenty years to find out I did not want to be a sports writer. And thirteen years to discover that I did not want to be married to my wife. Why had I been saved?

"It doesn't make sense," I said as we worked on a bottle in Joe's tent. "What am I going home to?"

Joe had his own problem. What was he going home to? When he had come to the question in the Army questionnaire, "What is your home address?" he had written, "Ten-dollar window, Hialeah." The officers had laughed and the line made all the columns but now, out here, it did not sound funny. Many things looked different: from a distance of ten thousand miles he saw Broadway clearly for the first time. He was going home to a saloon, a hotel room and two old trunks.

He had wanted or thought he had wanted success, money and fame. And he had gotten them, or vice versa. He had forgotten what Johnny Black used to say about fame. "Fame, Joseph, is climbing a greased pole for ten bucks and ruining a suit worth fifteen."

I'll be seeing you . .

Joe listened. A radio was playing in a nearby tent. *I'll be seeing you.* This was the lifeline out here, the hope of seeing loved ones again. He hummed the words and he thought of Letty. Before, they had reminded him of Tamara. *I'll be seeing you.* Was it Letty he wanted to see for the rest of his life? Only Letty? Would he be faithful to her? Did he really miss her? He had never missed anyone before.

When he had come to the question, "Who should be notified in case of your death?" he had given the telephone number of Max, his bookie. Joe E. Lewis, funnyman, Everyone had laughed except Letty. "You're living an act," she had said, "and acting your life." Was he?

I'll be seeing you . . .

This was a new experience for him. Until now, his only interest in songs had been how well they lent themselves to parodies. This was the first one he did not want to burlesque. He saw nothing funny in wanting to hold Letty in his arms again.

It wasn't the song. It had started in the hospital ward the day before. He had finished the show, a show he would never forget . . .

A boy with one arm pounded his iron bed to applaud him. A boy with no legs saluted him with his crutches. He stopped at each bed and wound up at the side of a pilot who had a Purple Heart with four clusters and the Navy Cross among his four rows of ribbons.

"I'll bet you'll have plenty of stories to tell the folks back home," Joe said.

The man who had fought his way back from a hundred hells looked up. "There's only one story I want to tell when I get back," he replied softly, "and only one person I want to tell it to. I just want to tell my wife how much I love her."

Joe looked at the wounded boy and envied him. He suddenly envied his world, a world in which love was a simile for life and not just a four-letter word. Then he realized that he had forfeited his right to envy: he had wanted no part of that world and had become famous ridiculing it. He had seen the selfishness and deceit of the pretenders and had mistaken it for the genuine. He had shored up his defenses out of cynicism and fear. It *was* fear. He was afraid to give himself to someone else. He had no faith in goodness. Or in himself.

Letty had not been afraid. She had gambled her wedding ring on him but he had lacked the courage to cover the bet. He, the man who had said, "You can't beat the odds by ducking them." But he had said that in 1927 when McGurn threatened him. At twenty-five he had not been afraid of death; at forty-one he was afraid of life. "Joe, marry me," she had begged their last night together. "Just *say* you will . . . please."

As he thought of her, a new fear gripped him. Was he capable of *loving* Letty? Could he love anyone?

Joe walked outside his tent. In the still, tropical night, save for the cicadas chirping in the moonlit jungle, he found what he had been looking for.

"Letty," he murmured, "marry me."

25   *Paper Doll*

It had been a rewarding experience and he would always be thankful to the men in New Guinea for giving him a new outlook on life. Their gratitude had embarrassed him. They had brought him many gifts, they who had so little: cookies from home, silver identification bracelets they had made, whiskey from their own stills. He would never forget any of them, but he would probably remember the bombing group in Dobadura longest. They would not let him leave until he had done every number he knew *twice* and, when he had finished, a corporal who had been selected as spokesman for the group thanked him.

"Mr. Lewis . . ."

"The name is Joe."

"Joe, we want to express our—"

"Knock it off, son." Joe was embarrassed. "Let's scare up some liquor."

"In appreciation for the wonderful shows you have given us," the corporal continued from a prepared speech, "and to commemorate your courage in sitting bravely through every air raid in our open and unprotected four-holer—"

"That wasn't courage," Joe interrupted. "It was dysentery."

"—we are officially naming the can after you."

The bombing group echoed its approval and thus was dedicated the most unique monument to an entertainer in World War II, the Joe E. Lewis Latrine.

The tour was over and he was back in Brisbane, waiting for transportation to San Francisco. The Major in Special Services, nursing a three-months grudge, kept him waiting. It was spite and Joe decided to go over his head but the Major had anticipated him. "You have been such an outstanding morale-builder, Lewis, that I have decided to extend your tour. You will report to Special Services in Sydney and continue entertaining in that area."

Joe would have remained in New Guinea for another six months but Australia was out of the question. There was less war in Sydney than in Des Moines, Iowa. The great capital of New South Wales, with its population of a million and a half plus the Allied forces, was the southwest Pacific's foremost pleasure resort for men on leave: its luxury hotels, night clubs, bars, legitimate and motion picture theatres, boxing clubs, et alii, were running wide open. A man who could not pick up a woman in the Hotel Australia lobby in less than five minutes any time of the day or night was a genius. They didn't need Joe.

"Your new orders are being cut," said the Major. "Check Amberly Field every hour for your flight. You'll be going out tonight or early in the morning."

That was Saturday afternoon. Joe moved fast but, with his supply of whiskey gone, he discovered that his popularity among the senior officers had waned. He could get no higher than a second looie.

Winterbottom was his last hope. "I *have* to get out of here, Tom," he said, "before those orders are cut."

"That's going to take some doing, Joe."

"And some booze."

Winterbottom came up with the ammunition and, in a little while, they were entertaining a Captain in Operations at the Officers Club on Amberly Field. As the evening and the grog wore on, the Captain became sympathetic to Joe's plight but said he was powerless to help him.

"We couldn't possibly get you out to the States before Monday even if you *had* orders," the Captain said. "Nothing is going out."

"Monday is too late," Joe groaned. "My orders to Sydney will be up by morning."

The Captain nodded. "The minute you're on the manifest, you're cooked."

Winterbottom sighed. "I guess you had it, Joe."

A Colonel came to their table and, after greeting Winterbottom, handed the Captain an envelope and told him to put it on the mail plane.

"Yes sir." The Captain saluted and introduced him, Colonel Gillespie—Commanding Officer of the Air Base—to Joe and Austin.

"Have a drink, Colonel," Joe said.

"Just one. I have a date."

Joe stole a glance at the envelope in the Captain's hand and noticed that it was addressed to Washington, D.C. He looked sharply at the Captain. "I thought you said there weren't any planes going to the States."

"There aren't. Just the mail plane."

"What time does it leave?" Joe had difficulty concealing his eagerness.

"O three hundred," Winterbottom answered. "Three A.M. in your language."

"Don't get any ideas, Mr. Lewis," Colonel Gillespie warned. "The mail plane doesn't carry passengers."

"Colonel!" Joe feigned hurt that his intentions had been suspected. "I have an important letter to send. I only have until Tuesday to reject this month's selection of the Book-of-the-Month Club." He started to refill the Colonel's glass but the Colonel stopped him.

"Thanks, old man, but only one before dinner." The Colonel rose. "I'll be back at 0400, Captain."

"By the way, Colonel," Joe said, "I'm leaving for Sydney in the morning and Tom is giving me a going-away party."

Gillespie's eyes darted to the supply of liquor under the table. "So I see."

"Just the preliminary. The main event will be at Tom's apartment later on."

The party had been conceived by Joe that moment but Winterbottom presciently picked up the cue. "I insist that you join us, Colonel," he said.

Gillespie reminded them that he had a date.

"Bring her along," Joe insisted.

"It might be midnight before I get there," the Colonel said as Winterbottom gave him his address.

"That's the shank of the evening," Joe said, "when the herring begin to marinate."

After the Colonel left Joe turned to the Captain. "How about you, Cap?"

The Captain shook his head regretfully. "I have to stay on the base until morning."

"Keep him company, Austin." Joe's tone of voice told Austin that he was to keep on drinking with him.

Joe and Winterbottom left.

"Can he stay with the Captain?" Winterbottom asked apprehensively.

"To play a drinker," Joe said, "Austin doesn't need a stunt man."

At 0255 the Captain lost his nerve. "I can't go through with it," he said. "I'll be busted."

"For what?" Joe asked. "You haven't done anything."

"That's it. Because I *didn't* do anything. You don't want me court-martialed, do you?"

"But you haven't anything to do with it! *I* talked the pilot into it. *Everybody* hitches rides in the South Pacific."

"But not to the States! I'm *ordering* you not to board that plane."

The motors were being revved.

"And I thought you were a standup guy." Joe threw the Captain a look of contempt. "You're no better than the Special Services Major downtown."

"I ought to knock your teeth out for that."

"Go ahead," Joe taunted. "The Major will see that you get the Distinguished Service Medal."

The Captain weighed the consequences against Joe's estimation of him. "Lewis, you better get your ass on that plane before I do knock your teeth out."

"This is a hell of a going-away party," Colonel Gillespie grumbled.

"Best going-away party we've had this week," Winterbottom dissented.

"But the guest of honor isn't here yet." The Colonel

looked at his watch. "It's 3:15, Tom! Haven't you any idea where Lewis is?"

Winterbottom nodded unconcerned. "He's on the 3 A.M. mail plane to San Francisco."

The plane sputtered into Fiji with a bad oil leak.

"You better stay here and wait for another plane," the pilot advised Joe.

"Hell, no." Joe refused to budge from his bucket seat. "I'll take my chances on this one. I don't want to become a native."

Back in the air, a few hours later, Austin suddenly pointed to a foreign object below. "Isn't that a periscope?" he shrilled.

The pilot scanned the sea. "It could be, but chances are it's a shark."

"Let's not take any chances," Joe said. "Fire all guns!"

"This is a mail plane," the pilot reminded him. "We don't have any guns."

"There must be *something* we can fire at 'em." Joe searched the plane, found nothing except the accordion. "It's better than nothing," he said, opening a hatch.

Austin dived for the music box. "No, Joe! It's irreplaceable, we still have some shows at Pearl Harbor."

Aroused to battle fever, Joe grabbed a canvas case. Austin leaped and wrestled him for its possession. "Our sheet music, Joe! Those are all our lyrics!"

"At least give me 'Ramona.' "

" 'Ramona'?"

"I don't use it any more."

Austin stared at him. "Are you off your rocker?"

Joe was serious. "I want to have the distinction of hitting a Jap sub with a sheet of music . . . But roll it up first, Austin."

They were on the last lap, Honolulu to San Francisco.

When the crew had changed at Pearl Harbor, the pilot again urged Joe to wait for another ship. "I honestly don't think this one will make it," he said.

"I've got to take it." Joe was afraid to stop lest he be picked up for violating orders and returned to Brisbane.

Austin watched him toss a handful of pills in his mouth. "What are you taking now?"

"Sleeping pills," Joe replied after he had swallowed the last one.

Austin shot up in alarm. "How many did you take?"

"Eight or ten. If we crash, I don't want to know about it."

Bones Remmer, a gambling man, brought a case of liquor to Joe's suite at the St. Francis Hotel. He poured a tumbler for Joe and put it in his hand. Joe lifted the glass to his lips but did not toss it down.

"Drink, you bastard," said Bones. "It's thirty-year-old."

The glass fell out of Joe's hand and he passed out. Some of the sleeping pills were still working.

A press conference was held the following day and Joe was asked to pose with an ornate Japanese sword he had brought back. Asked how he had acquired it, he replied, "I took it away from a Jap officer in Buna-buna."

The newspapermen smiled. Joe was drunk or lying or both.

"Oh, he was dead," he added, noting their skepticism.

"How did you know?" one of the newspapermen asked.

"I kicked him a little, that's how I know."

A commendation awaited him in Washington. "You must have laid 'em in the aisles at Loew's New Guinea," General Joseph F. Batley told him. "They say you're the best man we ever sent out there."

"I wish I could say as much for some of your officers in Australia." Joe was not joking, as General Batley quickly realized. "You have a few Colonels and Majors in the rear echelons who are more concerned about entertaining the brass in the Officers Club circuit than the enlisted men who are getting their rear ends shot off in New Guinea."

He put it on the line, with names. An investigation was launched and, as a result, the Special Services personnel in the southwest Pacific was reorganized.

He was eager to get back to New York.

"You might as well be the first to know," he told Austin. "I'm going to get married."

"It's about time," Mack responded impassively. "Letty?"

Joe nodded.

Austin broke into a smile.

Joe bristled. "What are you grinning at?"

"I was thinking what Cassie will say."

Cassie met them at the airport. After they had embraced, Joe looked around. "Didn't Letty come?"

Cassie looked at his expectant face and intuitively knew that his desire at last had conquered his fear. "No, Joe," she said, realizing that in another moment he would never again be the same. "She's on her honeymoon."

"No jokes, Cassie."

"Letty is on her honeymoon." Her heart was breaking for him but this had to be gotten over. "She got stuck on a guy the week after you left. He isn't a bad guy for a square . . ."

"I'll see about the luggage." Joe took the baggage checks out of Austin's hand and walked slowly toward the terminal. As he trudged, he heard a juke box playing the number one song on the Hit Parade, a revival of the song he and Johnny Black had introduced twenty years previously.

When I come home at night she will be waiting,
She'll be the truest doll in all this world.

I'd rather have a paper doll to call my own,
Than have a fickle-minded real live girl.

Cassie's eyes followed him. "Poor Joe," she said heavily. "He had to go twenty thousand miles to get dusted off."

26   *Lost Cords*

"Welcome to the Copacabana!"

The crowd applauded, whistled, pounded on the tables and laughed. The laughter increased in volume until it drowned out all other sounds. Joe had said nothing except "Welcome to the Copacabana." He had not mugged, he had no props, he was impeccably attired in dinner clothes.

An outlander, seeing Joe for the first time, looked around the room in astonishment. "What in the world are they laughing at?" he asked. "He hasn't said anything funny."

"He *is* funny," a Lewis devotee replied.

"He looks like a Limey bartender," the outlander commented.

"Copacabana . . ." Joe was on. "Translated into English, that means, 'Come and see us and bring lots of money.' Julie Podell has gone to great expense redecorating the Copa for my opening. In the bar he put in all new drunks. There's a lot of cheap talk going around that Podell is stingy. Well, may I say that nothing could be farther from a lie. Last year he produced a Broadway musical but this year he really gave the field of musical comedy a shot in the arm. He didn't produce any. And may I say that what Mr. Podell doesn't know about musicals is well worth knowing."

He turned. "I want to introduce our band leader, John Philip Souse." The Copa band leader took a bow. "And Austin Mack." Austin bowed. "When Austin graduated from music school he was voted the boy most likely to return. Seriously, Austin played piano for the late Texas Guinan and before that for the late minstrel star, Eddie Leonard." He scowled at Austin. "And I want to tip you off right now, Mr. Mack, you are not going to bury me."

He never carboned a line, there were constant variations of his basic themes.

"People ask me why I don't do an opening song. For one thing, it's risky. If the song is bad you're in trouble. If it goes over, the guy who wrote it expects to be paid. I bought a lot of new material, however. It hasn't been delivered yet but I hope you will bear with me for the next eight or ten weeks. The lyrics haven't been written, just the tunes, so I'll have to hum my first song." He hummed sixteen bars and stopped suddenly. "Right here is a hell of a laugh."

It was not easy to make people laugh in 1944. Many were self-conscious about drinking while men were dying in the Marshalls, on Leyte Gulf and on the beaches of Normandy. Then the roof caved in: the Government imposed a thirty per cent amusement tax. Hundreds of night clubs closed and twenty thousand entertainers were thrown out of work.

But not at the Copacabana. This night, as on all nights that Joe was on, the club was jammed to capacity. He went to the piano and lifted his highball. "Post time!" He turned to the crowd. "The thirty per cent Federal tax is a wonderful thing. Buying a drink is now patriotic!"

He spotted a customer coming in with three ravishing models. "Now there's a man who has the right idea. If it isn't rationed, don't hoard it."

Austin was playing the score from *Porgy and Bess*. Joe cleared his throat with a brace of vooms. "There's quite a controversy going on over my voice. One music critic, the gentleman of the *Etude*—or was it *Down Beat?*—got a little nasty and said that my voice was like combing a wire-haired terrier against the grain. Fortunately I have a good friend on the Houston *Press*, Paul Hochuli, and he came to my defense. Paul said that my voice reminded him of an all-clear signal in a floating crap game . . .

"I remember my first day at the conservatory. I sang half a chorus of the Pepsi-Cola commercial and the voice teacher said, 'I've heard enough. Now here's my price. I charge five dollars or ten dollars a lesson.' What's the difference, I asked. 'For ten dollars I stay in the same room with you.' He looked at me with pity. 'Do you really think there's a future for you in singing?' I said why not? Guy Lombardo is bound to run out of brothers . . . Guy didn't."

Austin was nearing the end of *Porgy*. "My first song is double-entendre and they're both dirty." He ignored the Gershwin cue and went into a parody of a Western ballad.

> *I'm out of the saddle again.*
> *She left me with just a great big yen*
> *And now the gruesome fact is*
> *At love I'm out of practice,*
> *I'm just an "alta cactus" again.*

"Joe's torch is showing," his brother Al said to Cassie.
"He'll be all right," she said.
Austin led him into "Thanks for the Memory."

> *Thanks for the memory,*
> *The night that I came home*
> *And found you weren't alone,*
> *You said he was a nudist who dropped in to use the*
>   *phone.*
> *Thank you so much.*
>
> *Many's the time you were willing*
> *And thrilling, darling, it was.*

But just when my love was fulfilling
You called me Moe and my name is Joe . . .

Broadway is illuminated by the torches of unrequited lovers. Joe lightened it with laughter.

He was drinking heavily on stage and off. "I drink to quiet my nerves," he quipped. "My doctor keeps asking me, 'How noisy can your nerves be?' He broke into his songs more often to bib with friends at ringside tables and, between performances, he continued drinking. "I enjoy my hostess work," he insisted, and it was true.

There were many nights that he seemed to be too drunk to sing but he always managed to stagger to the microphone and, guided by Austin's cues in their own bird language, he performed for more than an hour without repeating a line or flubbing one. "I studied for the bar," he said, "but my luck, I flunked in dry martinis. I still came out a C.P.A. A Certified Public Alcoholic. You know what an alcoholic is. Anyone who drinks as much as you do but you don't like him."

His voice became huskier and the strain on his throat greater but few were aware of it, except Austin, Cassie and Podell.

One night Podell was certain that Joe could not handle another drink. "You have the late show yet, Joe," he implored. "Don't drink any more and for God's sake, don't take another one on the floor. You'll fall flat on your face."

Joe fixed a bleary eye on his employer and friend. "You don't mean that, Julie. When I take a drink on the floor and say, 'This is my toast for the evening,' everybody drinks with me. So eight hundred people have to order another drink. That's eight hundred bucks. Now what were you saying?"

Podell was worried. "One of these nights, Joe . . ."

He was halfway through the third show and his second fifth.

"Drinking doesn't affect me." He went to a ringside table, a little unsteadily, and took the drink that one of the customers offered him. "Last night I was drinking all night and I was in great shape. The only trouble was people kept stepping on my fingers."

He returned to the microphone. Austin was cuing him into his parody of a George M. Cohan medley. "My next song," he announced, "was the theme of an unusual Western. The cowboy was smarter than the horse. Incidentally, do you think autos are just a gimmick to force down the price of horses?" He went into a maundering monologue on horses that he had not used in four or five years.

Austin instinctively knew Joe was in trouble. Not because of the routine. Joe often fished out of his remarkable memory a piece of material that had lain dormant for many years. Nor was it his apparent confusion, his groping desperately as though he was going down for the third time in his sea of whiskey. Austin had seen him flounder much worse and, when he seemed hopelessly lost, have him turn with a reassuring smile and boast, "I got in . . . and I'll get out." He always had. Joe's brain was clear. Clear enough. But Austin felt a foreboding chill of disaster, as if Joe was running down.

The crowd was laughing at his soddenness as much as his nonsense. "Boy, is he loaded!" a man's voice from the rear carried over the crowd.

"I will have you know, sir," Joe retorted, "I have so much alcohol in my system that last week I got a . . ."

The crowd saw and heard him slur, in a thickened tongue, something that sounded like, "last week I got a . . ." His lips continued to move but no sound came from them. The crowd laughed. Most people laughed at everything Joe said, even when they had to go back three or four times to get the joke. Not to have laughed the first time would have been long underwear.

"Man, is he *farblunged!*" roared a man at ringside. "He can't talk!"

The woman with him, obviously his wife, sneered. "Take a good look. That's you after three highballs."

The few who really knew Joe did not laugh. They were aware that something was frightfully wrong. Joe did not pantomime. He was *trying* to talk and could not.

". . . I got a hot-foot and burned for three days." He tried to say it again but he was as mute as that morning seventeen years past when, unaware that his vocal cords had been severed, he cried a silent "Help!" into a telephone.

There was a familiar trickle in his throat. He did not have to put his hand to his mouth, although he did. He knew it was blood. That's irony, he thought, I haven't an enemy, no one wants to hurt me, I'm standing here in front of eight hundred people, everybody is laughing and suddenly I can't speak and my throat is bleeding as if McGurn's knifeman was working on me.

It was ironical and shocking but not unexpected. There had been warnings, the first at Oro Bay in the South Pacific. He had been working without a microphone and had strained his voice. Austin commented on his increased huskiness. "Just a couple 'noodles' on the vocal cords," he explained. The days he did eight or nine shows were rough but it did not occur to him to cut down, it was rough for everyone down there.

The problem was to get off. If he could only say one line. "There's something stuck in my throat," he would say. "I think it's a shot glass." But he couldn't say the first syllable. He stepped back and reached for the drink on the piano. His lips formed the words, "Post time!" and he hoisted the drink. The customers understood and laughed. Then he turned to Austin and nodded in reluctant resignation.

Austin cued the band into "Chicago" and Joe trotted off the floor, the first performance in his life he had not finished.

The following day, Podell announced that Joe was "under the weather" and Phil Regan would fill in for him. The following month Podell announced that Frank Sinatra and other celebrities would carry on for him during his "indefinite absence."

Joe, according to the Broadway columnist in whom you reposed your trust, was suffering from laryngitis or leprosy, delirium tremens or the Big Bug. Actually, he was in perfect health except that he could not utter a word.

Instead of going to a doctor he used a tincture recommended by a friendly druggist. Austin painted his throat for a week and, when it showed no improvement, he went on strike. He and Cassie had to argue a few days longer before Joe would go to Dr. Max Som, a throat specialist. Once there, he did not object to an operation in which eleven polyps were removed from his larynx.

"When will his voice come back?" Austin asked Dr. Som after the surgery.

"I have no idea," Dr. Som replied.

"But you *must* know!"

"Lewis will know."

"Will it be days . . . or weeks?"

"It could be months, Mr. Mack. Let's be patient . . ."

"Months . . ." Austin did not like the tone in Dr. Som's voice. Was Joe finished? His throat had never been right since the slashing and he had abused it so many years with booze. It was a miracle it had held out this long. New Guinea finished it. Working fourteen to eighteen hours a day, outdoors at night, without a mike, had been murderous. Letty getting married had not helped . . . First Texas Guinan, then Eddie Leonard, now Joe. Austin was superstitious. In show business tragedy went in threes . . . "I

want to tip you off, Austin, you're not going to bury me."
It was a funny gag during the act. In Dr. Som's clinic it
sounded like a tragic prophecy—for both of them.

Joe's room at the Warwick was converted into a hospital-
casino-horse book in which he conducted all his business—
on five tracks simultaneously—by sign language and written
notes.

Toots Shor was a daily visitor. "How you feeling, Baby?"
he asked this day, a week after the operation.

Joe did not nod as usual. He scribbled a note, "Last night
I took a turn for the nurse."

A beautiful doll who belonged on a cover, even a magazine, came out of the bathroom. She was the new nurse but
her uniform did not convince Toots, nor did her credentials.

"You're coming to live with me," Toots told Joe. "You'll
never recover here."

Joe protested by writing large No's on his pad and shaking his head emphatically but Shor moved him to his home
in Deal, New Jersey. There, with an elderly nurse Toots
had selected, he convalesced, played gin rummy and waited
for his voice to come back.

The weeks passed and his speech did not return. Life
deals funny hands, he mused. You lose your voice, you work
like hell and you finally get it back after seventeen years—
only to lose it again. A philosopher would probably make
something of that, he only knew that he was as helpless as
he was during the black days of November, 1927, when he
lay speechless in Columbia Memorial Hospital. Instead of
Fogarty watching over him it was Shor. That was about the
only difference he could see.

As in a few other events in Joe's life, there are two ver-
sions of the circumstances in which he recovered his voice.
The more popular one was told to me by Austin:

"Joe was playing gin with some character in Toots' house

and he was a couple thousand points behind when the guy schneidered him. Joe hollered, 'No!,' and that's how he knew he could talk again."

"Austin's business is playing the piano," Joe says. "I tell the stories. It happened this way. I was baby-sitting for the Shors. I had to earn my keep some way. Barry Ellen, she was three then, suddenly woke up and leaned out of her crib. I thought she was going to fall so I hollered, 'Hey!' and for the first time since my last night at the Copa a loud 'Hey' came out. Little Barry Ellen couldn't believe it. She had never heard me talk. It was as if the cat had suddenly started talking."

Joe could say *hey* but he could not sing. He was out for eleven weeks and when he went back he was weak but a weak Joe E. was still the strongest drawing card in the country, his name a guarantee of capacity business, $55,000 per week.

It was the year the tide turned. The Jap fleet was destroyed in the Battle of Leyte Gulf. MacArthur moved into the Marshalls and the Philippines. Hitler lost Holland, Belgium, Poland, Rumania, Czechoslovakia, Hungary and Bulgaria. Patton's tanks were thundering toward Paris.

We were winning on all fronts, that autumn of 1944, all except in Joe's room at the Warwick. He was losing a minimum of $500 a day on the horses without leaving his radio that was permanently tuned to the Smiling Irishman broadcasting continuous reports on entries, odds, scratches, jockey changes, results and payoffs from coast to coast.

"Let's do a syndicated feature," I suggested. "Like Will Rogers used to do, one line a day."

"I'm not Rogers," he snapped but ultimately agreed to give it a try.

One quip a day from the funniest man in America did not seem a formidable task. It was impossible.

The only time the phone did not ring was when Joe was

talking on it, usually to place one or a series of the hundred or more bets he made each day, or to get rid of a dame, dames invariably calling two or three minutes before a post time. A constant stream of people poured through the room. On a typical afternoon his visitors would include Lester Lee, Jerry Seelen, Dan Shapiro, and other song writers with new tunes that were often old; Eli Basse, Coleman Jacoby and less gifted gag writers with alleged original material; press agents and leg-men for the columnists foraging for crumbs of gossip or a fast line; bookies and touts with sure things; Sam Bramson, his loyal liaison with the William Morris Agency, bringing the latest offers and figures; his brother Al or Murray with news of the family; friends from all parts of the country in New York for a visit, like Carl Leigh, the banana king, or Artie Samish, the unofficial Governor of California; pals like Dan Arnstein, who made his fortune in New York taxicabs; Sanchez, Swifty, Bert Wheeler and Eddie Duchin; promoters, gamblers, sports writers, and comics down on their luck; chiselers, handshakers, stooges and assorted *schleppers,* the retinue and impedimenta of a guy who makes good on Broadway and cannot say no to those who haven't, a guy in the chips who shares them. Through this motley crowd moved bellboys bearing telegrams and other messages from the outside world, and waiters toting trays of food and whiskey for the bona fide and barnacles alike. And over all of them rose the Delphic voice of radio's Smiling Irishman reporting which horse that Joe had not bet on was beating what horses he had bet on, and by how many furlongs, at Belmont Park, Hialeah, Churchill Downs, Bowie or Bay Meadows. Wherever they were running Joe was playing.

Midst this bedlam at four o'clock on an afternoon, a skinny, spindle-legged little man in a three-quarter length leopard-skin dressing robe sat calmly eating his breakfast, studying a scratch sheet and listening to the Smiling Irishman.

This went on until after six. Then he bathed, shaved and dressed, grabbed a quick coffee and did his eight o'clock dinner show at the Copa. At nine-thirty he reported to Shor's for dinner, drinks and gossip with the mob. His next stop was a newsreel theatre, then back to the Copa for the midnight show and drinking until the 2 A.M. show. He left around 4 A.M. and went to a restaurant on Fifty-fourth Street where he got six slices of French toast for a nickel. A man has to save on something. After the snack he drifted down the street and gossiped with cab drivers and thugs he knew on his nightly rounds. Then back to the Warwick with the early morning editions and the race selections. If he was on schedule, and he usually was, he finished ringing his first choices by 7 A.M. It was light, time to go to sleep if he wanted to get up by 3 P.M. There might be a good thing in the second or third at Jamaica.

Our syndicated column died with one of Joe's gluepots at Jamaica.

I could not compete with his routine.

A young girl named Martha Stewart thought she could.

27   *A Love Story (Hers)*

Joe E. Lewis, Joe E. Lewis, that's all I heard. Winchell's column, Ed Sullivan's, Earl Wilson's, you couldn't read any of 'em without Joe E. saying this or Joe E. saying that. A few cracks were kind of cute but most of 'em did nothing to me. The same with his picture, the one in the Carmen

Miranda turban. It was in all the ads for the opening with the line, "Seeing me at the Copa is the second best way to spend an evening."

Outside the Copa there was a poster of him at least ten feet high with blow-ups from the newspapers saying Joe E. is the King of Clubs, Joe E. is a Genius, Joe E. is The Funniest Man in the World and so on and so on. Nobody can be that good, I said. I admit I was a little prejudiced. Martha Stewart was in the show too though you'd never know it from the billing, unless you can read the bottom line on an eye chart. I wasn't Ethel Merman but I wasn't chopped liver either. I'd chirped with Glenn Miller and on the "Hit Parade," I could punch a song, if you call "Mairzy Doates" a song. They did in 1944.

I couldn't even get away from him in the dressing room. He was Topic A. You wouldn't think that kids in the Copa line had senses of humor as well developed as their chests, would you? They haven't. Mr. Lewis must be a lover, I surmised, this I got to see. Don't ask me how I had lived that long without seeing him but I hadn't. Not even in rehearsals because he didn't work with the production numbers.

I didn't even take off my make-up. As soon as I knocked off "Shoo Shoo Baby" I threw a wrap around me and found a place to stand in the back. I could take comics or leave 'em. Ten minutes of the best and I had it. I didn't *want* Joe E. to flop. I just wanted him to prove that he was human, like the rest of us, and not a genius. It was no disgrace to lay a bomb now and then. Hardly anyone lives up to his build-up, especially in our business. His was too big, even if he had talent . . .

The last thing I remember clearly that night was the band playing "Chicago" and Joe E. coming out. He sure took over. Fast. Everything he said and did was wonderful, even the lines that had sounded like nothing in the columns. I didn't know if he was a genius but he was the greatest thing I had ever seen on a stage. He hit me like no other guy ever had. I was in love. The kind of love that comes once in your life, if you're lucky. The kind you never get over, completely.

But I couldn't get near him. He said hello when we passed but he didn't see me. I thought he had a wife or something but it was worse, he wouldn't date anyone in the show. I should have let it go at that but not Martha—I wanted him and I was going to make him want me. Who was closest to him? Jorge Sanchez. All I had to do was cozy up to Sanchez. I did. I got to sit at the same table with Joe, and twenty other people, but he had no eyes for me.

I thought I'd play it smart. I wasn't pushing. Nothing was giving either. It's lucky I was in the Copa with him for sixteen weeks, I never would have gotten next to him. One night we were sitting around between shows and Sanchez said, "There's a new joint opening uptown, let's go." That meant everybody and he ordered a flock of cabs. Joe asked one of the girls if she would like to walk over with him. She laughed, thinking it was a gag. Joe asked another girl and she looked at him as if he had lost his marbles. I wanted to scream, "I'll walk over with you!" but I didn't. I was still playing it smart, I wasn't pushing.

A third girl said no and I could see he wasn't giving up, he was going to find out if there was a chorus girl in New York who would walk from one night club to another. At last he reached me and I was so excited I just nodded, I couldn't talk.

"Let's walk through the park," he said and we did. I don't remember anything we talked about. Probably Sanchez. The only thing that mattered was that I was with him.

The next night he invited me to dinner. He was so shy, like a boy asking for his first date. And do you know something, he made me feel the same way. I never thought I'd feel that way again.

We stopped at Sanchez' table on the way out. "What's this?" Jorge cracked. "Are you moving in on my girl?"

"I'm declaring myself," Joe said, and I noticed he wasn't smiling.

I was Joe's girl for almost two years before marriage was mentioned. My mother mentioned it. Often. I knew it wouldn't be easy to sell Joe. Easy? Just about impossible, but I promised Mom I'd try. Not for her sake but mine. I wanted to be Joe's wife more than anything else in the world. I wanted a home and children. Joe's.

What a campaign! I knew that the only way I could move Joe was through his friends. Joe's friends . . . *they're* the story of his life. He lives for 'em and he'll die for 'em. When I think of Joe's friends, all the laughs and all the tears, all the happiness and all the pain come back. To get the job as Joe's wife I had to audition for Sanchez, Marovitz, Arnstein, Austin and Cassie, Toots, Swifty Morgan, his brothers Al and Murray, Basse, Jacoby, Harris, Bramson, Podell and so many others . . .

I don't know how it happened but almost all of 'em wound up putting the pressure on Joe to marry me.

"It wouldn't work," he kept telling me. I had a feeling he hadn't gotten Letty out of his system but it was more than that. The average man needs a wife, or thinks he does, which is the same thing. Joe isn't an average man. He came back from that terrible slashing, all the way to the top, without a woman. All those years he couldn't talk and couldn't make a dime, he had no woman to hold his hand and he didn't need one. He was used to living alone. Sure he got lonely but he knew a lot of married people who were a hell of a lot lonelier than he was. Joe is a sensible man in most things. He honestly didn't think marriage was the answer. He knew himself. And I didn't. I didn't even know myself.

But I pushed it. When I sang "The Object of My Affections" and "Till the End of Time" in the show I was singing only to Joe. It didn't move him. He came back with "Don't Fence Me In." I couldn't match songs with Joe.

Then he got sick. Liver trouble. It had been a long time catching up with him.

I was sitting with him in the hospital and I was scared. The doctor had just warned him that he must never take another drink. Joe started to come back with a gag but the doc, who had seen him work a few times, stopped him. "And the only reason you see more old drunks than old doctors at the Copa," he said, "is because the old doctors are too busy signing the death certificates of chumps like you, usually for cirrhosis of the liver."

I took Joe's hand after the doctor left. "As soon as you're out of here," I said, "we're going to be married. You're going to have a home and live a normal life."

Joe looked at me. "I'm too old—and sick. You're too young."

I wanted to cry. Sure he was in his forties and I in my twenties but I had a little mileage, and I was nobody compared to him. He opened up a whole new world for me. Quite a world, while it lasted.

He recuperated in Miami Beach, and it might have been because his resistance was low or because he was on the wagon, but I finally got him to say yes. All right, Mother did, if you want to be technical. Only he wouldn't say when. "Let's ad-lib the date," he said and Joe's a guy you can't press.

Time passed and nothing happened. Two or three of his pals were greasing the skids under me. They kept telling him I was a chiseler and I was out to take him. Finally I went to Marovitz and said, "Abe, you're Joe's lawyer. Draw up a contract that says I don't want anything from him. Put in there that I'll pay my own living expenses and if the marriage blows up, God forbid, or anything happens to Joe, I can't ever claim a cent of his money."

Abe said it was unnecessary but I said it was or there never would be a wedding. I didn't ask him but he got hold of Sanchez and Seymour Weiss, he's President of the I Love Joe E. Association, New Orleans Chapter, and they had a long talk with Joe.

"She *really* loves you," Sanchez told him. "She signed away everything."

"She has to be a hell of a girl to want to live with you," Abe told him.

"Or crazy," Weiss said.

Joe didn't make any cracks. "Martha knows my faults," he said. "I guess we'll have to live together as man and broad."

We set a date and a few days before the wedding was to take place Joe called it off. "Sanchez is in St. Francis Hospital," he explained. "Appendix."

He saw how that bulletin hit me. "I'm sorry," he said, "but there couldn't be a wedding without Sanchez."

"I didn't know I was marrying Sanchez," I said as sweetly as I could.

The wedding was postponed two weeks.

Three days later, my mother packed her things and said she was leaving.

"Now what?" I asked.

"I can't stand any more," she said, "and if you're smart you'll come with me. Do you know what happened last night?" Then she told me that two men who had the room next to hers in the hotel had been talking loudly and she couldn't help overhearing one say to the other, "Why is Joe marrying a tramp like Stewart?" The other, according to Mother, replied, "He doesn't want to but her old lady put the screws to him." Then Mother said she heard the first one laugh and say, "Joe knows what he's doing. He's post-poned it because Sanchez got a sudden attack of appendicitis. Joe's got a lot of friends as good as Sanchez and—ha, ha—you never can tell when your appendix is gonna act up, can you?"

Mother left Miami Beach and I sobbed most of the day. I had honestly believed Joe loved me, maybe not as much as I loved him, but who's weighing? Joe was full of gags but I had never heard of him saying anything mean or doing anything unkind to anybody. I knew he wasn't crazy about getting married but very few men are and I didn't think he wanted to get out of it *that* desperately. The Joe I thought I knew would have come straight to me and said, "It's off." This wasn't like Joe.

I stopped crying and asked a few questions. The man registered in the room next to Mother's was Doc Marcus. Doc Marcus! The fog was lifting. Doc was a practical joker, one of the best in the business. A couple of Joe's pals who did not love Mother, nor appreciate her interest in Joe, had put Doc up to the rib. What about the second man, the one Mother heard him talking to? Doc had been alone. He's billed as a magician but he's a better ventriloquist.

According to one of *my* pals, Marcus watched Mother check out and then said to a couple of Joe's pals standing by, "Well, boys, I did my part."

Joe was unaware of the horseplay, which is a strange thing to say about Joe, but I can't say he was heartbroken when Mother scrammed. As far as the marriage, he was ready any time Sanchez was.

At last the date was set, March 31st, but I was certain something would interfere with my becoming Mrs. Lewis, like a tidal wave or amnesia. With Joe you never know what the punch-line will be except that it will not be the one you expect.

When we got around to picking the place, Joe said he

would like to be married at his hotel, the Lord Tarleton. That was all right with me until I found out that he didn't mean in one of the reception rooms or banquet halls but in his bedroom! He couldn't understand why no one approved. "I like it," he said, "it's a nice room."

Marovitz got the Sapphire Room of the Bel-Mar Hotel. The day after I sent out the invitations Joe broke the news that the Sapphire Room was out and the wedding would be held at the Tarleton. I think I lost my temper. At this point I had no objections being married in a diving bell or a tree-house, as long as I was married, but the invitations had gone out for the Sapphire Room. Why the Lord Tarleton?

"Because the manager of the Tarleton, Walter Jacobs, is a good friend of mine. And he says he's going to feel hurt if we're hitched at the Bel-Mar."

This was the end. "Who," I shouted, "are you marrying me for—Walter Jacobs?"

"I will not have you rap Walter in my presence," Joe said and went looking for Marovitz to solve the new crisis. Abe refused to switch the wedding but he kept Jacobs in the act by giving the Tarleton the wedding dinner.

Phone calls and telegrams kept coming day and night from all over. Joe Kennedy—*the* Joe Kennedy—rang up and asked if there was anything he could do. Marovitz remembered that the Ambassador controlled Haig and Haig Scotch, among other things, and said yes, Joe, you can send a couple cases of whiskey. He sent three cases immediately and it was none too soon.

Justice Frank Murphy was supposed to come down from Washington to marry us but at the last minute he wired—collect—that a case had come up in Supreme Court and he was sorry but he couldn't leave. "A case of what?" Joe shot back.

The wedding was out of Damon Runyon.

Everything was set, just like Joe's song about the groom. Almost. The Sapphire Room was "very spacious" but the bride wasn't exactly "sweet and gracious."

> *The crowd was very quickly growing*
> *By now the hall was overflowing*
> *But where, oh where, was the groom?*

The groom was outside, standing in the loveliest Florida thunderstorm you ever saw. Not that he couldn't get in, he *wouldn't.*

"Joe, darling, you're holding up the wedding." I tried to keep my voice down, I didn't want to frighten him away.

"There will be no wedding," he said, "until my guests arrive."

"Guests!" I exploded. "Who *else* could possibly come?"

"You'll see." He had that boy-stood-on-the-burning-deck look.

"Lover," I tried to sweet-talk him inside, "there'll be no room for the groom."

No answer. He kept looking up and down the street.

I thought I'd be cute and sing. I was soaked and my dress was ruined but I had little hope left of ever using it. "The butcher is in, the baker is in, your uncle who plays horses in Jamaica is in . . ." Then I left his lyrics. "Every bookie, bartender and creep this side of Fifty-second Street is in. *Come on!*"

The next thing I heard was horns.

"There they are!" Joe was grinning like a kid.

A fleet of taxis was splashing and skidding down the street toward us, every driver riding his horn. The first cab pulled up and Joe opened the door. A boy in uniform stuck his head out. "Are we late, Joe?" he asked.

"Martha and I have been waiting for you, son." Joe helped the boy out. The cab driver was opening a collapsible wheel chair and behind, all the way down the block, the other cab drivers were doing the same thing. I watched him as he gently helped the boys into their chairs and shook their hands and patted their backs.

When the last one was wheeled in, he turned to me. "Now we can get married," he said.

I broke up. This was my Joe, standing in the rain, keeping hundreds of people waiting—including a lot of big shots—so he could greet every one of the paraplegics he had invited from the Army Hospital.

It was happening at last. I was walking down the aisle to the "Wedding March" and it wasn't a production number at the Copa or a movie scene, it was for real. It was real, all right. The guests were *applauding*! I thought the organist would go into "Chicago" any second.

The rain was pounding on the windows and as Joe passed Warren Wright, the owner of the Calumet racing stable, he said out of the corner of his mouth, "Sloppy track."

"But it's a winning entry," Mr. Wright said. I hoped to God it was.

The ceremony lasted thirty seconds, I was told. I don't remember anything except that Seymour Weiss gave me away and Abe Marovitz was the best man and finally Judge Okra said, "Martha and Joe, you are now man and wife." I kissed my husband and somebody said I had to throw my bouquet of roses. I did and wouldn't you know it, Sophie Tucker caught it.

Immediately the place was a shambles. Waiters and guests ripped all the gorgeous flowers and rayon decorations from the walls, as if they were breaking a set on a movie lot, and it was just about the same thing. In one minute flat the Sapphire Room was converted into its regular use—as the Hotel Bel-Mar Cocktail Lounge—and the drinking began. I know how Cinderella felt when her golden coach suddenly turned into a pumpkin, but I guess I should have known that if I ever got Joe to marry me it would have to be in a bar.

There were a few fights, naturally. Sophie Tucker found a stranger behind a potted palm and slugged him. "I despise party crashers," she said.

"So do I," replied the stranger, holding his head.

"Then what are you doing here?" Sophie demanded.

"I'm Joe E. Lewis' brother-in-law," my brother replied.

A select few, Joe's twenty closest pals, were invited to the dinner at the Tarleton. One hundred and fifty closest pals showed up. Harry Richman, a smattering of Marx and Ritz brothers and Sophie put on a terrific show. "No Room for the Groom" was the theme, naturally, and for a finale everyone stood up and serenaded Joe with "Sam, You Made the Pants Too Long." Sophie pulled up her dress. She was wearing long pants.

If I live to be as old as I look, to steal one of Joe's lines, that day—March 31, 1946—will be the biggest day of my life. Even though it ended on April Fool's Day.

28   *A Love Story (His)*

Getting married was Martha's idea. I said it would be more fun to live in sin.

It never had a chance.

It's easy to say Joe drank too much and gambled too much. I drank too much too. I could cop a plea and claim I had to in order to keep up with him but that would be loading the dice. Joe was on the wagon the first year we were married, just a little wine, and he cut down his gambling. Uh-uh, it went deeper. His drinking and gambling weren't causes but effects. I don't want to sound like a skull-crusher, I'm just a little singer from Kentucky and I don't dig the psycho bit, that's not my idea of what couches are for. But I was Joe's wife for two years and I think I know a little about him.

Getting a contract at Twentieth Century-Fox didn't help. Maybe I was foolish to take it but it seemed wonderful at the time, I thought it was my big chance. As often as I could get away from the studio I'd rush to the airport, full make-up still on, and fly to wherever he was playing. But there were months of separation. And I was the one who was going to make a home for him and force him to live a normal life. Funny, isn't it?

It was so hilarious Joe did a whole routine on it.

"Everybody thinks I'm lucky to be married to a movie star like Martha Stewart," it went, "and they're right. I'm lucky if I see her once in a while. When I'm in Miami she is in Hollywood. And when I'm in New York she's still in Hollywood. People think my marriage is glamorous and thrilling. How thrilling can it be on a long distance phone? I'm a guy with no memory." Then, to the music of "Chloe":

> *All alone I toss for hours*
> *Though I take two ice-cold showers*

Still I feel that pounding in my head.
And while my heart keeps madly beating
A voice within me keeps repeating,
"Martha!—Martha!"
How can I do my routine
With three thousand miles between us?

Maybe it was crude but, to use Joe's way of talking, I had
to admit it wasn't funny. The second chorus was more subtle.

Through the black of night
While I got to punch for yocks,
You're just punching clocks
For Twentieth Century-Fox.
Here at the club I do the act on my own
But in my boudoir how can I act alone?
Every comic's wife helps hubby work up his show
But I must get worked up with girls I hardly
know . . .
Love is calling me but I'd rather be with you.

In case anyone hadn't gotten the point, Joe went on, "Phil
Harris has Alice around. What a team! They sing and dance
and clown. She's contented to play five or six shows a day.
From my wife I can't even get one matinee . . ." Then,
doing a take-off of Eddie Jackson's Bill Bailey, he moaned,
"Martha, Won't You Please Come Home?"

It got big laughs but for me it wasn't a laughing matter,
particularly his line about getting worked up with girls he
hardly knew. Joe sticks too close to the truth in his lyrics. I
could have quit Twentieth but I wanted to be another Alice
Faye. I wasn't. After a while my layoffs got longer and I
was glad, now I had no excuse for not being a full-time wife.
The first thing was to get a home. Joe wouldn't discuss it.
I nagged him for months and, when he decided to spend

the summer in southern California, he weakened. He wouldn't buy a house, that much he didn't weaken, but he agreed to rent one on a trial basis and see if he could get used to it.

It was a pretty little bungalow on Londonderry Place off Sunset and Joe was miserable from the moment we moved in. Every day when he got up he picked up the phone and automatically called for room service. Poor Joe was completely lost. I tried to make his breakfast but the eggs never came out right. The only thing he got out of my cooking was a routine.

"I miss Martha's cooking," he would sigh during the act, "as often as I can. I'll never forget the first time she invited me to her apartment. She fixed a real Continental dinner, all French dishes, Kreplach suzettes, matzoh balls under glass. For dessert, a Southern creation. Pastrami and cotton candy. And chocolate-covered oysters. It was right after that dinner that I popped the question. I said, 'Where is the bicarbonate of soda?'

"My uncle came to dinner one night and she made Welsh rarebit. I'll never forget my uncle said it was the best Welsh rarebit he ever had. How can I forget? Those were his last words." Then he would sing to "Music, Maestro, Please":

> *Tonight I mustn't think of her*
> *Bring more seltzer please . . .*

Joe always wound up eating breakfast at the drug store, he had to go there anyway to get his scratch sheet and the paper. I tried to remember them but I'm not Dunninger.

The house was like a prison to him. I thought it might work if he could get accustomed to it. I wanted a home and children. When I mentioned children he got hysterical. "What would I do with kids?" he shrieked.

Londonderry Place lasted almost four months. We went back into a hotel and Joe had his two trunks, his room service, his four freedoms and no dirty dishes in the sink. He was happy and why not? He was home.

For me it was hell. Could be I'm queer but I hate hotels and I like privacy, *some* privacy even if it's only five minutes a day. That's not too much to ask, is it? Try and get it with Joe. No matter where he is, it's always open house in his suite. We were together but still separated—by his pals. Every city a new cast of pals—plus Swifty Morgan. I can't remember *not* seeing Swifty around. Joe and I were never alone.

I better change needles before you get the idea I have nothing but gripes and that I'm not grateful for those two years. I am grateful. I loved Joe and he was good to me. He never said an unkind word to me and I gave him cause. He never argued. If he didn't agree on something, he just gave that funny little shrug of his and let it go at that. Joe never learned how to be small.

One day in New York, it was our first winter, he asked me to go out with him, he wanted to show me something. "Some other day," I said. It was snowing and I didn't want to dress. But he insisted. He had that pixie look when he's pulling a gag and I wasn't in the mood for practical jokes but he pestered me until I gave in.

There was a crowd outside the Warwick and Joe ploughed through the middle of it, me behind. Nothing can be this funny, I thought, but I mushed on. At last I saw what they were gaping at, a brand new custom-built Chrysler wrapped in cellophane with a red ribbon and an oversized Christmas card, "To Martha—from Joe E." The Copa had given it to him as a bonus for breaking all house records.

Joe drives a car like he does everything else. Distinctively. I think that's the word. One time we were driving from New York to Florida. The first day we only got to Trenton, New

Jersey. "We'll make it up tomorrow," he said. We got an early start, drove all day at better than seventy an hour and shortly after midnight pulled into Newark. "I have a hunch we're lost," he said. "I better find a shorter way to Miami."

He called a bookie—who else? After he talked to him, he came back to the car all smiles. "Everything will be all right now. Max said to play Route 1 straight and lay a little on Route 17."

Yes, he talks that way off the stage too. Joe *thinks* funny. Like the time we checked into the Southern Hotel in Baltimore. A house radio was playing "My Old Kentucky Home." "This *is* old," Joe said.

He was having trouble with his feet. They're flat, y'know. His arches were killing him and Jacoby got him to go to a foot doctor. Measurements were taken for casts and Joe was given an appointment for a fitting the following week. "It's going to cost you a hundred bucks," said the doctor, "but it'll be worth it."

Joe came back the next week. The nurse soaked his feet in soapy water. After she dried them, she left the room to get the casts. While she was gone, Joe put on his shoes and socks, handed the receptionist a hundred-dollar bill and walked out. "That's what I needed!" he said.

And that Swifty. You could write a book about Joe and him. Swifty peddles those awful ties to his friends. Joe gags that he got his start in life hustling Sulka labels for Swifty. One time they had a little falling out and we didn't see Swifty for a couple of weeks. Then he sent word that he was very sick and wanted Joe's forgiveness before he died. We rushed over to Swifty's place. He was in bed and looked a little green at that.

"I'm dying, old pal," he groaned.

Joe told him he wouldn't die for at least a week or ten days but that didn't cheer him up. He kept moaning that he was dying and he held on to Joe's hand. Even I felt sorry for the old gaffer. We stayed an hour or so and as we were going out the door, Swifty cried, "Joe, there's one last favor you can do for old Swifty before he shuffles off this mortal coil."

"Sure, Swift," Joe said, "what is it?"

Swifty cried a little and said, "Please reach into my dresser drawer—the top one—and get some ties. Leave the hundred bucks on the table."

One night, when we were living at the Wilshire Palms in Los Angeles, Swifty said he was going over to Benny Siegel's place and asked us to go along. We had been with Benny— Bugsy, but not to his friends—the night before in Las Vegas. Joe had given Benny a guest shot at the Flamingo, his first appearance in Vegas. "Let's go," Swifty said, putting on that old tweed cap of his.

Joe gave Swifty a hard look. "Can't you see I'm listening to 'Gang Busters'? Tell Benny we'll catch up with him later tonight." Joe wouldn't leave "Gang Busters" for *any-body*. Swifty went to Siegel's place but he didn't stay long, he said we'd all get together at Slapsy Maxie's later on. But we didn't. A few minutes after Swifty left Siegel's house, someone stuck a shotgun in the window and blasted Benny's brains out. I often wonder where we would be today if Joe hadn't been such a nut about "Gang Busters."

"Too bad," Joe said when he heard about Siegel, "but like they say on 'Gang Busters,' crime doesn't pay . . . Well, not like it used to."

"Gang Busters" and "Superman." That was his other favorite. I used to ask him how he could stand "Superman." "Great guy," he said, "never loses a decision."

There must be thousands of stories about Joe and horses but my favorite is one that has never been printed. He was playing at the Colonial Inn in 1946 or '47, I always get them mixed, and Mert Wertheimer, as a gag, gave him a horse. Ben Jones, the trainer, and Ted Atkinson, the jockey, led the horse on stage for the presentation. It was a spavined, twenty-year-old plug. Suddenly it reared and pinned Joe against the wall. Fortunately, Atkinson had just given Joe a jockey whip and Joe used it. The horse got nervous or something and defecated, I think that's the polite word, all over the floor.

"Stop ad-libbing!" Joe said. "If it hadn't been him," he told the audience, "it would have been me."

And how about the time he was invited to the White House? George Dixon, the Washington columnist, had picked him up at the airport. Dixon flashed his press credentials at the entrance to the White House and started to walk through with Joe.

"I'm sorry, gentlemen," the Secret Service man at the door halted them. "Special passes only tonight."

Joe pulled a paper from his breast pocket and waved it under the Secret Service man's nose. Noting the red border, the agent bowed. "Oh, I'm sorry, sir. *You* can go right in."

"Too bad, George," said Joe and strolled in, still holding his official-looking, red-bordered scratch sheet.

That was the night he met General Eisenhower. Joe looked at his uniform and said, "I don't know where *you* were during the war. I looked for you all over the South Pacific and couldn't find you. I know you weren't *there*."

Always laughs—or tears. Never anything in between. That was the trouble.

I suppose I've got to get to Joe's gambling sooner or later and I might as well get started. Nobody ever gambled like Joe. I've watched Nick the Greek and I've heard about Titanic Thompson and Arnold Rothstein and other high-rollers, but none of 'em gambled like Joe.

He lost $56,500 one morning at the Beverly Country Club in New Orleans, $35,000 at dice and $21,500 at cards. He blew it in less than three hours, from 3:30 A.M. to 6:15, after a couple of bottles. All he said was, "I work fast." The word got around and Earl Wilson asked him how he felt the morning after. "Broke," Joe told him.

He lost $6,000 on a horse at Hialeah, a stiff named Honest Knave of all things. Joe went for $22,000 that day. That night his act was funnier than ever.

"I go to the track for exercise," he cracked. "That's how I work off my superfluous cash. Today I bet on a horse named Honest Knave. I watched him run all the way around the track. It was the most aggravating forty-five minutes I ever spent. It would have been a photo finish but by the time he came in it was too dark to take pictures. Lucky thing the jockey had his whip with him. Otherwise the mosquitoes would have killed him. I don't say he pulled the horse but I do know that when the horse came down the stretch his bit was under his tail. That I know."

Then he sang a crazy song, "A Race Track is Where Windows Clean the People," and for an encore he did a parody on "My Old Kentucky Home"—"My Old Unlucky Home in Hialeah."

My old unlucky home in Hialeah. That $22,000 would have bought a house. I hadn't given up the hope of having a home, not altogether. But, like Joe says, you could commit suicide by jumping off a pile of his losing tickets, and on nights like those I wanted to.

What can you do when you're married to a gambler? Either you quit or you stand around and watch him gamble. One Christmas I gave him a wallet and on it I had engraved, "Remember, Joe, no horse can run as fast as the money you bet on him." But he never carried it. Joe doesn't use a wallet, it takes too long to get to your money. A man who plays gin for five bucks a point is not for wallets.

One time at Vegas he gambled all night until eleven the next morning. By this time he was blind drunk and $21,000 ahead of the tables. I wasn't with him but Billy Wilkerson was. He got Joe to bed, took all of Joe's dough except a couple hundred and deposited it with the manager of the casino for safekeeping. "Don't give it to Joe," Billy told him, "until tonight when he sobers up."

Two hours later Wilkerson walked into the casino. Joe, freshly shaved and dressed, was arguing with the manager for more credit. He had gone through his twenty thousand plus in twenty minutes minus. Yes, Joe worked fast.

Once, at the Mounds Club, I think, he wouldn't sign a contract until the owner agreed to give him odds of eight to five at the craps table on numbers six and eight instead of the six to five the customers got. The owner put it in the contract, as a gag. Big joke. Joe lost every cent of his salary, and then some, on six and eight.

Thank God he has Marovitz. If Abe hadn't saved his money for him, Joe would be in hock. He was playing at Slapsy Maxie's in 1946—or '47—his luck was sour and he borrowed $10,000 from a big-time gambler. When it came time to pay he didn't have it. He wired Abe and Abe said no. Joe called him and said that the gambler was a very tough party. "Not as tough as I am," Abe said. "Give it to him next year." He didn't send the ten, not a quarter.

Joe told him off. "You're acting as if it's *your* money!" Abe didn't budge. A couple days later Joe cooled off and sent him a dozen silk shirts. Marovitz is his lucky charm and he knows it. One night he was losing heavily at Ben Marden's Riviera, well over ten thousand, when Abe came up to the table. Joe asked him for money and for once Abe said yes, on the condition that they go partners and limit their losses to five hundred dollars. "And you better win," Abe said.

"I'll bend every effort," said Joe, "and I come from a long line of benders." He got his rushes on the first roll and won $7,500. "*Now* I have to have a partner!" he growled.

One night in Reno he put a twenty-dollar chip on ten the hard way. Double feebee came out but Joe wasn't paid. During the roll his chip had mysteriously disappeared. He was so blind he hadn't remembered playing the number. He gave the stickman a tip and walked out. One of the players at the table ran after him and caught him half a block away. "Mr. Lewis," he told him breathlessly, "I saw the stickman steal your twenty-dollar chip! Let's go back and get your money."

Joe gave the fellow a hard look. "Go away, you stool pigeon!" he said disgustedly.

Sophie Tucker's opening at the Beverly Country Club, that was one for the book. I ran out of cigarettes and Joe went for some. It took him ten minutes. I smoked one, tossed the pack aside and started to leave.

"Hey!" he said, picking up the pack. "You're smoking *all* of these. They cost me $900."

He was afraid to tell me the truth. They had set him back $9,000. At the dice table.

It sounds amusing when you rehash it years later or when Joe gags it up on the floor but it wasn't amusing to live with day in and day out. I don't get any kick out of gambling, and I didn't think we needed two in the family, so I played the bar. How many stingers can you drink? Too many. I was miserable and desperate. Why did this sweet, gentle, wonderful guy have to ruin his life and mine drinking all night and playing those goddamn horses, dice, roulette wheels and cards? When I took it out on him he said, "You knew I was like this. Why did you marry me?" He had me there. I married him because I loved him but love wasn't enough.

Nothing changed, it was just more of the same. The same old circuit. The Copa, the Colonial, the Chez, Mounds, Ciro's, Vegas. Once in a while a new joint but a dice box is a dice box and a roulette wheel is a roulette wheel. There were always twenty guys around him. And Swifty Morgan. I was just another guy.

Our second anniversary, it was pathetic. Joe took me to

Ciro's for dinner and gave me seven presents, including a heart-shaped diamond earring and pin set. He was sweet but we couldn't con each other, there was nothing to celebrate. We were just two years older, two years unhappier. He didn't need me. I was in the way, I fouled up his routine. That's one thing he couldn't stand, having his routine disturbed. Nothing must be changed or moved from its usual place. Like the tooth paste, the soap or the portable radio. Little things but that's all we had, little things.

And the drinking. He made up for that year on the wagon. He would drink all night and never have a hangover. I'd be a basket case. But he was heading for a crack-up. Nobody could drink that much. He had been worried after his liver trouble and had gone to six or seven doctors for checkups. Every one had warned him that he must quit belting.

"I finally found a doc with guts," he told me one day. "He says I can drink."

I didn't blame him as much as his "pals." I don't mean his few real friends like Marovitz, Arnstein, Sanchez and one or two others. I mean the hundreds of so-called "pals" who drop into whatever club he's working and insist that he drink with them. Some are dreadful oafs who want to impress a girl or their boss or somebody how well they know Joe, and some are well-meaning friends who sincerely like him, but the result is the same. If Joe stops at their table during or between shows they slip him doubles and laugh like hell when he staggers away.

Maybe that's the secret of Joe's success. Audience identification, they call it in Hollywood. I guess most men want to *be* Joe E. They would like to be able to drink, gamble and whore around all the time out in the open instead of only once in a while when they can sneak away from their jobs and the old lady. They would like to be amusing and clever when they're drunk instead of mean and belligerent.

Martha Stewart finally becomes Mrs. Joe E. Lewis, March 31, 1946, in a Runyonesque wedding at a Miami Beach bar. Judge Abe Marovitz of Chicago (right) was the best man.

"I can't remember when Swifty wasn't around," Martha Stewart recalls of her marriage to Joe. The ubiquitous Harry (Swifty) Morgan (right) accompanies the Lewises, this time at the Stork Club.

Joe and his Four Freedoms: a scratch sheet, the newspapers, his mail and breakfast in bed at 2 P.M.

Joe with Gene Tierney, motion picture star, and Alfred G. Vanderbilt at the Piping Rock in Saratoga Springs, N.Y., in 1948.

They would like to be able to blow six thousand on a horse and make jokes about it. They would like to be brave bulls instead of scared jackals. I'm sure that's it. They want to laugh at their inhibitions, their frustrations, their ulcers and their creditors but they can't. Joe E. is the only man in the world who can make a living, let alone seven thousand a week, laughing at the law, conventions and respectability. That's why they worship him. He's proof that it *can* be done and there's some hope left for them. It's a national cult. I must have met a thousand of Joe's "pals" who looked me straight in the eye and told me they were in the Commonwealth Hotel on their way to Joe's room when he got cut up.

"They're killing you, Joe," I told him that night at Ciro's on our second and last anniversary. "They get crocked once in six months and it doesn't hurt 'em, but you have to get stinkin' *every* night, to satisfy your 'dear pals.' You can't go on this way . . . and neither can I." It wasn't a threat. I didn't mean it to be. His friends *were* killing him by making him drink with them.

He wasn't an alcoholic, he could quit. Joe drank to relax, because under the laughs he's as insecure as the rest of us. He can't stand being out of work three days. He'd go crazy if he couldn't do his act. He wouldn't know what to do with himself. He can't stand being alone. That's why he drank so much. He didn't require liquor, it was friends he had to have, and he thought the only way he could hold them was to play the drunk seven nights a week. It's tough to be that lonely, that desperate for people around you.

"You're going to die to please your friends," I warned him.

That had a great effect on him. He didn't say anything for a minute, then he looked at me. "Martha, my drinking goes back a long time. When I was still in high school I was voted most likely to dissolve."

What do you do with a man like that? Like I said, either you quit or you sit around waiting for a miracle to happen. I got tired waiting.

The blowup came in Vegas. It started out just like any other night. He was at the dice table trying to prove how many times four can come up hard and I was at the bar trying to prove how many stingers I could drink before *I* dissolved. I saw him every hour or two and begged him to quit but he said he couldn't, he was too far behind. At nine o'clock the next morning he was still behind. Twenty thousand. Quite a distance.

I had put away sixteen stingers, according to Cassie, who was looking out for me and keeping score. And I *felt* pain. Twenty thousand dollars' worth. That would have bought a wonderful house . . .

My dream house. Every night I dreamed of a different house but before I woke up every one turned into a nightmare house. Its windows had no curtains or even glass, only signs with $2, $5, $10, $15 Combination and $50 over them. And Joe was standing in front of *all* of them, like one of those mirror shots. The walls, floors and ceilings were covered with green baize numbered one to thirty-six, half red and half black. The furniture was cubist, all the tables and seats in different sized dice. I was in a king's size bed alone but I couldn't sleep because roulette-wheeled chariots kept pounding over the covers and the last one was always Honest Knave being driven by Swifty Morgan.

"You've had enough, Martha, let's go home . . ." I heard Cassie's voice and I felt her hand on my arm. Cassie meant well but she didn't understand. She was married to Austin, not Joe. Austin wouldn't bet that Easter comes on a Sunday if you gave him three to one. Austin drank a little but he wasn't a bottle man. Cassie didn't need a home. Austin was her home.

"You've had enough, Martha, let's go home . . ." Home?

A two-room shack behind a gambling joint, that's a home? I didn't care if it was El Rancho Vegas and if it was called a bungalow, it was still a shack. I didn't want to go there alone while Joe was still burning up all my beautiful houses on the hard four. It wasn't right. Cassie led me out into the most gorgeous sunrise I ever saw. Except that it wasn't sunrise; Cassie had thrown my pink cloth coat over my head.

Oh, was I ill. Joe came in at 11 A.M. and looked at me. I was a mess. "Serves you right," he said. "You've ruined your robe." Seymour Weiss had given us twin ice-blue silk robes as a wedding present and we were nuts about them. I looked at mine and bawled.

A few minutes later I staggered to my feet and started packing.

"What do you think you're doing?" Joe asked.

I told him I was leaving and getting a divorce.

He saw I was serious. "You can't do it."

"And why can't I? This is no marriage, it's a drunk."

"At least postpone it a while," he begged.

Joe had never asked for a favor since we started going around together. Was there some hope? Had he waited until the last minute to tell me he needed me?

"How long a postponement, Joe?" I had made it easy for him, all he had to do was declare himself.

"Until after I play the Copa."

I thought I'd flip. Until after he played the Copa? Starry-eyed, romantic Martha, I thought he was going to say, "Forever, darling," and take me in his arms. I'd played too many Technicolor musicals.

"What's the Copa got to do with our divorce?" I asked. "Has Julie Podell joined the Church?"

"If you can see your way clear," he said, "I'd appreciate it. Eli Basse has written three songs about you. They set me back a couple thousand and I'd like to get some use out of 'em."

I wanted to laugh and cry at the same time. "We'll arrange something." I continued packing.

"Hey, you forgot this." He handed me the robe I had ruined.

"That's not mine."

"Of course it is. You just took it off."

"I'm sorry, Joe, that's your robe. I packed mine."

"You packed mine!" he howled and went for my suitcase. He found the twin robe, freshly laundered, and took it. "You ought to be ashamed of yourself, Martha."

"Joe . . ."

"What is it?" he asked, holding on to the clean robe.

"Look at the breast pocket, Joe."

He looked. "No!" he screamed.

"Yes." The monogram was *M*. In my confusion a few hours previously, I had put on *his* robe instead of mine. Mine wouldn't have fitted him even if I had wanted to give it to him. And I didn't want to. I loved that robe.

Joe looked at the other robe as if he had lost his dearest friend. His face became harder than I had ever seen it. "Get your divorce," he said, "the sooner the better."

There was a terrific sandstorm but I got a plane out that afternoon. Half an hour later, I was told, Joe heard the drone of a motor. He looked into the stormy sky and saw a plane flying low. "I hope that ain't her back," he said.

We were divorced June 15, 1948. I asked for nothing and I got nothing, except the car Joe had given me for Christmas. Maybe I couldn't hold up my end of the marriage but I could stick to the agreement I had signed.

Joe was wonderful. He told all the columnists that he alone was to blame. "I promised Martha I'd stop gambling and I didn't. She couldn't reconcile herself to horses by day and dice by night, and I don't blame her." He was serious and asked them to play it straight but he ended on a gag. "It's the first time a wife ever named a horse as a corespondent. Boys, I swear I never went to bed with Citation."

Warren Wright's sure thing—the "winning entry" of March 31, 1946—was an also-ran. I came into Joe's life singing "Till the End of Time" and I went away torching "I'll Walk Alone." I was broken-hearted that horses, dice, roulette—and even that blue robe—meant more to him than I did. But I'm not kidding myself, my time with Joe was the best part of my life.

30   *Bill of Divorcement (His)*

Marriage is no good in show business unless you're Lum and Abner.

31   *Alone*

The divorce seemed to have had no greater effect on him than the marriage.

It had.

His routine of living was unchanged but he was not. Little things irritated him that had not bothered him before. He became increasingly impatient, even in his act. The first time it came in the open was at the Latin Casino in Philadelphia, less than three months after Martha left. He was singing his parody of "Riders in the Sky."

> *Will there be a race track up in Heaven?*
> *Because I'll never get even in this world,*
> *I can see . . .*

"You sure won't!" a heckler bellowed.

Joe stopped. "I can't talk to you now, pal," he said gently. "Where are you going to be later? I mean in about fifteen years." There was no retort and he continued his song.

> *If I thought my luck would change when I'm im-*
> *mortal*
> *I wouldn't have to leave this earth a nervous wretch*
> *Because I won't feel strange up there in Heaven's*
> *portals*
> *I'll see my horses that all died in the stretch.*

"You sure will!"

Joe spotted the heckler. He was heavy-set, about forty, the same nuisance who had interrupted his show at the Copa several times the previous month.

"It's amazing!" Joe studied his man. "Three heels in one pair of shoes."

"Funny! Funny! Who writes your material—Bob Hope?"

"Pardon me," Joe riposted, "but are you the victim of sex experiments?"

"You ought to know!"

Joe's face darkened. The audience was laughing with the heckler, not with him. This had never happened before. Or was it his imagination? Had he become edgy since the split-up? Or was his liver acting up? He did not know. He knew only that no one had ever annoyed him as much as this heckler.

"Brother, I worship the very ground that's coming to you." Joe did not smile as he spoke.

They met a few minutes later, and again the following

morning, in Magistrate's Court. The heckler—Martin Steinberg, a Brooklyn builder—had charged Joe with assault and battery. Joe called him on both counts and raised him one, a complaint of disorderly conduct.

Steinberg, who had been patched up at Mt. Sinai Hospital, testified that Joe had invited him into the kitchen of the Latin Casino, and then had slugged him and knifed him.

"Knife?" Joe was on his feet. "I don't even carry a pencil."

The magistrate, Keller H. Gilberg, asked Steinberg if he had done anything to provoke the alleged attack.

Steinberg's bruised face broke into a smile. "Mr. Lewis knows me. I'm what they call a heckler. I heckle loud. That's my style." He beamed, then his expression turned to hurt and surprise. "I don't know what caused Mr. Lewis to hit me. I love him! I follow him all over."

Joe took the stand. "I don't know this bum," he testified, "except that he's been lousing up my act for weeks. Last night he followed me into the kitchen, and he spit and swore at me. So I belted him. Do you think I should have kissed him?"

David Kraftsow, the Assistant District Attorney, asked for a dismissal of charges against Joe.

Steinberg was found guilty of disorderly conduct and paid a fine of one dollar plus $2.50 costs but the prosecutor refused to drop the charges of assault and battery and his bail was set at eight hundred dollars.

"Oh, Mr. Lewis, this is awful," Steinberg groaned. "I don't have the eight hundred."

Joe stared at him. "You don't expect *me* to pay *your* bail, do you?"

"Of course not. I have the money but not in cash." He took out his wallet and produced a plane reservation. "If you'd advance me the money on this ticket . . ."

Joe inspected the ticket and let out a howl. It was on a flight to New Orleans two days hence, the day Joe was scheduled to open at the Beverly Country Club in New Orleans.

A year later, on Joe's return to the Latin Casino, he was served with a subpoena to appear before the Grand Jury. He appeared but refused to prosecute Steinberg. Instead, he paid twelve dollars court costs and asked the Jury if he could be excused, it was noon and he had not yet gone to bed.

Steinberg gave up his contracting business and bought a night club, the Las Vegas on Fifty-fourth Street, New York. Joe went to it several times, to heckle his heckler, but never found him in.

One night a customer interrupted Joe's act with a loud, obscene remark.

"Please sir, watch your language," Joe chided him. "Remember there are musicians present."

The customer continued his vulgar monologue.

"He's drinking tonight and carrying a torch," Joe told the audience. "His wife left him in a fit of good taste."

That did not stop the abuse, either. Joe walked to the customer's table, picked up a cup of hot coffee and hurled it into the foul-mouth's face.

Another night, a boor who had not been house-broken became vulgar during one of Joe's songs.

Joe glared at him. "You can go home now," he said, "your cage is clean."

The boor continued to recite all the four-letter words in his vocabulary.

"Perhaps," Joe said, "you would like the microphone?"

"You're f——well right I would!"

Joe took his portable microphone to the boor's table. "Here," he said and slammed the mike into his mouth. No four-letter words came out, just teeth.

Many nights he would remain in his dressing room between shows to avoid pests. The standard bore would wrap his arm around Joe's neck, force him to have a drink, and then go into an inane conversation that rarely varied from city to city.

"Joe . . ."

"Yes?"

"I'm going to see Tom."

Joe had no idea who Tom was but experience had taught him that to ask would only prolong the agony. Instead, he responded, "Say hello to Tom for me."

"I will, Joe old boy . . . what else shall I tell him?"

Joe wanted to get away but the pest had a combination armlock-strangle and he had been the 1930 heavyweight wrestling champion at Lehigh. "Tell him to save his money," Joe said dully. He didn't want to encourage this boy.

"Ho! Ho! That's terrific! From *you*, Joe! And to *Tom*, of all people!" By now Lehigh was crying with laughter. While he was wiping his eyes, Joe extricated his head from the armlock-strangle.

"Oh, Joe, you *slay* me! But seriously, is there anything *else* you want me to tell Tom?"

These idiots irritated Joe now. They never had before. Not as much, anyway.

He was changing and so was his act. He lifted his sights above the bar, the dice table and the tote board, and he became aware of other worlds. He was commenting trenchantly on the affairs of the upper-case Operators who gambled continents and with millions of lives. "You got to be wise before you're witty," Josh Billings said. Joe was becoming witty.

Westbrook Pegler, an intimate friend from his Chicago days, had been aware of the transition in Joe's style for some time. In January, 1946, he had commented in his syndicated column:

"It is a strange thing to me that, although Joe E. Lewis made his reputation with the low-downest, dirtiest humor you ever heard, his best audiences were really nice and respectable men and women and I don't mean just mink trade but people who live right and go to church and don't even think along the lines of that humor, much less talk that way. It seemed that he hit them with a blackjack and stunned them and they lost their inhibitions and went along with Joe.

"But in the last year or so I have noticed that he has done less of that and has become a real good political satirist which I believe is a new line in night club comedy.

"Just to show you, one night recently at the Copa in New York, facing an audience that was pretty well along and hard to hold, anyway, he went on for more than an hour entirely in a satire about President Truman, starting with Mr. Truman's piano playing, and not even a smudge of dirt, and left them hollering for more."

He had opened a new frontier but he did not neglect his other domains. His raw material now came from the news— drama, society, sport and gossip as well as the front page— and no event was too momentous or too trivial for comment.

When the great thoroughbred Stymie was retired after winning more than $900,000 in purses, he sang—

> *If I broke my leg they would shoot me,*
> *Nobody would salute me,*
> *They would bury me with my face to Pimlico.*
> *I'd be out of circulation, but Stymie's on vacation,*
> *He's retired with my dough.*
> *While I'm working for Uncle Sammy*
> *He's sitting on his fanny,*
> *No more running in the mud, he's now in stud.*
> *All that grazin' and feedin'*
> *Comes from money I'm needin',*
> *And those thoroughbreds he's breedin' with my blood.*

South Pacific became the biggest hit on Broadway. Joe saw it, came out of the theatre and shook his head. "I don't know," he said, "*I* liked it! I guess it's all a matter of taste."

Austin played "Bali Ha'i" and Joe sang—

> *She and I started drinking*
> *First some Scotch and then some rye.*
> *Bye and bye this Chinese maiden*
> *Velly high, velly high.*

Austin cued him into "One Enchanted Evening." "One Enslanted Evening," Joe began and he ended the medley with "I'm in Love With a Wonderful Rye!"

The take-off was well received, except in *The New Yorker* magazine, whose critic reported that Joe's poor voice had not done justice to the music.

"Some nerve," Joe wrote Harold Ross, the publisher of *The New Yorker*. "What does he mean, a poor voice? I have *no* voice at all. Why don't you pay your writers more money so they can see *South Pacific?* This poor lad did not know it was a parody."

Ross chuckled and added the note to his file on Joe for a Profile, a project that was interrupted by Ross' death.

His longest-running gag ended in 1949 when he posed for a photograph that he had promised fifteen years previously. Joe Louis had retired as the undefeated champion of the world: he had been the titleholder longer than any man before him, eleven years and eight months, and had defended his crown against more challengers than anyone in history— twenty-five. And Joe had bet against him every time, except when he fought Schmeling.

Joe E. introduced his nemesis at the Copacabana and joked about the hex he had put on him.

"I believe," Louis responded, "this is the first time that

a Negro has been in this fine club." He shook Joe's hand. "I thank you, Mr. Lewis, for my people."

"You're welcome," Joe E. said, "and if anyone hits you, you call me."

"JOE E. LEWIS ON THE WAGON!"

The story in the New York *Post* was published as straight news. Earl Wilson, in an exclusive interview, claimed that Joe had told him he would never take another drink.

"I might even crusade against liquor," Joe was quoted.

If it was true, this was the greatest blow to bacchanalia since John L. Sullivan took the oath. Joe did not deny the story. He would not repudiate a newspaperman regardless of what was printed about him and it is likely, during a lost Lent, that he had said he would carry on for Andrew Volstead.

Joe's sole comment came a short time later in a new song.

I'm afraid I'm going normal and it's driving me in-
*   sane,*
People stare at me since I've stopped playing dice and
*   gin,*
I've even shopped around for a girl who'd like to
*   settle down,*
A sure sign that sanity is setting in.

I went to one of those guys
To be de-psychoanalyzed.
He said, "Close your eyes,
Relax, now what's your weakness?"
I said, "Doc, I'm at a loss,
I just refuse to play a horse."
He said, "You're suffering from Dementia Preak-
*   ness."*

The people that I know, about me they're worried so,
Because they know what brains I've got
And where I've got 'em.
So if I go nuts some day,
I know all my friends will say,
"Poor Joe E. Lewis, he blew his bottom."

I'm torn by two emotions,
First I'm sad and then I'm blue
Ever since my personality split in two.
Half of me always wants me to go to bed early
And the other half of me wants to know with who.

All sorts of crazy thoughts I've started thinkin',
Like givin' up my gamblin' and my drinkin'.
If I ever find my senses I'll become a mental case.

He continued to gag about Martha in his act. Not to have
mentioned her, to his way of thinking, would have been an
admission that he missed her and wanted her back. That
would have been out of keeping with his professional character. Joe E. had to preserve his reputation for having no
inhibitions, publicly.

"A man doesn't know real happiness until he's married,"
he jested, "then it's too late. Martha tells everybody we split
up because I never took her out. That's not true. I took her
to the track every day. My late hours bothered her too. The
first time I came home at 8 A.M. she hit the ceiling. She
was a poor shot. We were always fighting. Fight, fight, fight,
every day except for a half hour to listen to 'Life Can Be
Beautiful.' But I'm sorry we got divorced. I had my heart
set on having three kids. Just three. The Almanac says every
fourth child is a Hindu.

"Little things keep coming back. Like the way she did my

laundry. My shirts would come back so white. Especially the blue ones. Or the time I came home and she was crying because the dog had eaten a pie she had made for me. 'Don't cry,' I told her, 'I'll buy you another dog.' "

It was a cover-up. He missed her greatly and it was a blow to his pride, and to his hopes, when Winchell reported that Martha had selected his successor. Joe saw her at Shor's and wished her luck. All news, good and bad, had to be discussed on his forum and, in his late show, he commented:

"I saw Martha tonight and asked her what her new boy friend was like. 'Nothing like you,' she said. 'He's healthy. He has muscles like steel rails, shoulders like boxcars and he's as powerful as a locomotive.' I asked her, 'What track does he run on?' "

Martha remarried in haste and divorced post-haste. The rebound had little bounce.

Joe did not deviate from his routine, on or off the stage. He had developed his act, in form and precision, to its highest degree of perfection. The only records he could break were his own.

Joe Louis was an ex-champion now, beaten by Ezzard Charles and knocked out by Rocky Marciano. Joe Lewis was the champion.

He drew $328,000 in six weeks at the Copacabana, an all-time high. Joe had converted a third-class cellar that had never had a name act into America's foremost night club, a showcase for Durante, Martin and Lewis, Frank Sinatra, Tony Martin, Danny Thomas, Sid Caesar, Lena Horne, Nat (King) Cole, Billy Eckstine, Peter Lind Hayes and Mary Healy, Kitty Kallen and Eddie Fisher, among other outstanding talents.

When Jerry Lewis lifted Joe's routine of taking drinks from ringside tables, Joe smiled. "I don't mind," he said, "but it may make the boy a drunkard."

The grand ballroom of the Waldorf-Astoria Hotel was crowded to capacity the night of November 3, 1950.

A lot of Scotch and water had passed under the bridge in the twenty-two years since Joe's last testimonial banquet. The money, he was told, would go to the Friars Club building fund—but it was still a benefit for him. He needed friendship as much as he had needed money in 1928.

More than twelve hundred people paid $53,000 to honor Joe. Bernard Baruch had purchased his own ticket and sat at an adjoining table to another elder statesman, Swifty Morgan. Sanchez came from Havana, Marovitz from Chicago and Harris from Los Angeles. Pegler made one of his rare public appearances and his arch-enemy, Quentin Reynolds, was the master of ceremonies.

"Above anyone else, Lewis has the gift of inspiring laughter," Reynolds extolled him. "He makes men laugh at solemn pretensions, he makes them laugh at fools, he makes them laugh at each other and in their common laughter they become brothers again. When men are laughing, there is no room for evil in their hearts."

The highest and the lowliest of Broadway, the champions and the never-wases, Newport dowagers and Harlem madames mingled with the elite of Hollywood, Washington's top diplomats, billionaires from Texas and the aristocracy of Chicago's underworld.

Joe E. belonged to all of them.

Sophie Tucker, the indestructible, sang as lustily for him as she had at the Oriental Theatre in Chicago a generation previously. The little girl he had discovered at the Trocadero, Judy Garland, came from California to serenade him with the songs she had sung for him on her first audition. Frank Sinatra and Toots Shor did a slapstick comedy act climaxed by Sinatra hurling an oversized custard pie in Shor's face. Eddie Cantor, Danny Thomas, George Burns and James Barton added their tributes. Milton Berle, the

Abbot of the Friars, presented Joe with a life membership and said, "His every breathing moment is devoted to doing things like a champion."

The last toast was made and the last song was sung after a three-hour show, a song written for the occasion and sung by Tucker, "We All Love You, Joe."

"I don't know how to tell you how much all your speeches affected me," Joe responded. "After all, there are ladies present. Some of the things you have said here have all but ruined a bad reputation that has cost me thousands of dollars to build up. Still, I am grateful for your generous gesture in giving me this banquet. It was also nice to give me a life membership in the Friars Club, even though after all those long speeches the value of a life membership has been cut in half. It's still nice."

He turned to Abbot Berle. "Thanks, Milton." Joe turned away. "Waiter!"

A waiter hurried to the dais.

"Take good care of Mr. Berle tonight," Joe told him. "Give him everything he needs. A knife, fork, napkin—pencil—everything." He turned back to Berle. "I really didn't mean that crack, Milton. I want you to believe me. And the only way you can believe me is by breaking the pencil."

Joe looked at the crowd and his eyes became misty. "Thanks for all the nice words," he said humbly. "I'm glad you said them while I'm alive."

It is loneliest at the top. There is no place to go except down. In his case there was not even the stimulation of competition. There were no contenders because there was only one of his kind. It was impossible to imitate or duplicate him. McGurn's knifeman had carved only one masterpiece.

It was, in the words of Dickens, "the best of times, it was the worst of times . . . it was the spring of hope, it was the winter of despair." He, like his America, had faced his Armageddon and they had both won—or had they lost? He had won the love of thousands and had lost the only two women he had ever wanted.

The world was trying to find its peace with threats, ultimatums, blockades, conferences, declarations and pacts. He was trying to find his peace with a scratch sheet, a dice box, a bottle of whiskey, a joke and a song. From now on, he knew, one year would be the same as the last, only lonelier.

The lights were going out . . .

Jimmy Walker had been a Number One, until he had slipped and gone down the drain. Runyon wanted to cover his funeral. Three weeks later, Damon went to his own funeral. Joe and Damon had had lots of laughs together, before Damon lost his voice and everything else. Runyon had been a Number One too. And he had died broke, his illusions gone with his money, his ex-wife, his home, his prize fighters, his horses, his wardrobe, his power and his fading byline. The Big Bug had devoured all of the props, and then the man who had collected them. Mark Hellinger, who had written so many columns about him, had been the next. Dead at forty-four. Five years younger than Joe. His pal Eddie Duchin was gone, dead of leukemia at forty-one. Eight years younger than Joe. Then Jolson went, with all his fame and all his millions, alone in a hotel room, with his piano player.

His stage was emptying.

I'm a lucky bum, he thought. If I hadn't been cut up I would have been just another comic. The knife sharpened my brain, made me think. Made me slow down too, improved my delivery. It took fifteen years but that's not so long, after you've lived 'em . . . Lucky that fuse blew out. He hadn't thought of that fuse since it blew out, in the early '30's. It happened on radio station WMCA in the old Hammerstein Building one Sunday night. He was introducing a new song, reading the lyrics from a song sheet, when the lights went out. He didn't know the words but continued the song, ad-libbing the lyrics. He never sang a song straight again. He had learned the art of parody, by accident. Thanks to a worn-out fuse. I'm a lucky bum, he thought.

It was 6:30 A.M. He picked up the morning paper, asked Charley the cab driver who he liked at Belmont, and continued along Madison Avenue. It had been a big night at the Waldorf and like all nights, big and small, he would wind up at the Warwick alone, with his two trunks.

Joe E. Lewis, Single. That was his billing and his biography. There was a girl now and then, always young, always pretty, always a stranger. Not too often, though. He had to space them. The young ones could kill you, and he would be fifty years old on his next birthday.

Fifty . . . He shuddered. Who wanted to be fifty, except a guy seventy? Fifty . . . that's when it takes twice as long to rest and half as long to get tired. He smiled. He would have to put that line in the act.

Letty had called it. The act had become his life. And his life had become the act.

the fifties

JOE'S

*"The last ten years went fast,
the next ten we'll go fast."*

JOE E.

The ides of March, 1951, and Senator Estes Kefauver had overtaken Joe's good friend, Frank Costello.

"Mr. Costello," shrilled Rudolph Halley, Chief Prosecutor for the Senate Crime Investigating Committee, "you have admitted receiving eight thousand dollars a year from Phil Kastel of the Beverly Country Club in New Orleans. What did you do to earn that money?"

Costello replied carefully, "I'd go out and look for an act and if it looked good—like Joe E. Lewis—I'd call him up and tell him we needed him."

Halley smiled contemptuously at the gambling overlord. "Does it require an expert to pick out a headline star like Joe E. Lewis?"

Costello's hands, the New York *Journal-American* reported, "fluttered suppliantly as if praying for a right answer." Costello went to prison and the Beverly Country Club went out of business, as did several other gambling blinds masquerading as night clubs, including the Colonial Inn in Miami Beach and the Mounds Club in Cleveland.

The heat was on, and Joe put it to song to the title tune from the Broadway musical hit, *Wish You Were Here.*

> *They're not letting the boys make book this year,*
> *Wish you were here.*
> *Because I thought I'd get back what they took*
> *Last year.*
> *The handwriting on the wall brings no joy*
> *Since they rubbed off the name of Kilroy,*

And I shed a tear because it says very clear,
"Kefauver was here."

Everyone laughed except Joe. Kefauver had ruined his schedule.

Operators like Costello and Kastel, eager to attract Joe's select following of high rollers, had been happy to pay him $7,500 a week for as many weeks as he would give them, especially since he usually left his salary, and interest, on the tables. Now the gamblers' comedian had lost his gamblers and he had to look for new markets, without game rooms.

Pittsburgh . . . Houston . . . Galveston . . . Reno . . . San Francisco.

He looked over the itinerary Bramson had made for him, and he was apprehensive He had never appeared in these cities or even in the surrounding territories. There would be no waiting claque of old friends—as there were in New York, Miami Beach, Chicago and Hollywood—his faithful Hamelinites who would laugh before he said a word, and request the songs he had sung for them every year for twenty years or more.

Pennsylvania . . . Texas . . . Nevada . . . Northern California.

This was the hinterland. Its favorite comedians were Bob Hope, Jack Benny, Eddie Cantor, Groucho Marx, Jimmy Durante, Milton Berle, Fred Allen and Pinky Lee—funnymen who had entertained them in movies, radio and now television, the mass media of entertainment in which he was unknown. He was essentially a comedian for the chi-chi set. How chi-chi was Pittsburgh or Galveston? How would his smart and sometimes gamy material react upon people accustomed to a high content of corn in their humor, people who went to work instead of to bed at 7 A.M.?

The first stop was the Carousel in Pittsburgh.

"Joe E. Lewis busted an old skepticism wide open," *Va-*

riety reported. "Although he's been in show biz thirty years, this is his first time in Pittsburgh, a real ripley. Owners here have long insisted that Lewis' brand of stuff is strictly for the sophisticated gambling and racing centers, and not for insular, strait-laced communities like western Pennsylvania's leading metropolis.

"Bunk, pure bunk. Could be that none of them up until now wanted to shell out the kind of dough Lewis is getting, or more likely that he was content with his regular New York-Miami-Las Vegas-Chicago-Hollywood-Atlantic City run, and didn't need to add any new stopovers. At any rate, now that he's finally hit Pittsburgh, they're not going to let him pass up the place in the future.

"For Joe E. proves there aren't any boundaries for his brand of class, and that the hepsters are universal. For more than an hour, Lewis had them eating out of his hand with quickies, tales, parodies, cuffo bantering and his usual assorted mixtures. It's no longer strictly a question of material with Lewis, for the style is the important thing.

"The guy has charm—that's the best description of it—a warm, friendly, affable, pixieish, slightly Rabelaisian kind of charm that puts an unmistakable stamp on everything he does, whether it's good, middle-ground or even somewhat indifferent. Lewis always seems to be having such a good time up there himself, giving off the impression that this is fun and not work, that nobody out front can fail to catch the contagion.

"The ad-lib quality of the whole turn gives it the sort of freshness that cafes seldom see these days. Socko is hardly the word for his Pittsburgh debut. It's downright explosive."

His next conquest was Texas.

It made no difference where he played—the Studio Lounge in Galveston, the Adolphus Hotel in Dallas or the big Shamrock in Houston—the result was the same. He broke the record of every room.

One night in Galveston, he ended a show with a throw-away line, "Good night, ladies and gentlemen, and I want you to know that I am available for weddings, private parties, graduations and meat-market openings."

A stranger barged into his dressing room. "Mr. Lewis," he said, "I want to hire you for a little party I'm giving a few friends."

Joe smiled. "That was just a gag, podner."

"I like your gags, Mr. Lewis," said the stranger. "The party is a week from Sunday at my home in Dallas. I'll send my plane for you."

"I told you it was a joke. I only work in night clubs."

"The decorators will take care of that." The Texan chuckled. "My living room is bigger than a lot of these clubs. By the way, will ten thousand be all right?"

Joe did a take. "*Ten* thousand?"

The Texan misconstrued Joe's shock. "I'm not going to haggle, Mr. Lewis. Let's call it twelve thousand five for the night, and expenses. How about it?"

Joe shook his head. "My fee for private parties is ten thousand. That's enough."

One evening, on the floor at the Adolphus, Joe was discussing Topic A in Texas. "Money isn't everything," he said. "It can't buy poverty. For that matter, a man worth ten million is just as happy as a man worth eleven million."

"That's what you say!" a customer shouted.

"It's nice to be with friends," Joe commented, "even if they're not my own."

"You said it!" the heckler bellowed.

"One wonderful thing about this audience," Joe went on. "Eventually it leaves."

The heckler became louder and more insulting.

Joe glared at his critic. "You make a perfect stranger," he said. "Even Dale Carnegie would turn you over to Ripley."

The next day, Joe was invited to a cocktail party given by one of the wealthiest oilmen in Texas.

"Remember me, Joe?" his host asked when they were introduced.

Joe was embarrassed. "I'm sorry, sir, but I don't."

His host beamed. "I'm the guy who kept topping you last night!"

San Francisco was a repetition of Pittsburgh and Galveston.

"Joe E. Lewis brought a breath of the 1920's, an air of the Scott Fitzgerald aspirin age, to the Fairmont Hotel," William Hogan wrote in the San Francisco *Chronicle*. "He is a pixie personality, but with urbane earthiness, a Runyon character who sings. He is from the era of Jimmy Walker, high-toned speakeasies, Paul Whiteman and the mobs."

"Add San Francisco as another hot-town on Joe E.'s sawdust trail," *Variety* reported. "He sets the customers to gibbering in their drinks and leaves his worshippers satiated with the conviction that they have lived again. At last they no longer have to travel to New York, Las Vegas and other points to get their fill of Lewis nectar."

He formed new friendships and renewed old ones. One night, during his act at the Riverside Hotel in Reno, he recognized an old pal at a ringside table but could not recall his name. "I know this man's name as well as my own," he said aloud. That did it. His memory responded and he addressed the customer properly, "Hiya, Joe."

Joe E. had become a national character. His life was dramatized on the CBS television network by Red Buttons and the Lewis magic that had touched Judy Garland, Deanna Durbin and Mary Martin brought Buttons stardom and his own show on CBS.

Reader's Digest and other magazines quoted him, especially when he lampooned politicians. He needled friends and foes equally.

Among Joe's friends was Averell Harriman. On his first visit to the wealthy diplomat's mansion in New York, a buffet supper was served in one of the drawing rooms but Joe could not find it. He tarried at the bar in another salon all evening.

"You got a nice place here, Av," he told his host as he was leaving, "but I don't think you'll make it pay. You don't serve enough food. And those paintings on the wall . . ." Joe shook his head. "Stick up a couple nude broads."

When Harriman was campaigning for the Presidential nomination at the 1952 Democratic Convention in Chicago, Joe was one of his stanchest supporters. He plugged for him in his show at the Chez Paree and helped his old sparring partner, Franklin D. Roosevelt, Jr., Harriman's campaign manager, distribute buttons, pennants and literature.

One morning during the hysteria of the pre-balloting stage, Joe stepped out of an elevator in the Hotel Blackstone and was greeted effusively by Harriman, who was standing in the lobby with a group of his supporters. Harriman wrapped his arm around Joe's shoulder and introduced him to his friends.

"I missed you last night," Harriman said.

"Last night I was campaigning all over town for you," Joe said. "And I got stiff."

Harriman's face darkened. His eyes were riveted on Joe's unadorned left lapel.

"Joe! Where's your campaign button?"

"Today I'm sober," Joe replied and walked away.

The crack reached the rabbit ears of Westbrook Pegler, who was covering the convention, and he asked Joe's permission to print it. Joe refused. Pegler was one of his closest friends but he would not sacrifice one friend for another.

Pegler, not a Harriman admirer, was eager to use the gag

but knew it was futile to argue with Joe. Almost anyone else would confirm an amusing line he had authored, for the publicity value of a favorable mention in Peg's column, but not his pal Joe. Once, during a drinking bout, he had promised Joe he would write a piece about him.

"I'd rather have one line from Winchell," Joe had replied, "than your whole column." Winchell's niche in Pegler's affection adjoined Eleanor Roosevelt's.

Pegler had laughed and written an entire column on Joe, a solid rave.

"Who reads it?" Joe had gibed.

Pegler's presence in Chicago for the convention meant an extra shift for Joe. They made their nightly milk-route after his last show at the Chez, an itinerary of the low resorts on the North Side, the stamping ground of their youth. They usually walked, in a manner of speaking, from one deadfall to another, but one morning in the past Joe had ridden majestically down Clark Street on a pushcart they had appropriated and that Pegler, having lost a bet, had been obliged to push.

"That night," Pegler recalls, "we holed up on the North Side and were sitting in a booth with some bums of both sexes when, it being summer, I felt moist and reached my right hand inside my jacket to scratch myself on the tit.

"With a roar of alarm, Joe half leaped across the table, grabbed my hand out and bellowed, 'Never do that in here.' The chivalry in that place carried little holsters in that position usually containing a pistola called a Spaniard."

They were boon companions, the relentless crusader who fulminated against sin and the elfin Debureau who advocated it.

"One night, although it was really along about four in the morning," Pegler recounts, "we got into a spell-down with a well-digger in a place on Clark Street and this well-digger spelled both of us bow-legged with one hand tied behind him, and a nice-looking, rather stout barmaid named Agnes refereed.

"This girl said she was a high school graduate and I guess she was, all right, but the well-digger said he had barely tagged grammar school and just spelled by ear. You meet some very unusual and interesting people in such places at such times."

One morning at 10 A.M., Robert Ruark tells the tale, Joe and Pegler were searching for a Turkish bath. "Suddenly Joe turned to Pegler and said, 'You got a reputation for guts. I wish to see how brave you are. We will now go stick up this bank.'

"'Lead on,' Pegler is alleged to have remarked, 'we will heist same.'

"Joe pulled his overcoat menacingly around his neck and swaggered up to the bank dick. He had his hand shoved deep in his pocket. 'This is a stickup,' he said. 'You go in that bank and bring me back five G's. No monkey business.'

"The bank dick looked at him for a long moment. He spoke.

"'Tsk, tsk,' he said. 'Oh, Mr. Lewis, you're drinking again.'"

Pegler avers that the account is true, except that Joe did not order the policeman to grab five grand. "Joe distinctly said one hundred thousand," swears Pegler.

"If Truman had made two more speeches," Joe commented after the Republican landslide, "Ike would have taken Canada."

The ex-President, Joe claimed, applied for the job as his accompanist and, though he had once serenaded him at a National Press Club banquet with a plea, "Mr. Truman, Why Don't You Be Human and Play the Piano for Me?," he had had a change of heart since the election, as he explained in song.

Dear Mr. Truman, though you're at liberty,
My act is all filled up with Mack and 4-star
   Hennessey.
In the meantime, don't call me, I'll call you.
I'm sure that you could handle the position.
From the way you ran the country up till 1952
I always knew that you were a musician.

When the folks began to cry
That their taxes were too high,
To each one you did reply with Music! Music! Mu-
   sic!
And here's a good suggestion, if you've got your fu-
   ture planned,
And a musical career is your ambition,
With those State Department guys you could organize
   a band
That would give Phil Spitalny competition.

"President Eisenhower is doing a wonderful job," Joe commented after the new administration had been in power six months. "Ike has surrounded himself with great advisers. Ben Hogan, Sam Snead . . . Next year there will be a golf club in every garage."

His comments, on Democrats and Republicans alike, became more incisive. He had become the keen political satirist Pegler had prophesied he would be more than seven years previously.

When Stalin died and Malenkov took his place, Joe confided to his devotees, in the confidential manner of a Drew Pearson, what had actually taken place inside the Kremlin. "Molotov was supposed to get Stalin's job, but at the last minute they had to bring in Malenkov. Molotov refused to sell his General Motors stock."

His interest in global affairs increased, but he did not neglect the livelier arts.

One night, when Dr. Alfred Kinsey's report on sexual be-
havior and misbehavior had become a best seller, Joe announced, "If Dr. Kinsey is in the room, I'd like to say I
don't know where it's all going but I'm not getting my
share. Still, in my book, he's okay."

Christine Jorgensen inspired a song which Joe dedicated to
the doctors of Copenhagen, "They're Breaking Up That Old
Gang of Mine." Contemplating what would happen if he
changed from Joe to Josephine, he sang—

> *My voom will lose its boom*
> *My key will range above high C*
> *But I sure dread the day*
> *When Austin Mack looks good to me . . .*

He parodied the passing show, from the song hit, "Diamonds Are a Girl's Best Friend."

> *When oysters and clams don't affect your condition,*
> *Doc Diamond is a man's best friend.*

—to the Gentlemen of Distinction in the liquor advertisements:

> *Men of Distinction are so in demand.*
> *In the bedroom he's never a bore*
> *For instance, when they score,*
> *They say they've tallied,*
> *Men of Distinction are grand.*

—to the British movies in a hymn by Eli Basse—

> *Why don't those British films have English titles*
> *So Americans can understand the plot?*

I don't mean to be a crank
But I'll be frank, J. Arthur Rank,
Your British actors they don't talk so hot.

When a guy says, "Blymie blast those bloomin'
*   Jerries,"*
Can't you print the English meaning down below?
What do they mean when they say, "Carry on"?
Is a privy seal the key that locks the john?

And why do they shout "pip, pip" before they sing?
To me two pips can only mean one thing.
I do my own translating and that's why I assume
That a lady in waiting is a lady who's trying
To get into the powder room.

You've got a House of Rothschild, and history records
You've got a House of Commons
And you've got a House of Lords.
Egad, m'lad, how come so many houses without
*   broads?*
*   (to "God Save the King")*
But there'll always be a Brooklyn,
Where English is spoken,
And as long as there's an England,
English will be spoken—broken.

Television ultimately became important enough for him to acknowledge, and he dedicated a song to Faye Emerson, "The Lower the Neckline, The Higher the Hooper."

Though Uncle Miltie with money he's filthy,
Like Cantor and Hope, I declare
Those guys are three aces, but on TV three aces
Can't even beat a small pair.

The lower the V-necks, the higher the TV checks,
A fact we just cannot ignore.
With talent they're choosy,
They won't hire a chanteuse
If her voice is not a perfect 44.

So Mr. Paley, I'll play a ukulele,
I'll go with Jack Haley or I'll sing "Eli Eli,"
But I'll never wear a low-cut gown.
Tattoos are ugly, I'll never wear a low-cut gown.

"Television is here to go," he announced. "It will never replace the old-fashioned keyhole. And what about the poor bar owners who can't afford television sets? One I know had to put in live wrestlers." Then he explained in song why he would never be on a network, "Because You Can't Drink VO on TV."

I don't like steady work unless I'm unsteady.
I'm "Happy go Lucky," when I drink Old Kentucky!
They're so strict with a gag,
You can't say broad or a hag.
Give me those old night clubs, where a fag is a fag.

He lifted a highball from the piano top for a toast.

Here's to your networks, CBS and NBC,
You can keep television because I like privacy.
When I do a matinee, there'll be no cameras on me!
Please close the transom . . . I'm too sexy for TV.

Television's Vice-Presidents in Charge of High Dudgeon would have taken umbrage if the barbs had come from any other entertainer. Instead, CBS made him a fabulous offer

"The Elmo Lincoln of the keyboard," Austin Mack, Joe's accompanist for 17 years, and Milton Berle in Joe's dressing room at the Copacabana, New York. *Photo by Bill Mark.*

"The horses I follow follow other horses," Joe warns Cary Grant as Jorge Sanchez, wealthy Cuban sugar planter, looks on at the new Las Vegas Race Track in 1953. This is the only track in which Joe has not gone broke. He did not have time, the track went broke first.

"For my next number, in a voice that has kept me out of motion pictures for twenty-five years—" Joe E. at El Rancho Vegas, June 1955. *Photo by Dave Lees.*

to make his television debut on Ed Sullivan's "Toast of the Town."

Joe was genuinely surprised. "I'm still trying to get on radio," he said.

The skeptics were positive that he had made a mistake this time. Many of the greatest names in show business had tripped over the coaxial cable. It was not an indictment of their talents, only that their styles were incompatible with television. The Cassandras quoted Joe's own words. He couldn't drink VO on TV, he couldn't call a fag a fag, he couldn't clean up his act for Uncle Miltie's nephews and nieces. At Lindy's they were laying seven to five Joe could not get up in time for the show.

Joe appeared on the show sober, his material was as chaste as Mary Margaret McBride's, and he was such a brilliant success that Sullivan brought him back for a second show and a third.

"Just think, Joe," Sullivan reminded him on the stage, "this is your third time on 'Toast of the Town.' "

"And just think, Ed," Joe responded, "I haven't been paid for the first time."

"Don't worry about the money. Just play ball with me. You won't be sorry."

"That's what I have been doing, Ed. Playing ball. Tonight opens my one hundred and fiftieth inning. And according to my latest Hooper rating, seventy per cent of the people in this studio are not listening."

The crowd roared and Sullivan withdrew.

"There he goes," Joe said, "the Smiling Irishman. The greatest smile since Ned Sparks. He lights up a whole room just by leaving it. I used to know Ed when he was a greeter at Forest Lawn Cemetery. He had to quit the job, it was too dangerous. They tried to bury him three times."

The crowd gave him a big hand, ad-libbing without the customary applause cards.

"Not too much applause, please," he implored, "this happens to be a very old theatre." He became confidential. "I'm appearing under a handicap. First of all, I just got up. Do you know what it means to eat oatmeal at seven o'clock at night? Another thing, I'm not used to working in a place that is cluttered up with sober people. But I'll do anything for Sullivan. He might be stingy with other actors but when he comes to me, I'm no exception."

He had to get laughs without championing drinking, gambling, or moral turpitude, and he did. His approach to world news was novel to a public educated by John Cameron Swayze.

"There's one nice thing about living in Russia," he said. "It's impossible to lose an election bet. I'm not afraid of the Russkys, and believe me, they will never invade our country. They couldn't find a place to park."

He converted his raffish humor to the canons of television and it lost little of its amusement.

"I saw a swell murder mystery on 'Suspense' the other night," he recalled. "A witness said that the victim had been shot, strangled, poisoned, machine-gunned, then tied and thrown in the river. The detective listened and said, 'Hmmm. Tell me, were any of his friends practical jokers?'"

The audience howled and Joe went into a jig. "I learned dancing from Arthur Murray," he said. "Later I found it was more fun with a girl."

Joe yawned. "I didn't get my rest last night. I certainly envy you people in the audience who are sound asleep." He signed off with a special song, "Darling, You Forgot to Turn Off the Electric Pad and Now I'm the Toast of the Town."

The response was tremendous and NBC requested his earliest availability to appear on the "Colgate Comedy Hour." Joe E. had discovered a new medium and vice versa.

The early '50's had brought many things but their greatest rewards and penances were yet to come. He would become the most honored man in his profession. He would become gravely ill, and he would continue to entertain people while he fought for his life. He would be reunited with Martha, for a time.

And he would play his third act as if it were his first.

33   *Anniversary*

On April 1, 1953, Joe's pals bought twenty-five pages in *Variety* at four hundred dollars a page to commemorate his thirtieth year in show business. Not since Mark Hellinger's wake had there been such an effusion of love.

As he read the special edition, there was a rush of memories and emotions.

The Friars Club page saluted him as "The Nicest Guy in the World."

He wished that he deserved the words. And, he thought, how long ago it was, and yet what a short time, since Johnny Black had taken him to the Friars Club for the first time and said, "Joe, someday you will be a member."

Another valentine, "From One of the Younger Set," carried no name, only a nose.

Was it a quarter of a century since he had tried, so miserably, to follow Jimmy Durante, Eddie Jackson and Lou Clayton at the Parody Club? It was.

"To my Sweetheart—Love," read Sophie Tucker's page.

Sophie. The last time she had come to the Copacabana, he had introduced her as "The Judy Garland of the Stone Age." When she had refused to respond, he had gone on,

"But I admired her war work. For a time, though, I was afraid the Confederates had captured her." She was the most remarkable personality he had ever known in his profession, and the warmest-hearted.

"Next to Joe E. Lewis," Eli Basse confessed in his ad, "I love Joe E. Lewis best."

Eli had been an obscure hoofer when he met Joe. "Lewis taught me everything I know about show business," he admitted, "how to drink and play horses." Joe had brought out Eli's native wit, and now he was the best comedy writer in his field.

"Horses love him—people love him—God love him!" Hy Ginnis of the Trade Winds in Chicago composed for his four hundred.

A fine parlay, Joe thought.

"To us you have been a star for more than thirty years, and always will be," Judge Abe Marovitz, Edward Barrett and Ray Maloney toasted him from Chicago.

Little Abe had been a good friend, maybe the best one. He had kept him from a thousand follies and had taught him many things, like his rule about gossip. "Before you repeat any gossip," Abe told him twenty years ago, "be sure it passes three golden gates. Is it true? Is it important to repeat? Is it kind?" Joe had tried to remember.

"Cheers to a great human being," Judge Bernard A. Frank of Miami Beach echoed.

"Roses to our boy!" was the Chez Paree's garland.

"We know from personal experience," Jake Freedman and Jack Entratter added from the Sands in Las Vegas, "there is no business like Joe business!"

"*Zul zein mit glick* (May it be with luck)," wished Martha Raye, "my ever lovin' Nick Condos (whom she divorced a few months later) and our daughter Melodye. We all sing your praises."

Jack Benny, Bob Hope, Danny Thomas, Ted Lewis,

Arnstein, the Sanchezes, the Shors, Seymour Weiss, Ben Marden, Podell, Jock and Betsy Whitney, and scores of others added their testimonials. Seagram's Whiskey proudly boasted that it is "Known by the Company It Keeps," and Hildegarde, assisted by Anna Sosenko, was inspired in verse.

> *As long as there will be a sky,*
> *A flaming sun, a moon on high,*
> *A world of people loving laughter*
> *You'll make them laugh forever after.*

> *From "Sam, You Made the Pants Too Long,"*
> *In every line of every song*
> *You're wry, you're sly, so warm and witty,*
> *Why, dear Joe E., you're even pretty!*
> (l'envoi)
> *Whether East or West, North or Dixie,*
> *You'll always be our favorite pixie*
> *Darling,* je vous aime beaucoup . . .

Abel Green, the editor of *Variety*, reviewed Joe's career in five columns of type, and concluded in part:

"Joe E. Lewis is a show business phenomenon whose work, almost literally, is his play and vice versa, because he's doing what comes naturally. Almost a gypsy in reality . . . he is at home in all the gayer cities of America, and could virtually call seventy-five per cent of them his home. His homes away from home are what dissipates the legend about the necessity to call something, some place, his home.

"Underneath his avowed vagabondia is a realistic awareness that the business of being a fool brooks no foolishness. The mobs and the snobs, the effete set and the muggs, the borscht belt and the Texas oil tycoons, all dig his stuff. By gearing his material to the heps he also knows how to perform for the squares or, at least, the so-called not so initiate. That's where his pixie personality proves potent because, in even more rarefied atmosphere, he has gotten away with some slick nifties which, under other auspices, would be pedestrian. What is one man's B.S. Pully comes out ultra-sly divertissement with which only a Lewis seemingly can get away.

"His capacity for friendship is as much a part of his basic box-office appeal as his talent. There is no minimizing his wide personal following, some of it almost bordering on a cult. Result is that Lewis can do no wrong, be it with the press or pundits. In certain key cities as much as ninety per cent of his draw is personal, or customers who feel that they have an almost personal relationship with him. It is said that Lewis, by phone, could raise a couple of million if he wanted to go into the racetrack, bistro or any other business."

Julie Podell watched Joe turn the last page of *Variety*. "Where can you go from here?" Podell asked.

"Jamaica," Joe said, picking up his scratch sheet. "It opens today."

April 1st. If Martha hadn't left, he thought, they would be starting their eighth year of marriage today.

The reaction to *Variety's* accolade to Joe by his fellow comedians was significant.

"Dear Greeney," Groucho Marx wrote Green. "I rarely write fan letters because it's hard to find anything worth praising. But after reading your outline on Joe E., I want you to know that I took my secretary in hand just to let you know what a magnificent appraisal this was of a wonderful guy."

"Joe E. is an absolute master at comedy gag timing," said George Burns. "He's got that certain sense of being able to twist a risqué story, by perfect timing, into a terrifically funny, harmless comedy line."

George Jessel had stated unequivocally in his book, *So Help Me,* "Joe E. is the only comedian with originality to come up within the last ten years."

Jessel had learned first-hand. One night, during World War II, they appeared on the same TV show at St. Alban's Navy Base Hospital on Long Island. The sailors were slow to warm up. Each time the master of ceremonies, a Captain Walker, rose to introduce a performer, the men froze.

At last Joe came on. The men gave him a polite hand, little more than they had Captain Walker.

"I'm happy to be here," he began, "and I'm especially glad to see Captain Walker."

An undertone of resentment was heard.

"Don't get me wrong," Joe added. "My friend is the Captain's daddy. *Hiram* Walker."

The sailors roared and, from then on, they were Joe's.

Jessel stood in the wings and watched the magic. "Why didn't I think of that?" he wondered.

Three weeks after the testimonial issue, the Friars named Joe as their Abbot. When they had called him "the nicest guy in the world," they had meant it. They knew Joe, and they remembered . . .

They remembered a day in 1941 that he had walked into the Theatre Authority in Chicago and had put down a sheaf of fifty-dollar bills. "See that the girl goes first-class," he said. "If you need any more, call me." He glared at the man behind the desk. "And if you ever mention that it came from me, I'll have your job." The girl was Helen Morgan, the once wonderful singer, who had just died. Joe had hardly known her, but he had heard that she had not kept enough money from her $2,500-a-week days for a proper funeral. Helen Morgan had been an entertainer. That was all Joe needed to know.

They remembered when Bill (Bojangles) Robinson had died.

"Are you going to Robinson's funeral?" a friend had asked Joe.

"No," Joe replied. "I was with Bill when he was alive, when he needed a friend." Robinson had died without money or friends, except for one or two like Joe.

One night, at a benefit, Robinson was introduced as "one of the great Negro dancers of all time." Everyone applauded except Joe.

"Why do you always call Bill the great *Negro* dancer?" Joe asked the master of ceremonies. "I don't know whether he's black or white. All I know is that he's great."

The Friars remembered.

They remembered when Joe was making his comeback at the Green Mill in the early '30's. "We're dropping the chorus line," the manager had told him, "and you're getting the $250 extra a week." Joe was in debt, but he turned down the extra two and a half. "I'm no better than those kids," he said. "They stay or I don't."

They tried to remember a mean thing he had said, or an unworthy act he had committed, or an enemy he had made. None came to mind. Joe was a friar in the Franciscan tradition. No change of circumstance could alter his conception of friendship.

On the night that Joe was installed as Abbot, Berle presented his successor in an incredibly long introduction, even for Milton. Joe stood next to him, shifting his weight from one foot to the other. Berle, who had been expected to remain the Abbot in perpetuity, obviously was holding on to his mantle as long as possible. Each time that Joe thought Berle was handing him the microphone, and he reached for it, Milton switched hands and recalled twenty additional funny things that had happened to him on his way to the club.

At last Berle gave up. "Joe," he said, "you are the new Abbot of the Friars but remember, I'm the Abbot Emeritus." The Friars had given him the title as a balm to his pride. "Do you know what Emeritus means?" Now he handed Joe the microphone. This was not a rehearsed bit, except on Berle's part. He was challenging Joe, throwing a curve that he was positive Joe could not hit. How could he know what emeritus meant?

"Emeritus," Joe replied without a pause, "is when you run out of the money."

"How does he do it?" Berle asked with sincere respect, and envy.

How does he do it?

"Humor can be dissected, as a frog can," says E.B. White, "but the thing dies in the process. It has a certain fragility, an evasiveness which one had best respect. Essentially it is a complete mystery. A human frame convulsed with laughter, and the laughter becoming hysterical and uncontrollable, is as far out of balance as one shaken with the hiccoughs or in the throes of a sneezing fit."

Man laughs to be free, free of his tensions and the fears that cause them. Lewis, like every outstanding practitioner of nonsense from Aristophanes to Chaplin, instinctively knew that the surest way to release man's tensions is by satirizing the frustrations of life, most effectively with the sadistic, self-inflicted cut.

"Anyone who thinks I don't need a psychiatrist," he says, "needs one himself."

The clowns are the unloved. Medieval court jesters were hunchbacks. The Grimaldis, Fieldses, Durantes and Grocks have been lonely punchinellos who reduced life to its deepest absurdity by viewing it through the prism of their infirmities. A man hates what he laughs at, Spinoza said, but in making themselves ludicrous the clowns ridicule the world, and in their moment of brave, pathetic laughter, they momentarily forget their loneliness.

As do those who come to laugh at them.

Mankind, said Chesterton, has always regarded reason as a bit of a joke. Accordingly, Lewis Carroll's wonderland was populated by insane mathematicians; in Thurber Country, "sixty minutes of thinking of any kind is bound to lead to confusion and unhappiness"; man constantly invents new forms of gambling in which to escape the rational; and Joe E. Lewis earns more than $250,000 a year for going to a night club, telling a few jokes, singing a few songs and drinking a few carloads of whiskey.

How original is Joe? First answer, how original is any man? He does not conceive all of his own material, only a part of it, but he inspires almost every line and, like a shoemaker using leather, he rubs it, presses it, stretches it with his teeth, fashions it and polishes it until the finished product is his, unlike any other.

His is a talent unique, envied by every performer, great and small, who knows that Joe is totally at ease *only* when he is on stage. Danny Kaye was genuinely jittery before his debut at Ben Marden's Riviera a few years ago. "You played there eighteen weeks," he said to Joe. "What's the room like?"

"Nothing to worry about, Danny," Joe assured him. "In the first show they eat and don't pay attention—so don't knock yourself out. At the midnight show they're all drunk—ignore 'em."

"Is that *all?*"

"There must be an easier way to make a living," Joe said, "but I doubt it."

He picked up the morning paper and headed for the Warwick. Julie Podell must be getting old, he mused. Imagine,

Julie asking, "If you had it to do all over again, Joe, what would you do?"

If I had it to do all over again, he thought . . . I wouldn't have the energy.

34   *A Day with Joe*

In the summer of 1953, on Joe's arrival in southern California for his annual sojourn at the Mocambo night club and the Hollywood Park race track, I decided to set him down on paper.

"Come up for breakfast and we'll talk," he said on the phone. "Make it early. One-thirty . . . Oh, wait a minute, how will I know you? Wear a brown coat and blue slacks. I'll be in shorts."

Going up on the elevator of the Beverly Wilshire Hotel, I remembered a line Mel Heimer of the New York *Journal-American* had written in a series of articles on Joe back in 1945. "Getting a fact out of Lewis," Heimer had said, "is like pushing mercury to the wall."

I stopped in the hall and listened. A radio announcer's shrill, "They're off and running at . . ." had always been an unfailing radar beam to his door, but not this day. The corridor was still. Luckily, I remembered the number of his room.

His door was unlocked, the room strangely silent.

Breakfast for two was on a bridge table. Joe was sitting alone, attired solely in aquamarine shorts adorned with scarlet and saffron horseshoes, four-leaf clovers and dice rolled to seven.

"Yussel!" I shouted. It had been three years since our last reunion.

Without a word, or a glance from the television set that commanded his attention, he pointed to the other chair.

"How are you?" I asked.

He put his finger to his lips and gestured to the television screen. A film, *The Great Flamarian* starring Erich von Stroheim, was beginning. For the next hour and a half, Joe did not say a word. His eyes never left the twenty-year-old picture of a mad vaudevillian who substituted a real bullet for a blank and killed his unfaithful wife during their stage act. Joe left the room once, for ten minutes, but he first turned the set so that it was on a direct line with his seat in the bathroom.

At last the Great Flamarian came to his deserved end, and Joe said hello.

"About the book . . ." I said quickly, before the next program could begin.

"Hiya, Joe." Swifty Morgan shuffled in, leaning heavily on his gold-headed cane. "My leg is killing me," he groaned. He sat down and took a hunting knife out of his pocket. "If the pains keep on," he said, drawing his thumb along the edge of the long, sharp blade, "I'm gonna slit my throat."

"You know Art," Joe said.

Swifty turned to me. "What are you tryin' to con Joe out of?"

"He wants to write the story of my life," Joe said.

"To hell with Joe's life," Swifty growled. "Write mine. Just come up with the money. But you got to promise to put *all* my larcenies in it. God, I feel awful. I'd give a guy a hundred if I could move my bowels."

Joe grinned. He loved the old rogue. "Art was one of Runyon's boys."

Swifty scowled. "Runyon left nothin' to his friends, just Patricia. I gave him more stories . . ."

"You got yours, Swift," Joe said.

"I got two-seven-five for the *Lemon Drop Kid,* and one-two-five-o for the *Return of October*. That's money?" He glared at me. "I'm not givin' you anything. Joe! Get dressed, I'm ready to eat."

Joe dutifully went into his bedroom to dress.

Swifty struggled to rise from his chair. "Give me a hand," he groaned, "I'm an old man."

I helped him to his feet. He walked to the desk, read Joe's mail and inspected Joe's wallet. "Short again," he said. "Need any ties?" he asked me. "How did you like those shorts I gave Joe?"

"Swift," Joe called from the other room, "tell him about the time I had a toothache."

"Toothache? My leg is murdering me. I tell you, I won't last the week."

"What about Joe's toothache?" I asked.

"It was fifteen below zero."

"Where?"

"In Chicago, where the hell would it be fifteen below zero? Joe, are you gonna let this dummy write your story?"

"It was fifteen below zero in Chicago," I prompted.

"There was a cab strike on and Joe had to get to a dentist. He had a toothache—remember? So I flagged a car and told the driver I was an F.B.I. agent, and had to get downtown right away. He didn't believe me at first, but when I told him that Joe was a four-time loser who had just escaped from Statesville, he said hop in."

Joe was in the doorway. "Imagine anyone taking Morgan for an F.B.I. man."

Swifty chuckled. "When we got out I said to Joe, 'Take care of the cab. Where you're goin' you won't need any money.'"

Joe's eyes were clamped on the television screen. An attractive young singer was selling a ballad.

"Pretty girl," I remarked.

"They're all pretty," Joe said.

"You're a hypocrite," Swifty said. "How about that broad in Dallas last month?"

"What broad?"

"The one who was giving you a bad time during the show. You roughed her up pretty good."

"But she was drunk!" Joe's abhorrence was unfeigned.

"You shouldn't talk to broads like that, drunk or not."

"All I said was, 'Madame, I don't go over to your counter at Woolworth's and annoy you when you're working, do I?"

"I know what you said. Let's eat."

Joe smiled. "That was the one who hollered she had lost on Native Dancer in the Derby."

Morgan nodded. "And you told her she had lost before she bet, goin' away."

"Let's take a walk," Joe said after he had fed Swifty.

We walked around the block that girds the Beverly Wilshire Hotel. On the third lap, we met Ted Sherdeman, a producer at Universal-International Studio.

"I'm glad the case is settled, Joe," Sherdeman said.

"So am I," said Joe. "Say hello to Leo."

"I will," said Sherdeman and left.

"What case?" I asked.

"Universal made a picture last year and called it *No Room for the Groom*. They didn't even ask my permission, and I own the title. I told Marovitz to sue 'em for a million bucks. Yesterday, Leo Spitz, who runs Universal, called me up and asked if I would come over to see him, he wanted to settle. Leo is an old friend of mine and I went. 'You're not going to hold us up for a million dollars, are you?' he asked me, and I said, 'Oh, I guess not. Give me a bottle of whiskey and we'll call it even.' "

"How come?"

"What could I do? Leo was at Cedars of Lebanon Hospital, and he didn't look very good."

On the fifth trip around, a middle-aged man in shorts, an Hawaiian sports shirt and a worried look came up.

"Joe! I haven't seen you in two weeks."

"That's a coincidence," Joe said. "I haven't seen you in two weeks."

"Have I got troubles. I drop fifty-eight hundred at Vegas, and borrow four G's on my life insurance. This morning my wife is cleaning the desk and says, 'Where's the policy?' I tell her it's down at the office, but she takes one look at my kisser and knows I'm lying. What do I do?"

"Be like me," Joe said. "Don't bet."

On the seventh lap, my legs began to buckle.

"Let's go see Mike," Joe said. We had passed Romanoff's Restaurant six times. I had feared that Toots Shor had broken off diplomatic relations with His Royal Highness and it was out of bounds.

Prince Michael embraced Joe, and escorted us to a center table.

"There's a man with class," Joe said, as the hardiest of the Romanoffs excused himself to greet a studio paladin. "Back in the '30's, when Mike was strapped, he asked me to loan him a buck for gas. I offered him a fin, but he wouldn't take it. 'I want to borrow one dollar,' he said, with real dignity, and that's all he would take. A man shows his class when he's broke."

Like loaning his last ten thousand to a man he has never seen before, I thought.

"Is there enough material for a book?" he asked.

"A book, a Broadway show and a picture. It could be better than *Guys and Dolls* because it has more heart."

"Do you really believe it?"

I was certain. I had written twelve pictures in the past four years, half of them at Metro-Goldwyn-Mayer. I thought

I knew a good story and I had been thinking about Joe's since 1943.

"It can't miss," I told him. "Make 'em laugh and make 'em cry. It has never failed, from Dickens to Runyon."

He shook his head. "It hasn't a finish."

"I'll find one."

"If you do, I know three or four major companies that will make the picture. Schenley . . . Calvert . . . Seagram . . ."

"I'm serious."

"If you ever write the book," he said, "please say that all I ever wanted to do was entertain. And put this in, it's very important. Performers don't make people laugh. *People* make people laugh. One laughs and the others follow."

He was in a rare, reflective mood.

"The sons don't take the places of their fathers," he went on. "They don't know cabareting. The Gay Nineties must have been the best. They took their time about living—and dying. Today everyone rushes. In the old days they waited a week for a stagecoach. Today, when they miss the first section of a revolving door they blow their tops."

"Imagine what it will be like fifty years from now."

"There will always be a tavern in the town," he said. "There has always been one since George Washington's time. There will always be guys who made a million, or lost a million, who want to remember. There will always be people getting engaged, or married, always a guy losing a wife or a girl, and either way they drink. I knew a man, he was a lawyer, who sat at the same table every night of the week except Friday for ten years. Fridays he went to the synagogue. I don't know why he came but he must have had a reason. Radio, television and even the movies may go but the tavern will remain."

He suddenly grimaced. "Let's go."

In his room, he took a relief for hyperacidity.

"How long have you had ulcers?" I asked.

"Three years."

"You've lost weight."

"Twenty pounds. I'm down to one-forty. Diabetes."

"What about booze?"

"I've cut down."

"Why don't you cut it out?"

"I like to drink while I'm working. It gives me energy."

"And ulcers."

"I don't drink as much as everyone thinks. I can't work if I drink too much. Nobody can. I stop when I'm too drunk."

"Could you do the act sober?"

"I did it for over a year! Nineteen forty-six."

"I remember. You're better drunk."

That irritated him, not the criticism but the implication. "Jim Barton had the greatest drunk act in the business," he said with a note of envy, "and no one thought *he* was a drunkard or expected him to get loaded every night. It was accepted as an act—like Jack Benny being stingy or Don Ameche being a lover." He looked at his watch. "If we play our cards right, we can catch the last two races."

The last two races caught Joe, for seven hundred.

Henry McLemore, the columnist, came by and introduced his wife to Joe. "Honey," he said to her, "I'm not easily impressed but here is the most lovable, the most unique, the only one of his kind in the world."

"Maybe that's what's the matter," said Joe.

"What about Martha and the marriage?" I asked on the way back.

"We were drunk most of the time."

I waited for him to continue. That was all he had to say.

"How about the rich one, Letty?"

"We were friendly."

I waited. "What else?"

"What else is there?" He lapsed into another silence.

"That's going to make a great chapter."

Joe nodded. "Let's go to Chasen's, Lackey's waiting."

Al Lackey had been married to Sophie Tucker for twenty-one years and divorced from her for thirteen years and he had not recovered from either experience.

"Sophie is an amazing woman," he said as we ate dinner. "When her brother died, she wired her friends, 'Suffered irreparable loss. Have you read *Some of These Days?*' " *Some of These Days* was Sophie's currently published biography.

"How's your new wife?" Joe asked as he finished his dinner of three thin slices of roast beef, a lettuce salad without dressing and one Scotch highball.

Lackey groaned. "You won't believe it, Joe. I just found out yesterday she doesn't even know what *lox* is."

"Joey!" Louella Parsons had just come in. "Joey," she pouted, "You're unfaithful to me!"

"When, darling?"

Louella waggled a bejeweled finger at him. "You know, you bad boy. But I still love you, Joey." She continued to her table.

"Joey!" Louella was calling across the room. "Be sure and listen to my radio program tonight. I have an exclusive about that new love in your life."

"I will, Louella," Joe promised.

Dave Chasen sat down with us and talked of the old days when he had been on the stage with Joe Cook. "How's your pal Sanchez?" he asked Joe.

"Not so good. Jorge has melancholia." The rest of us smiled. "It's on the level," Joe said.

"How did he get melancholia?" Chasen asked.

Joe shrugged. "He was just moping around, and he got it."

"Irving Berlin's in town," said Lackey, changing the subject. "You're a friend of his, aren't you, Joe?"

"I've done more for Irving than any singer in show business. I've never sung one of his songs. We made an agreement after I heard him sing 'Oh, How I Hate to Get Up in the Morning.' He promised never to sing one of mine, either."

We ate in silence a few moments. "I always meant to ask you, Joe," said Chasen. "You never had a middle initial when I first knew you. Where did you get the E?"

"I borrowed it from Lizabeth Scott."

The waiter plugged in a phone. Charlie Morrison, the boss of the Mocambo, was calling Joe.

"Don't worry, Charlie," he reassured him, "Doc Mitchell says I can work."

"What's that about?" I asked when he had finished.

"I had pains in my back and shoulders when I got in yesterday. The doc and the boys over at the Finlandia baths fixed me up."

I pointed to his empty whiskey glass. "That fixed you up."

Joe paid the check and we stood up to leave.

"Don't forget my radio program, Joey dear!" Louella called out.

We went back to his room, and he immediately turned on the television. The news, comedians and singers had no interest for him. He tuned in a half-hour mystery drivel, and watched it intently.

"Time for Louella," I reminded him.

He switched on a portable radio and listened, at the same time watching the television drama. After fourteen minutes and forty-five seconds of her fifteen-minute program, Louella announced excitedly:

"Exclusive! There is a new love in the life of Joe E. Lewis! She has followed him to California and her name is . . ." She mentioned a name I had never heard before.

"Who is she?" I asked.

Joe was puzzled. "I think it's a broad I knew in Chicago . . . or was it Cleveland? Haven't seen her in a long time."

"Is she in town?"

"I wish she was. Turn up the television. I can't hear."

He began dressing at 9:40. Inserting his cuff links still gave him the most trouble, there being no sense of touch in his right hand.

He reluctantly turned off the television at 10:10. It was time to go to work.

His face was contorted with pain as we drove to the Mocambo.

"The back?" I asked.

He nodded.

Harry Harris and his wife were waiting at the club. Harry was worried. "Are you all right, Joe?" he asked.

"Never felt better," Joe lied, and went to his dressing room.

"Swifty says you're going to write a book about Joe," Harry said as we waited for the show to go on.

"I hope."

"It won't be easy. There's never been anybody like Joe. Has there, Velma?"

Harry's pretty wife shook her head.

"I've known him almost thirty years," he continued. "He never walked three feet in any direction that he didn't want to go. He's the most self-sufficient man I've ever come across. He has learned how to live alone, because he's game."

"And shy," Velma said.

"His shyness is caused by loneliness," Harry went on. "He's always looking for people, people he can help."

"Why did you split up?" I asked.

"In 1943 I got tired of writing comedy songs. I had been at it twenty years and I wasn't getting anywhere. They all sounded like my first song, 'I Had Someone Else Before I Had You and I'll Have Someone After You're Gone.' It was fun when I was in my twenties, like writing a song for J. C. Flippen while he waited. But not in my forties. I told

Joe why I was quitting, and that I was going to take a crack at the movies. 'It's a good idea,' he said. 'You might need this while you're doing it.' He slipped me twenty-five hundred dollars."

The band was playing "Chicago." Joe was on.

"To those who have seen me before, 'Hello,' and to those who have never come before, I say, 'Cowards!' The Mocambo caters to a restricted clientele. You can't get in without money. And, I might add, you can't get out with it. Sometimes the checks go so high they yodel." His eyes roved to the glass aviary that occupied an entire wall, and the scores of canaries and parakeets flitting inside. "And if Charlie Morrison doesn't pay me all my dough this time," he said, "I'll throw an alley cat in there."

A year or two previously, when a fire had threatened to raze the Mocambo, Joe had opened his show with a tribute to his feathered friends. "It was only the stalwart kidneys of those birds that kept this joint open." Now he dedicated a song to the girl who took care of the aviary.

> *She's got chanticleers and dicky birds,*
> *Intelligent and tricky birds,*
> *That make the fellows follow her around.*
> *Her crow is black and shiny*
> *And her hummingbirds are tiny,*
> *But she's got the biggest parakeets in town.*
>
> *And every night when she gets into bed*
> *She puts each one on a pillow,*
> *They sound like Bing*
> *When they begin to sing,*
> *Tit willow, tit willow, tit willow.*
> *Imagine on her wedding night*
> *When hubby dear turns out the light.*
> *Next morning he wakes up with such a frown*

As he goes to caress her, he sees them on the dresser,
The biggest parakeets in town.

Joe was racked with pain, from his liver, his kidneys, and
his ulcers. The spasms came faster and the stabbing lancets
more piercing. He started to perspire. The show had just begun and it was opening night, he had to pace himself for the
next forty minutes or he would not last.

"Ladies and gentlemen, Austin Mack." Austin took a bow.
"Mr. Mack has been with me fourteen years. I can't believe
it. I can't remember breaking two mirrors." Austin was cuing
him with Cole Porter's latest score. "And now," Joe went on,
"I'd like to sing a song from, you'll excuse the expression,
Can Can."

"Post time!" someone shouted.

They were ahead of him. He looked at the drink on the piano. It would go down hard tonight. Every drop would burn
but he was expected to empty the glass, and many others.
The customers had paid to see him get drunk.

He threw down the drink but he could not mask his distress. "I may not look well," he covered up, "but I feel awful.
I must be sicker than I think. My insurance man took back
all the blotters. Some mornings I'm so weak I have to use
both hands to brush my teeth." The lines were there but he
was not. The magic was missing, and the crowd knew it.

"You look at me as though I have no talent," he tried to
thaw them, "and may I say that tonight you have very good
eyesight." A hurt expression came into his face. "Honestly, I
can't understand why you're not laughing. It's disrespectful.
What was good enough for your parents should be good
enough for you."

There was a ripple of polite applause. "That's more like
it," he said. "When I work, I demand a deathly hush. Just a
few intellectual nods." He stopped and turned to Austin.
"Austin, open up your heart and give me a cue." Austin con-

tinued his Cole Porter concert. "Last night I dreamed I met my perfect mate," Joe went on. "A centaur. Half woman and half horse." That brought a few laughs.

"Thanks, folks," he responded. "If I make good tonight, Mr. Morrison has promised the next show he'll turn on the mike." The crowd was still cold. "Lots of comics have dead-pan deliveries," he commented. "I have a dead-pan audience." If they did not warm up soon, he thought, he would have to do "Sam, You Made the Pants Too Long."

He lifted another drink. "Today is a very important day in history. Exactly one hundred years ago tonight, Eli Whitney went to the Cotton Club and drank some gin. Eli Whitney. Behind every famous man is a woman. Antony and Cleopatra. Napoleon and Josephine. Heinz and a tomato." The crowd responded a little to his manic mood, and he continued in the vein.

> *Once I knew a little girl*
> *Who was ten, going on eleven.*
> *Now she's a woman thirty-nine*
> *Going on twenty-seven.*

There was no reaction. Age is not a laughing matter in Hollywood. He kept punching.

> *Thirty days hath September,*
> *April, June and November*
> *All the rest have thirty-one*
> *Except Jane Russell, who has a perfect forty-six.*

"Falsies don't kid anybody," he added. "They're so obvious they couldn't even fool a baby. I saw a girl in one of those tight-fitting sweaters a little while ago. The wool looked sexier on a lamb."

Nothing happened. "I know you're not laughing," he said, "but let's not make a crusade. You should have seen the audience I had in Reno last week. Laugh, I thought they'd never start."

He had one arrow left. Money was always a sure-fire subject in Hollywood.

"Some of us make big money," he admitted, "but how much can you wind up with after taxes and gambling? Having money may not get you friends but it'll get you some high-class enemies. I don't want to take it with me, I just want enough to get me there." He reached into his pocket and took out a shoestring. "See this shoestring? It looks small. Let me tell you, it's not as small as it looks. I know the head of a major movie studio who ran a million dollars into this."

There was a lull. "That's the last joke I buy from the men's room attendant. There's only one thing I can do now. I'll have to ask for a vote of confidence."

He was in physical agony, and the show was dying. Suddenly, he was greeted by the boozy voice of a heckler.

"I don't mind Bronx cheers," Joe said. "It's the spray that gets me."

The heckler gave him a reprise.

"Sir, you're not disorderly," Joe lashed, "you're just distilled."

The heckler became louder. Joe peered through the crowd and recognized his critic. He was the aging juvenile, Sonny Tufts.

"You're going places, Sonny," Joe snapped, "and I wish you'd start right now."

Tufts was enjoying the attention he had attracted, and he continued heckling, unmindful that he had to compose his own dialogue.

Joe measured the broad-shouldered, blond booby. "Physically, you resemble a man, Sonny, but mentally you're like a yo-yo."

Tufts wanted to remain in the act, and he booed.

"Come on down to Malibu Beach tomorrow," Joe sallied, "and I'll give you a lesson in drowning."

That brought a big laugh. The show was off and running at last. Joe E.'s magic had come back. From then on, he could not say anything that they thought was unfunny. It had always been that way. As he had said, "Performers don't make people laugh. People make people laugh. One laughs and the others follow." The trick was to make the first one laugh. He played percentage. You had to catch a Sonny Tufts now and then.

"Heckle me, Sonny," he pleaded after a momentary lull twenty minutes later. "Make me a big hit again."

An hour later, they were still yelling for more. "May the good Lord take a liking to you," he signed off, "but not too soon."

A lean, weather-beaten man in his fifties sat at a ringside table and joined in the applause.

"He's terrific, isn't he?" one of the two younger men at his table enthused.

The lean, weather-beaten man's eyes crinkled. "Do you think he's good now? You should have seen him before he was cut. That's when he was *great*."

"Did you ever hear him then?" the younger man asked.

"A few times . . ." He had not always had a lumber mill in Oregon. He had not always run forty thousand feet of timber a day. He had not always been a benign old codger with grandchildren to play with. He used to pack two pistols, and he was known from the top of the North Side to the bottom of the Levee as John Fogarty of the Rendezvous, a game guy who feared no man, including Machine Gun Jack McGurn.

Joe stopped at Fogarty's table and embraced his old friend. "Thanks for coming, John."

"It wasn't my idea," Fogarty rasped. "The kids wanted to catch you."

Joe smiled. John had not changed. He would give you his life, but he would needle you with his last breath.

"Great show, Joe! . . . Wonderful, Joe E.! . . . Joe! Here's your drink!"

He was hemmed in by well-wishers, but at last he escaped to his dressing room. He locked the door, took some pills and sank on the couch, exhausted.

I found Cassie Mack in the bar, and I asked her to have a drink.

"I don't drink," she said. "They drink enough."

Swifty Morgan passed. "Don't tell him nothin', Cassie," he said, "unless he comes up with money."

"Our Joe is very funny," Cassie said with the love of a sister for her favorite brother. "He'll lose fifty thousand dollars at a dice table without batting an eye, but he has to wear a shirt twice. Say he puts on a clean shirt for his last night at the Copa, and then lays off to dry out in Hot Springs. He'll fold the shirt very carefully, put it away and say, 'This is for opening night at the Chez, three weeks from Tuesday.' He's very serious about that. He won't send out his laundry until he has twenty dollars' worth."

Estrelita, a Cuban singer, and her husband, Grant Withers, an old-time movie star, stopped to say hello.

"The first time Estrelita applied for a job on Joe's show," Cassie said when they left, "she admitted she was only thirteen years old. 'I'm not superstitious,' Joe said and okayed her. One day he was playing gin with Withers, and took him for three hundred. Withers didn't have it, but offered him a hundred on account. 'Forget it,' Joe told him, 'until you make another picture.' "

Austin joined us. "Swifty says you're doing a book on Joe," he said. I nodded. "Be sure and mention the time Frank Costello came into the Colonial Inn and gave Swifty the elbow to shake hands with Joe. Morgan cooled him. 'Costello,' he said loud enough so the busboys in the kitchen could hear, 'I knew you when you first came around and wore earrings.' "

We chatted about the mechanics of Joe's act.

"He buys about twenty songs a year," Austin said, "from the best writers at the top prices. About ten are good, if he's lucky. He keeps around sixty in the active book but holds on to all of them, except when he gives a couple to some poor guy down on his luck."

"And never tell him not to sing a certain song," Cassie said. "He keeps trying, year after year, with some hopeless duds. That's Joe. He'll stay all night with an audience, no matter how small, to win it."

"Put in something about his driving," Austin said.

"Austin's brother Roy loaned him his car back in the '20's," Cassie recalled. "Joe took it and drove in the street-car tracks all the way to where he was going. He thought that's how you're supposed to drive. Coming back, he honked his horn all the way. 'I couldn't find the light switch,' he told Roy. 'You sound like a jerk who never drove a car before,' Roy told him. 'I never have,' Joe admitted."

Austin remembered something he thought should be included. "We were playing Galveston and Joe was looking out of the window of the Hotel Buccaneer. A pretty girl passed and Joe gave her the eye. An hour or so later she knocked on the door of his room. 'Sh-h-h-h,' Joe shushed her and handed her a twenty. 'See you tomorrow.' He started to close the door but she stuck her foot in. 'The manager says you're checking out tonight," she said. Joe got tense. 'Can't you see I'm listening to "Gang Busters?" ' He was really indignant and got her out of there. Joe sure likes 'Gang Busters.' "

"And the time at Niagara Falls," Cassie recalled. "My home is in Buffalo but I hate the Falls. One time we stopped there for a visit. Joe was late. When he caught up, he asked me if everything was all right. 'I'm okay,' I told him, 'but I don't know about Austin.' He looked around. 'Where is he?'

he asked. I pointed up to the little car crossing the Niagara gorge on that one cable. 'In there,' I told him. Joe started shaking. 'You shouldn't have let him go, Cassie!' he said. 'What if—if something happened?' I tried to calm him. 'Don't worry about Austin,' I said.

"Joe nearly went crazy until the cable car came back. Then he grabbed Austin and said, 'Don't you ever do anything like that again. What would have happened to my verses?' You see, Austin memorizes the first lines of Joe's verses. All the cues are in *his* head."

We talked about their early days and I asked Austin how much Joe had received for their first engagement at the Earl Theatre in Philadelphia, 1938.

Austin stiffened. "I never knew Lewis' price," he said, "and I never wanted to. I still don't. It's none of my business. When he got more, I got more. I've never asked any questions, and we've never had a contract or even talked about it. No matter what happens, he gets it up there every week."

Joe was back in the room. A stranger stopped him. "Mr. Lewis," he said, "you don't know me, but I'm a friend of Sam Ruby. Sam told me that if I ever came across you, to say hello."

Joe shook the stranger's hand. "How is Sam?"

"Fine."

"I'm glad to hear that," Joe said and he recalled the time, a few years back, when he had read a newspaper story that Sam Ruby, a prominent Chicago car dealer, had dropped dead. His friend, Sam Ruby, was a prominent Chicago car dealer, and he was grief-stricken. An investigation, however, revealed that the dead man was another Sam Ruby. Relieved, Joe wired his pal, "Dear Sam, I knew you when you were alive. Let's keep it that way."

Joe talked and drank with friends for the next hour and a half; he made a date with Billy Wilkerson to play gin rummy Saturday; he promised to have dinner at Joe Schenck's home

Sunday; he finished his late show at 2:15 A.M. and at 3:10 we sat down at the Beverly Wilshire Drug Store, where Joe ate an egg salad sandwich and drank a glass of half cream and a half milk.

"I drink milk for my ulcer," he said, "and whiskey for me."

James Cruze, the once-great director, stopped to say hello. "What's new, Joe?"

"My tax man says that if you spend a hundred on a girl and don't score, it's deductible."

He finished, and drifted to the drug counter. "Give me some Bill Corum blades," he told the clerk, "a couple tubes of Eddie Cantor tooth paste and a bottle of Arthur Godfrey seltzer."

The clerk nodded. Joe's insistence on plugging his friends had compelled the clerk to identify products by the names of the entertainers who advertised them on radio and television.

Joe inspected his purchases. "This isn't Arthur Godfrey seltzer," he said, pushing it back. "No ringers."

"I'm sorry, Mr. Lewis," the clerk said, "but Mr. Godfrey changed sponsors this morning."

The spastic newsman outside the hotel handed Joe a morning paper, and Joe stuffed a bill into his canvas pouch.

As we walked through the lobby to the elevator, he turned to the sports section. "Too bad," he said.

"What's too bad?" I asked.

"The horse they named after me. Lost again today." Joe E. Lewis, an alleged thoroughbred by Challenger II out of Lovely Night, was adding little luster to its name. It had run out of the money again in Hialeah. "And in a thousand-dollar claimer," Joe said.

"Breakfast tomorrow," Joe said. "About two."

"What's playing?" I asked.

"Charles Ray and Clara Kimball Young."

The elevator doors opened. "Good evening, Mr. Lewis," the operator greeted him.

"Good morning, Dan." As the doors closed, Joe reached into his pocket. He never went up without slipping the operator a bill.

Wilshire Boulevard was desolate and still, from Beverly to the sea. The fourteen hours I had spent with Joe unraveled, and I was more convinced than ever that he would make a good book. A little mercury had been pushed to the wall. I had asked many questions, and I had found many answers, but Joe had asked the most important one:

What would I use for a finish?

35   *Curtain*

It was summer, 1954.

More than a year had passed since I had begun the research, and suspended it, to write four films in Italy. My notebook was filled with data and memorabilia on Joe, but I still did not have a finish. Now I was flying back from Rome, in quest of the missing line without which his story would have no meaning.

We had corresponded regularly during the year.

His Christmas present had been a picture of a horse. "Hang this on your bathroom ceiling," he wrote, "so you can have something to look at when you gargle."

His Yuletide greeting had read, "A Happy New Year as far as I'm concerned."

A few days later, a load of calendars, ten years old, was delivered. "You'll make a fortune with these," he wrote, "if 1944 comes back."

When he heard that my disk had slipped, and that I was on my coccyx for a few weeks, he wrote, "I hope the enclosed will buck you up." Attached were twenty $100 parimutuel tickets on gluepots that had run out of the money.

A letter from Texas, in February, was typical.

"Received your Magna Charter in Dallas," he wrote, "where I'm working at the Adolphus Hotel and, on the side, looking after a piece of an oil well I bought last year. It will produce 500 barrels a day—no oil, just barrels.

"Business has been very good. Last night it was so crowded there were only two empty seats and they were in the men's room. Oh, I am very subtle. With me you never see jokes coming, but you're awfully glad to see them go.

"You ask how I'm feeling. I'm just getting over a severe case of whiskey. Actually, I'm about the same, a hundred and fifty pounds of solid bone and Serutan. I'm so weak I couldn't fight my way out of a paper bag, but there's not much chance of me being caught in a paper bag.

"Regarding your questions about my early days, I was known as the Grand Old Man of Kindergarten Six. We had progressive education, even then. One year in the first grade, two years in the second, three years in the third, and so on. I went from the third grade to the first, the only kid in the history of P.S. 184 to skip two grades backward. They finally got me a tutor, a graduate from U.S.C., University of Southern Comfort.

"I was a pretty fair athelete, though. I broke the school record in the high jump the day I backed into a javelin. Seriously, about the only thing I learned was that two and two are four the hard way. My teacher used to keep me after school every day. Both of us were expelled at the same time. My father wanted me to be a sex maniac, but I couldn't pass the physical. Like I always said, you can lead a horse to water, but teach him to lie back and float, and you have something.

"In all modesty, I was cut out to be a genius but somebody forgot to put the pieces together. I have three brothers who are just the same. Instead of getting a college education, they used to fight. They were so tough that any one of my brothers could lick the other three.

"Answering your question about my drinking, I've been loaded only twice this winter, January and February. I had a physical last week and the doctor said I had too much blood in my alcoholic system.

"It was okay in Miami Beach but the bellboys are tip-crazy. One day I sent down for a deck of cards and the bellboy came up fifty-two times.

"When you write the book, don't forget my war record—especially at Chateau Thierry when I was crawling on my belly and the machine-gun bullets were zinging all around me. One of the toughest night clubs in Chicago, that Chateau Thierry.

"Not much news. Austin passed away last week, but I haven't the heart to tell him. The newspapers are still making a fuss about Communists and flying saucers. I don't know why. A Commie is just a guy who thinks everything is perfect in Russia. But he would rather stay here and rough it. As for flying saucers, if you want to see flying saucers, just pinch a waitress.

"By the way, I hear they have some great Italian restaurants in Rome. Don't miss 'em.

"You haven't been missing much on television. There's a new show, 'Stop the Money.' They give away music. But the commercials! The other night I heard an announcer say, 'Our cigarette is the only cigarette that contains desulphatized shemogan. More than a thousand doctors have said, "We don't know what the hell that means." ' Jack Eigen has his own show now. Listening to him has made an atheist out of me.

"So you're living in the Rossellini apartment. Some class, but I don't do so bad with my sunken butler and my duplex maid. I don't envy anybody except oysters. They only have to be good from September to April.

"After that last line I'm gonna quit. I have to write this, all you have to do is read it. Say hello to Marta and Luciano.

"P.S. As you know, I'm a pretty patient guy. I've been waiting and waiting. Do you think something could have gone wrong with my Pyramid Club?"

I reread letters, notes, clippings, lyrics and impressions until a pleasant voice interrupted. "Fasten your seat belts, please. We land at Idlewild Airport in five minutes."

That afternoon, in the William Morris Agency offices, high above Broadway, a thin, gray-haired man told me about the Joe E. he knew.

"I've been with him twenty-five years," said Sam Bramson. "Not once has he questioned a booking, salary, billing or advertising. If I didn't call him, I would never hear from him. He does all his business at the National City Bank, on the ground floor of this building, and he has never been in the William Morris office.

"Joe makes up for a lot of un-nice people in this business. He never brags. He never raises his voice. He leaves show business on the floor. He pays his commissions by return mail. He gives his play to little out-of-the-way joints that need the business, buys drinks for everybody so he can build up the check. He wants everybody to be happy. He even goes around chilling beefs between the columnists.

"He passes up two or three days' work between spots, which amounts to plenty a year, because Austin won't fly. 'It's because of his religion,' Joe says. 'Austin is a devout coward.' Once Joe canceled two weeks' work to put on a dinner for his pal, Dan Arnstein. Gave up fourteen thousand bucks."

"Where does he go from here?" I asked, seeking a clue for the finish.

"Where does he go from *here?*" Bramson was shocked by the question. "Julie Podell's got him ten weeks a year at the Copa for life. That's an annuity!"

I closed my notebook.

I walked down Broadway, past an elderly bootblack's stand, and I remembered a night in 1944 that Joe had stopped for a shine. He was in his work clothes, a double-breasted dress suit and black tie.

The bootblack looked up, noticed the tuxedo and asked, "Waiting tables?"

"Sure," Joe answered. "Can't you tell a waiter when you see one?"

" 'Course I can. Used to be one myself."

When the shine was completed, Joe handed him a dollar tip.

"My, my," said the bootblack, "where are you working?"

I continued along Broadway. Joe's face leered at me from Lindy's window on a picture autographed, "This was taken when I was much older."

I wanted to see him when he was much younger. Perhaps I would find the end at the beginning. I flew to Chicago, Joe's Chicago of the '20's.

This was the Levee, this was the hurly-burly South Side. This was Twenty-second Street, between Wabash Avenue and State Street, but where was the Midnight Frolics? Where was the tonk in which Joe had sung "Eddy Steady," "Yes, We Have No Bananas," "Ain't We Got Fun?" and "Oogie Oogie Wa Wa," four shows every night, for $115 a week?

"It was over there." The middle-aged cab driver pointed to a junk yard, between a gasoline station and a place called the Square Deal Cleaners.

"You're nuts," cut in a bulbous-nosed derelict, who had

stopped to listen. "The Frolics was over there. I used to get stiff in the Frolics every night." He pointed a palsied finger across the street, toward a shack named Bungalow Beefburgers.

The elevated rattled overhead. I left the cab driver arguing with the wino, and I retraced the miserable slum that had been the gaudiest tenderloin in Capone's empire.

Around the corner on Wabash, next to the Miracle Speedy Five Minute Car Wash, I found a landmark. Fire had gutted the ancient, four-story brick building, but the mark of Cain remained. On the scorched door, in blistered red, were the once proudest numerals in all Chicago: 2222.

The windows were opaque, painted green with a patch of orange. On the bottom of the door was a sign, Quick Service. I walked inside.

It was a long room, dark and dismal. The front part of it was used for sleeping. There was an old iron bed, a broken couch, a backless chair, and a television set. In the rear, a middle-aged Negro woman was washing clothes. Behind her, four little colored children were playing. Two girls were shrieking as their fortunes changed in a game of jacks. A boy was blowing on a harmonica, furiously. The youngest, a baby of two or three, was pounding the floor with a hammer, and bawling.

The woman seemed oblivious of the clamor, apparently deaf except to the radio at her side. A quiz show was on, and a contestant was receiving an orchid, a gold watch, a fur coat, an electric washing machine and a one-week vacation to Hollywood. The woman at the tub beamed.

I left after five minutes without having been noticed. I had been in Big Jim Colossimo's joint, the Four Deuces. Here, Capone had been a mop-boy at twenty-five dollars a week. Here, his hundred-million-dollar syndicate had been born. Here, Colossimo had been killed. Here, Joe had met Capone, and had taken his first step up in the arts.

It was gone now, as if it had never existed. Nothing was left, except the four red deuces on the door. Even Twenty-second Street had died. It was now Cermak Road.

My next stop was up on the North Side, at Broadway and Lawrence Avenue.

It was an ordinary bar, as standardized as its tens of thousands of counterparts throughout the land. In the window, next to a box of faded pink paper flowers, was a sign: "Scotty Highlanders—No Cover Charge—Lilyan Cole Nightly at the Hammond Organ." Inside, a Stan Kenton record was spinning on a one-hundred-record player. Four people were drinking, three of them beer, at a long bar on one side of the narrow room. Only one of the booths that lined the other wall was occupied, by a young couple, intently tapping the beat of the music.

Was this the place I was looking for, this little cocktail lounge, in the center of a respectable suburban community, alongside the Peter Pan Style Shop, snack shops and the Palladium Ball Room, Dancing Friday, Saturday and Sunday?

It was the place where Joe's story had begun. The door in the back led to the little office where Joe had told Danny Cohen, "I'm leavin'." This was the Green Mill, Machine Gun Jack McGurn's Green Mill. Now it had Lilyan Cole nightly on the Hammond organ.

I went on, as Joe had gone twenty-seven years before, from the Green Mill to the Rendezvous.

The Rendezvous had vanished; 511 Clark Street was a deserted place, its front boarded. No one on the block remembered it.

"That was a long time ago," said the butcher who ran the Fresh Cut Up Poultry Market next door. "There have been so many joints in there, just the last ten years."

I looked across the street. Up there, on the roof of the gasoline station, three of Fogarty's men had covered Joe on his opening night, one of them through the sights of a sawed-off shotgun.

Next door was the Blue Ribbon Bar, then the Trojan Laundry, and the Victory Club Lounge. Beer joints, hamburger shacks, tenements, but not a vestige of the Rendezvous.

I walked the two short blocks along Diversey Parkway to the Commonwealth Hotel. Davidson Bakery . . . Super Market . . . Golden Rule Cleaners . . . Gertrude Kopelman, Suits and Dresses, Fifty Percent Off . . . North Side Cleaners . . . Diversey Bootery . . .

Here, McGurn had threatened Joe, "You'll never live to open." There, shortly before dawn on that November ninth, McGurn's car had pulled up. That was the doorway where Fogarty had covered Joe with two guns. "It's time to come back now," McGurn had said. That was 1927. Now, Gertrude Kopelman's suits and dresses were fifty percent off.

The Commonwealth Hotel was twenty-seven years older. I revisited the room where Joe had gotten it. It was like a million other threadbare, single hotel rooms that had been used by countless tens of thousands. It told me nothing. Mrs. Lauterman and Casey, the elevator man, were unremembered names out of a forgotten past.

Now, to "State Street, that great street . . ."

The room, about twenty feet square, was empty. The windows were filthy. The floor was littered with rags, crumpled newspapers, nails, half a can of paint thinner, seven empty soda pop bottles, and a blueprint.

A blueprint of Yesterday. This was 738 State Street, once a flower shop, where Dion O'Bannion had provided everything for a funeral including the corpse, ultimately his own.

Across the street the sidewalk was lined for more than a block with sweet-faced young women in white caps and gowns, graduates of the Catholic Hospital, filing through the portals of the Cathedral of the Holy Name, to receive their diplomas.

A generation of nurses had wiped the blood of Hymie Weiss from the pavement.

Another of Joe's markers remained.

Cab driver 818 drove me to the Werber Storage Company, and the David Fix It and Swap Shop, on North Clark Street. Inside, the small office was lined with paintings, on consignment, the clerk informed me. Behind, the two-story building was filled with storage vaults.

Storage vaults, indeed.

"I guess you know about that place," I remarked to the cab driver, a young man in his early twenties.

He looked at the building. "What's to know about a warehouse?"

"Ever hear of the St. Valentine's Day massacre?" I asked.

"Who hasn't?"

"That was before you were born."

"I've seen the pictures. All them guys on the floor of a garage, with the blood running out of their heads . . ."

I pointed to the Fix It and Swap Shop. "That was the garage, son. Number 2122."

Joe's Chicago was as extinct as Carthage. Standing at the crossroad to Nowhere, there in the still warehouse where seven men had been slaughtered, where Joe had missed being the eighth by a few minutes, I knew that the answer to his story would not be found in death but in life.

My next stop was California.

It was 9:50 P.M. Joe should have been dressed but he was still in his shorts, and he was sprawled across his bed, in the Beverly Wilshire Hotel. His face was pale and drawn, and he was clawing the covers. The pains were almost unbearable.

Harry Harris, the only other person in the room, moved toward the phone.

Joe turned on one side. "Stay away from that phone," he ordered.

"You can't make it, Joe," Harry said. "I'll call Charlie Morrison . . ."

"You'll call nobody." He struggled to his feet, and started to dress.

"You can't go on this way, Joe."

Joe ignored him. He had had two bad hemorrhages in the past eight weeks, but he had not told anyone.

"Will you do me one favor?" Harry pleaded.

"I'm going on tonight," Joe said as he put on his shirt.

"I know that, but will you go see a friend of mine tomorrow?"

"Another doctor?"

"He lives next door to me. Morris Wilburn. A hell of a nice fellow. Let him take a look at you."

"Why? He'll only find ulcers."

"Maybe he can help you."

Joe had another seizure, and doubled up in agony. "All right, Harry," he said.

Two days later, Dr. Wilburn studied the x-rays and turned to Joe. "Lewis," he said gravely, "you have as bad a case of duodenal ulcers as I have ever seen. Four rips." Joe knew what was coming. "That means total abstinence."

"For how long?" Joe asked.

"As long as you live."

Joe's face darkened. "I'll make a deal with you. If I cut . . ."

"I can't compromise," Dr. Wilburn interrupted. "From what Harry tells me, you have tremendous will power. You can give up liquor."

Joe stood up. "We'll talk about it," he stalled.

"I'll catch you at the hotel later," Harry told him. "Morris wants to give me a check-up."

Joe knew he was lying, but he let it pass. He had had a

strong feeling, while Wilburn was talking, that he had not told him the whole truth. His suspicions were confirmed, in his mind, the following day when Abe Marovitz wired that he was flying in from Chicago.

Two days previously, Abe had called. He was leaving for Ireland and he had said good-bye. Now, suddenly, he had decided to come to Hollywood first. That was unlike Abe. Another thing, he kept thinking, why had I suddenly decided to drop everything in Italy, and fly halfway around the world to see him? He was certain that Abe's unexpected arrival and mine were more than coincidence. What had Dr. Wilburn told Harry, and what had Harry told us?

Did he have the Big Bug?

"Ulcers don't bother me," he chortled in his show at the Mocambo, that night. "I have a new insurance policy. It has a clause that I get fifty thousand dollars if I'm tomahawked by an Indian uprising." He took the Scotch highball from the piano top, and lifted it to the crowd. "I've ruined my health," he said, "drinking to the health of others."

Marovitz and I watched him from a ringside table.

"You've done a lot for Joe," I remarked.

"He has done much more for me," said the little gray-haired judge. "He taught me humility. Joe is the only man I have ever known without envy, jealousy or hate. One time a politician made a nasty crack about him and I wanted to take him on. 'Call him up and thank him,' Joe told me. By example he shamed that man into being nice.

"We were sitting in a hotel lobby one day and he overheard two girls talking. One was sad because she had seen a bracelet next door that she wanted very much but could not afford to buy. Without a word Joe walked out, bought the bracelet and handed it to the girl. He didn't even ask her name.

"Joe must get rid of a thousand a week in small touches, to down-and-outers who wouldn't eat but for him. Only he knows who they are. He dies when one of his charities is found out.

"One day we went to the Broadway Synagogue for mourning services for his father. 'I'd like to donate two hundred and fifty dollars,' he whispered to the shamus, 'but it must be anonymous.' The shamus nodded, and went to the altar. 'A donation, two hundred and fifty dollars,' he announced in a loud voice to the congregation, 'Anonymous, by JOE E. LEWIS!'

"Put in the book that Joe has never lost a friend. That his house is always in order. That he's the best son a mother ever had, and the best friend I ever had." His eyes were on the stage. "And that he has amazingly good common sense, except when it comes to drinking."

Joe was finishing another drink at the piano. "I never stagger," he boasted. "I fall in a straight line."

The crowd was roaring, unaware that the man who was making them laugh should have been in a hospital.

"Austin," he said sternly, after stopping in the middle of a song, "what is the next line?"

"If I'm asleep, wake me," Austin prompted. "If I won't, make me."

Joe nodded approval and turned to the audience. "I knew it but now and then I have to give him a loyalty test. For my next song, 'The Night Is Young but You're Too Old, So Let's Play Canasta, Baby.' "

Joe beamed at Marovitz and introduced him. "My old friend from Chicago, Judge Abe Marovitz." Abe took a reluctant bow. "The Judge taught me the value of money," Joe went on. "I've been rich and I've been poor. Believe me, rich is better." There was a twinkle in his eye. "Before I met Marovitz I was broke. Today, thanks to him, I'm independently bankrupt."

Marovitz laughed and drew a slip of paper from his wallet. "That's the first one," he said proudly. The first of the twenty-year policies he had forced Joe to buy had matured that week. In his hand was a check for eighty thousand dollars.

"He's fixed for life," Abe said.

"He sure is." I was thinking of Joe's four duodenal ulcers, and his diabetes.

Three hours later, we were at the Beverly Wilshire Drug Store. Joe's snack was cottage cheese.

"Listen to this," the man on the stool next to Joe told his girl, and read an item in the morning paper. "According to the American Medical Association, the number-one killer in the United States is heart disease." Joe listened. "Cancer is second, hypertension third and diabetes fourth."

Joe shook his head gloomily. "I'm out of the money again."

"Are you going on the wagon?" I asked a few minutes later as we waited for the elevator.

"I can't," he said, like a condemned man. "Drinking is a part of the act."

"You mean you're not as good an actor as you are a drinker?"

His answer was a look of hurt.

The biographer is a hunter, and the spoor led me to Las Vegas.

My time in the United States was almost spent, I had to return to Europe. The pursuit had begun, by chance, in the New Guinea jungle, eleven years ago, and it would end in the Nevada desert in a city dedicated to chance.

Was that my story, the majesty of chance?

Every turn of the whirring roulette wheels, every click of the dice, and every shuffle of the cards said yes. You can't win, but you keep playing. You can't get out alive, but you keep breathing. Man's breath is short but his plans are long. Freedom of will is only an illusion of human pride, but you imagine that you are the captain of your soul. Everything is six to five against, as Runyon used to say, but you keep hoping.

There is no end to any story, but you keep searching.

Chance was a partial answer, as it was a part-time god, for Joe as well as the rest of us. Chance determined in what bed you were born, and in what bed you would die, but you chose the ones in between. Chance had made a killer's knife miss Joe's jugular vein by the breadth of a hair, but chance had not healed the wound. Courage, and the love of others, were not allies of chance. Faith, not futility, had won his battles, and had kept him an entertainer instead of a hoodlum, a genuine artist in a world of sham.

Night came. The chase was almost over, for Joe and for me.

He sat in his dressing room at the El Rancho Vegas, waiting to go on.

He looked around the bare walls of the cubicle. It had been different the year before. August, 1953, had been a good month. He and Martha had been together again, not as man and wife, but the next best thing. They had been on the same show. He had worked on Beldon Katleman, who finally agreed to give her two weeks, but he had held out for four. Martha had needed the job, and he . . . no, he would not admit that he had needed her. Let anyone draw his own conclusion. They had shared this dressing room those four weeks, as if they had still been married, but he had not touched her.

He had wanted to. He had talked big. "You owe me one," he had reminded her, an unfinished embrace of their last night together. She had laughed, "I'll pay you someday," and that's how something you feel deeply becomes a foolish, running gag. Fifty-two years old, and he was still shy.

It was as it had been, almost ten years ago, when they had

been together at the Copa. Even when she beefed that the music was off.

"We're divorced, don't you remember?" he had told her, with a smile. "Take your complaints to Katleman."

Martha had wanted less from him than anyone else, he now realized, and she had gotten less.

There was a knock on the door. "You're on, Mr. Lewis!"

Joe buttoned his coat, straightened his tie, adjusted the red carnation in his lapel, and brushed the thinning hair from his temple with the palm of his hand. "You're on, Mr. Lewis!" The words echoed. He had been on a long time, thirty-five years since the night he had sung "Macushla" and had won a gold medal at the Fylo Club. Thirty-five years and thirty-five thousand performances, and he had never been as nervous as he was tonight.

He was afraid.

Through an open window he heard the familiar sounds of the casino. The squeals of delight and the groans of defeat. The laughter and the silence. "The number is eight," a stickman called. "Eight. Four and four the hard way. Get your bets down . . ." The games had lost their lure for him. He had seen too many desperate faces around those tables, too many unhappy faces. Everyone was trying to prove something, to himself or to someone else. Even a guy who knows his way around, as he did, has to tap out.

The band was playing "Chicago."

"Sorry I'm late," he began, after he had run on the stage. "I just walked back from the track. A little meeting of the Last Horse Club. I must apologize for my appearance too. Out here in the dude ranch country I'm supposed to wear a cowboy oufit and chaps. Chaps, you know, are the kind of pants you look at and say what a silly place to run out of leather.

"It's good to be back at El Rancho again. The last time I was such a hit, they held over my money. I wish I could af-

ford to work here more often. It's a relaxed town. The natives take things so easy. Your money, your stocks and bonds,
everything. I just heard about the dumbest crook in the
world. He was trying to rob people on the way *back* from
Vegas.

"First, I want to thank Mr. Katleman for bringing me
back. Whether business is good or merely sensational, he has
always faced the future with a frown. I must say for him,
though, no matter how much he loses on the tables, he man-
ages to make a pretty shabby appearance. And he's generous.
I know Bel would like to loan me a little if I was short, it's
just that he's got all his money tied up in money. But I like
to come here, for sentimental reasons. I like to visit my
money."

He spoke with the slight, overly precise diction of a drunk
who is trying to camouflage his condition and is failing
through the disloyalty of a thickened tongue and a befogged
brain.

"There are many interesting people here tonight, and I'll
begin by introducing them." He looked over the crowd,
which was studded with Hollywood celebrities. "I can't see
anyone now," he said, "so on with the show. And believe
me, there's no business like Win, Place and Show business.

"My first song—in a voice that has kept me out of movies
for twenty-five years—is about a terrible dream I had last
night. I dreamed that my girl and Marilyn Monroe fought
over me, and my girl won. Did you see Marilyn's picture,
Don't Bother the Knockers? Maybe it was *Don't Bother to
Knock.* That was the one which showed her in a negligee,
panties and bra. You know the kind, a documentary. There
was a psychiatrist in it. Worked for Alcoholics Anonymous,
twenty-five bucks a week and all he could drink. He had the
personality of an untipped waiter. The kind who is never at
a loss for something to say which he is sure to regret. When
he introduced himself to Marilyn, he said, 'I'm Dr. Schultz,

P.H.D., M.D., B.B.A.' For a guy who is supposed to be educated, that's a funny way to spell Schultz. Seriously, when I was visiting Twentieth Century-Fox last week, Zanuck asked me to make a movie with Marilyn. I said no, Darryl, but I'll make a calendar with her."

Joe teetered a little. He had to grope for words. "Austin Mack, the illegitimate son of Senator Kefauver. Even though Austin never studied music at Julliard, you can tell it." Joe's glazed eyes focused on the baskets of flowers displayed on each side of the stage. "I can't understand why they're here," he said. "You can't bet on 'em."

The crowd was laughing continuously.

"Post time!" He picked up the drink from the piano top, and turned to the audience. "Smart act." He gazed at the glass. "This is the only prop I use. I drink my Scotch straight and my gin horizontal." He gulped half the drink, and grimaced a little. "I don't particularly like drinking," he said, "it's just something I do while I'm getting drunk."

Joe paused and listened, swaying almost imperceptibly.

The crowd laughed and applauded. They watched him in amazement and envy, as they always had. The undertone of comment was unchanged.

"He's stiff already! Tight as a tick!"

"How does he do it, night after night?"

"With ulcers yet!"

"Man, has *he* got a load!"

Joe stood rigidly, in a kind of suspended emotionalism.

Then he heard Austin's voice behind him, soft and joyful. "You did it, Joe."

He had done it. Cold sober, without a drink for four days, he had convinced the crowd that he was intoxicated. He had recreated himself with an illusion that the audience had been unable to discern from a drunken Joe E. It was his greatest performance. The drink on the piano top had been tea.

He took another swallow and held up his glass. "Would you believe it, ladies and gentlemen," he said solemnly, "this is tea."

The crowd howled. The unbelieved truth had gotten Joe the biggest laugh of the night.

Within him the coil of fear unwound. He was free at last. He had separated himself from his alter ego.

The gardens were peaceful and sweet-scented in the moonlight.

This was his home now. Each season he managed to spend more time here. This year it would be for six months, from April to October, with only a few weeks off for short engagements at the Mocambo and the Riverside in Reno. New York and the Copa were all right for a couple of months in the fall. He still enjoyed Miami Beach in the winter and Chicago in the spring but the rest of the year he wanted to keep for El Rancho. Bel Katleman was his closest friend now, he had never worked for a better man. The pace was slower. He was slower. There was nothing to do during the day except sit by the pool and play gin. The desert air was dry, and the sun felt good on the belly.

"Joe . . ."

He stopped, and held his breath.

Martha stepped out of the shadows on the crosswalk. "Wonderful show, Joe."

"Why didn't you tell me you were in the house?"

"Opening night, I knew you were busy."

"I wasn't busy."

They looked at each other and for a moment all was still.

"I met your new girl, Joe."

"Kitty Kopet?"

"She told me she wants to marry you. 'Don't expect any help from me,' I told her, 'I love him too.' "

He was ill at ease. Didn't Martha know she was the first and last Mrs. Joe E. Lewis?

"Sorry to hear about the ulcers."

"I can't say you didn't warn me."

"You used to say you got 'em from me."

"I was only kiddin'."

Martha smiled sadly. "We're even. I got a spastic colon."

"Serious?"

She shrugged. "Serious, shmerious, you're sick. How about you? . . . I worry about you."

"That's foolish. Any time you wake up in the morning you're way ahead of the game. It's nothin' worse than ulcers. They checked."

There was another silence.

"You were right about the house, Joe."

He looked at her questioningly.

"You know how much I had my heart set on a house. I finally bought one. It took every cent I could get my hands on, but it was mine. Something I had wanted all my life." She shook her head. "Nothing. I got rid of it, at a loss."

"I'm sorry, Martha."

"Why should you be sorry? You were right."

He looked at the only woman he had loved enough to marry. Over her shoulder he saw the outline of a bungalow. The bungalow. Was it six years since she had walked out of it? Nineteen forty-eight. It was six. It's funny how the cards fall, he thought. She had left him because he drank and gambled all the time. Now he couldn't drink and he didn't want to gamble. It's not always the wrong person, he realized, it might be the right person but the wrong time. Not who you marry, but when. Timing. Everything was timing, whether it was with a girl or a gag.

"Staying here?" he asked.

She nodded. "On the other side."

He hesitated. "Want me to walk you home?"

She hesitated. "You don't have to . . ."

The hopeful look on his face vanished. "Good night, Martha."

He walked away slowly, forlorn. She had disappointed him. He had hoped she would have remembered their first night together. The night at the Copa that Sanchez had wanted to go to the opening of a new club, and Joe had asked three or four girls to walk with him. He had wanted to ask Martha first, but he had been too timid. He had had his eyes on her for a long time . . .

"Joe . . . !"

He turned.

Martha was running up the path toward him.

"I didn't mean to hurt your feelings," she said, her voice breathless and quavering with emotion.

"I only wanted to walk with you," he said. "You were my wife . . ."

They looked at each other, two lonely people in a lonely world, as from a window of the casino a stickman called, "Four is the point. Four. Two and two, the hard way—"

The point of no return.

EXIT

November the tenth.

On this day, in 1918, a kaiser named Hohenzollern bowed his head and the first of the world wars ended. On this day, six years later, a hoodlum named O'Bannion fell among his flowers and a new war began. On this day, in 1927, a comedian named Joe Lewis regained consciousness, and a man was reborn.

After a while every day is an anniversary.

It was November the tenth, 1954.

The long vigil would soon end, one way or another. "How is he, Doc?" Dan Arnstein asked Dr. Milton Porter as he came out of the room.

"Still in an oxygen tent, still unconscious."

"So long?" Arnstein was distraught.

"He came to for a few seconds, opened his eyes and asked, 'Who won the fifth at Jamaica?' I smiled and told him, 'You'll be all right' but it didn't seem to cheer him. To the contrary. 'Never mind that,' he said—and passed out." Dr. Porter shook his head. "What a horse player—even under ether!"

Arnstein grinned. "I had a horse running at Jamaica today. Murph's Deb, a filly. She won the fifth—and Joe had two hundred on her nose . . ."

The mists of anesthesia lifted and, twenty-seven years to the day, Joe again found himself in a hospital room, this time the Harkness Pavilion of Presbyterian Hospital in New York. Once again he had faced a knife.

His eyes widened and he stared out of the window at the city of his birth. A look of wonderment came into his gentle, scarred face.

"What do you know?" he murmured. "I made it again."

INDEX

ABOUT THE AUTHOR

ART COHN was born in New York City on April 5, 1909, but left two days later for Schenectady, where he spent his first sixteen years. He moved to the West Coast, spent ten years as a sports writer in Long Beach, California, then seven years as sports editor of the Oakland *Tribune*. During the war he was sent to New Guinea by International News Service as a war correspondent, then to the Middle East. His career as a foreign correspondent ended in Ceylon, where he had a run-in with a British admiral.

In 1947, the late Mark Hellinger gave Mr. Cohn his first assignment in the motion picture industry, and since that time he has had a varied and successful career as a screen writer. His first product, *The Set-Up*, was awarded the International Critics Grand Prix at the Cannes Festival in 1949. He collaborated with Roberto Rossellini on the screenplay of *Stromboli*, and has written many other successful films for major studios here and in Italy. He has just completed a book of reminiscences of his days as a sports writer and editor.